BUSINESS
Superbrands

AN INSIGHT INTO SOME OF BRITAIN'S STRONGEST B2B BRANDS 2009

superbrands.uk.com

Chief Executive
Ben Hudson

Brand Liaison Directors
Fiona Maxwell
Claire Pollock
Liz Silvester

Brand Liaison Manager
Heidi Smith

Administrative Co-ordinator
Alice McSeveney

Head of Accounts
Will Carnochan

Managing Editor
Laura Hill

Author
Karen Dugdale

Proofreader
Anna Haynes

Designer
Claire Boston

Other publications from Superbrands in the UK:
Superbrands 2008/09 ISBN: 978-0-9554784-4-4
CoolBrands 2008/09 ISBN: 978-0-9554784-5-1

To order these books, email brands@superbrands.uk.com
or call 01825 767396.

Published by Superbrands (UK) Ltd.
44 Charlotte Street
London
W1T 2NR

© 2009 Superbrands (UK) Ltd

superbrands.uk.com

Printed in Italy

ISBN: 978-0-9554784-6-8

Contents

Endorsements

We are very pleased to be including comments from several well respected industry bodies and thank them for their support of the programme.

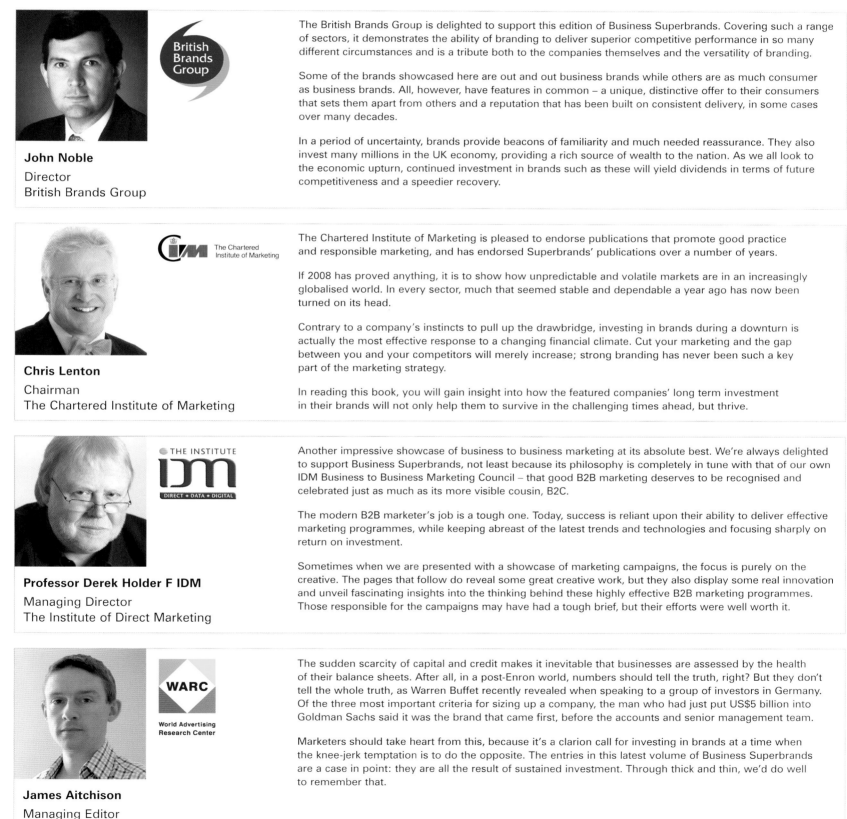

John Noble
Director
British Brands Group

The British Brands Group is delighted to support this edition of Business Superbrands. Covering such a range of sectors, it demonstrates the ability of branding to deliver superior competitive performance in so many different circumstances and is a tribute both to the companies themselves and the versatility of branding.

Some of the brands showcased here are out and out business brands while others are as much consumer as business brands. All, however, have features in common – a unique, distinctive offer to their consumers that sets them apart from others and a reputation that has been built on consistent delivery, in some cases over many decades.

In a period of uncertainty, brands provide beacons of familiarity and much needed reassurance. They also invest many millions in the UK economy, providing a rich source of wealth to the nation. As we all look to the economic upturn, continued investment in brands such as these will yield dividends in terms of future competitiveness and a speedier recovery.

Chris Lenton
Chairman
The Chartered Institute of Marketing

The Chartered Institute of Marketing is pleased to endorse publications that promote good practice and responsible marketing, and has endorsed Superbrands' publications over a number of years.

If 2008 has proved anything, it is to show how unpredictable and volatile markets are in an increasingly globalised world. In every sector, much that seemed stable and dependable a year ago has now been turned on its head.

Contrary to a company's instincts to pull up the drawbridge, investing in brands during a downturn is actually the most effective response to a changing financial climate. Cut your marketing and the gap between you and your competitors will merely increase; strong branding has never been such a key part of the marketing strategy.

In reading this book, you will gain insight into how the featured companies' long term investment in their brands will not only help them to survive in the challenging times ahead, but thrive.

Professor Derek Holder F IDM
Managing Director
The Institute of Direct Marketing

Another impressive showcase of business to business marketing at its absolute best. We're always delighted to support Business Superbrands, not least because its philosophy is completely in tune with that of our own IDM Business to Business Marketing Council – that good B2B marketing deserves to be recognised and celebrated just as much as its more visible cousin, B2C.

The modern B2B marketer's job is a tough one. Today, success is reliant upon their ability to deliver effective marketing programmes, while keeping abreast of the latest trends and technologies and focusing sharply on return on investment.

Sometimes when we are presented with a showcase of marketing campaigns, the focus is purely on the creative. The pages that follow do reveal some great creative work, but they also display some real innovation and unveil fascinating insights into the thinking behind these highly effective B2B marketing programmes. Those responsible for the campaigns may have had a tough brief, but their efforts were well worth it.

James Aitchison
Managing Editor
World Advertising Research Center

The sudden scarcity of capital and credit makes it inevitable that businesses are assessed by the health of their balance sheets. After all, in a post-Enron world, numbers should tell the truth, right? But they don't tell the whole truth, as Warren Buffet recently revealed when speaking to a group of investors in Germany. Of the three most important criteria for sizing up a company, the man who had just put US$5 billion into Goldman Sachs said it was the brand that came first, before the accounts and senior management team.

Marketers should take heart from this, because it's a clarion call for investing in brands at a time when the knee-jerk temptation is to do the opposite. The entries in this latest volume of Business Superbrands are a case in point: they are all the result of sustained investment. Through thick and thin, we'd do well to remember that.

About
Superbrands

Superbrands presents expert and consumer opinion on the UK's strongest brands. The organisation promotes the discipline of branding and pays tribute to exceptional brands through three annual programmes: Business Superbrands, Superbrands and CoolBrands.

Each programme features a dedicated book, national media supplement and website. By identifying the country's strongest brands and telling their stories, Superbrands provides consumers with a deeper appreciation of the discipline of branding and a greater understanding of the brands themselves.

Each brand featured in this, the seventh volume of Business Superbrands, has qualified for inclusion based on the collective opinions of the independent and voluntary Expert Council and more than 1,500 business professionals. Full details of the selection process can be found on page 136.

Superbrands was launched in London in 1995 and is now a global business operating in more than 55 countries worldwide.

The Business Superbrands Award Stamp

The brands that have been awarded Business Superbrand status and participate in the programme are given permission to use the Business Superbrands Award Stamp. This powerful endorsement provides evidence to existing and potential consumers, media, employees and investors of the exceptional standing that these Business Superbrands have achieved.

Member brands use the stamp on marketing materials, including product packaging, advertising, websites and annual reports, as well as other external and internal communication channels.

QUALITY   RELIABILITY   DISTINCTION

better work, better life

As a global leader in HR services, with a network that spans more than 70 countries, Adecco is a well-positioned and informed career partner for businesses and individuals alike. Aiming to set the standard for best practice in the recruitment industry, Adecco is committed to developing and maintaining prosperous relationships and to realising its vision of 'better work, better life'.

Market

The Adecco network includes 900 staff in 190 offices throughout the UK and Ireland, while the worldwide network under the Adecco Group banner comprises more than 37,000 employees across 7,000 offices.

As one that is closely linked to the health of the economy, the recruitment industry has, until recently, benefited from a favourable economic climate; turnover reached an industry high of US$27 billion between April 2007 and March 2008, while the number of staff employed in the industry exceeded 100,000 for the first time (Source: REC Annual Industry Turnover & Key Volumes Survey). The most notable growth in the UK market was seen in permanent placements, up 21.7 per cent. The REC survey also showed the number of temporary and contract workers to have fallen by 1.8 per cent over the period.

Achievements

Adecco is a regular commentator on the employment market, providing insight into the recruitment industry and the way in which it contributes to the economy and society as a whole. Recent activities include hosting a roundtable in partnership with the Financial Times to discuss the impact of the credit crunch on the recruitment industry and the labour market, and providing the keynote address at the 2008 Recruiter Annual Forum – presenting on the importance of customer service and initiating discussion on how to continue to raise industry standards.

2008 proved to be a year of business recognition for Adecco. Its placement as 274th among the 2008 Fortune Global 500 cemented its status as one of the world's largest companies, while Adecco UK and

Ireland was ranked second in Recruitment International's Top 100 Report of 2008.

Product

Adecco sources permanent, temporary and contract positions from across a wide range of sectors including secretarial, office support and administration, financial, retail, industrial, hospitality and contact centre staffing.

As a business, however, Adecco is evolving – not only in reaction to the current financial pressures but in recognition of how its customers' needs are changing. For clients, this involves greater testing, screening and development of workers, more efficient business practices and ongoing expert guidance. Tools such as Competency Based Interviews (CBI), Adecco Aftercare and e-recruitment services are utilised to ensure clients have access to a consistent pool of appropriately skilled workers.

In turn, job seekers benefit from their own personal Adecco consultant, who helps to keep them informed and to make the best possible career choices. The online

Candidate handbook   Client handbook

1919	1957	1964	1977	1996	1997
Alfred Marks, Adecco's original trading name, is the first recruitment agency to be formed in the UK.	The ADIA Group is founded in Switzerland. The recruitment firm grows rapidly, subsequently expanding into France, Austria and the US.	ECCO is founded in France, quickly becoming the country's largest provider of temporary employment. By 1996, it is Europe's largest personnel company.	Alfred Marks joins the ADIA Group.	The ADIA Group and ECCO merge, forming ADECCO. The combined operation comprises 2,500 branches around the world.	The Adecco name first appears on the UK high street.

AdeccoXpert system provides access to complementary training programmes and testing facilities for developing skills further.

Recent Developments

In 2008, Adecco UK and Ireland strengthened its management team with the arrival of Christian De Conti as managing director. De Conti joined the newly appointed CEO Catherine King, bringing with him more than 10 years of Adecco experience from across the globe – namely that of sales and business development director for Adecco Italy, senior vice president of Adecco North America and country manager of Adecco Venezuela.

Other notable developments within the Adecco business during 2008 include initiatives to improve the working lives of its candidates, clients and internal staff; the introduction of client and job seeker aftercare services, for example, as well as improved incentive systems and a greater emphasis on training and development programmes for Adecco employees. One such initiative, Adecco's Culture programme, explored the 'candidate journey' in order to help consultants deliver and sustain effective candidate-led service. The two-day training course was rolled out across the entire branch network.

Demonstrating its commitment to supporting its staff in their own career development, the Adecco Management Development programme was also launched. The scheme encourages personal growth and provides consultants with the skills to progress their career, as well as equipping branch managers for senior management roles.

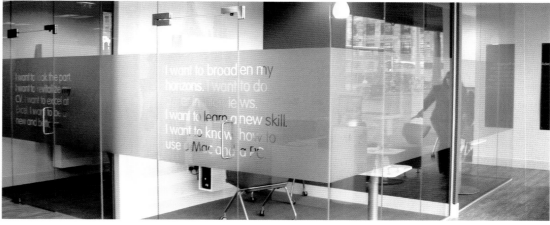

Promotion

Founded in 2006, the Adecco Institute leads the way in research in the field of employment and acts as a platform through which to drive awareness. From governments and academics to employers, unions and employees, the Adecco Institute facilitates discussions among all stakeholders on the broad topic of 'work' and how it impacts individuals, regions and organisations.

Through primary and secondary research as well as thought pieces, conferences and events, the Institute provides a forward-looking and fact-based perspective on innovative approaches to help organisations and regions raise employability, productivity and employee satisfaction at work.

Brand Values

As the world's largest employment services group, Adecco is underpinned by a commitment to providing more for its candidates, clients and colleagues. Conscious of its global role, Adecco has taken significant steps to redefine itself and is moving forward with the aim of placing a greater emphasis on the customer and employee experience – one that is encapsulated by the company's vision of 'better work, better life'.

adecco.co.uk

Things you didn't know about Adecco

Adecco's roots lie within Alfred Marks, the UK's first recruitment company, which was formed in 1919.

The name 'Adecco' came from the merging of its two parent companies in 1997, ADIA in Switzerland and ECCO in France.

Through Adecco's extensive global network, a total of 312 people are employed every minute.

During 2007/08, the number of staff employed in the recruitment sector rose by 7.5 per cent.

Adecco is a Fortune Global 500 company – 274th in 2008.

2000	2005	2006	2008
Adecco acquires Olsten Staffing, becoming the biggest recruitment company in the US.	After a strategy review, Adecco makes a commitment to realign itself across six professional service business lines.	The Adecco Institute is founded – a research centre focusing on thought leadership in the field of work and exploring its impact on society.	Adecco is ranked second in Recruitment International's Top 100 Report.

Allied Irish Bank (GB)

Our business is business banking.

Allied Irish Bank (GB) continues to strengthen its brand through its firm foundation of providing each customer with tailored solutions and support for all of their business banking requirements. Listening and continuously responding to customer needs, combined with relevant innovation has built the brand to what it is today. Allied Irish Bank (GB)'s business is business banking.

Market

Amid a period of immense change in global financial markets, Allied Irish Bank (GB) has maintained its position at the forefront of relationship banking by responding quickly to market conditions and keeping customers fully informed of developments.

Offering a full range of products and services for growing and expanding mid-corporate businesses, Allied Irish Bank (GB) is a specialist business bank. The Bank operates and has developed specialist teams in its key

sectors which include healthcare, medical, education, hotels and leisure, public sector and charities, environmental services and the professional sector.

Responding to market demand, the Bank has extended its Private Banking offering with an increased focus on personalised asset management for high net worth individuals. The Bank continues to establish itself as 'first choice' for businesses by providing an alternative to traditional high street banks. It aims to achieve these goals through expert

counsel and a continued commitment to its key business principles of: providing a tailored service to its customers; developing long term relationships; local bankers who are interested, knowledgeable, experienced and fully involved with all decisions; short lines of communication and speedy decision making; and a branch management team who work closely with centralised specialists.

Achievements

Allied Irish Bank (GB) regularly tracks customer opinion using detailed customer satisfaction surveys. A recent survey found that 94.8 per cent of customers interviewed were satisfied with the quality of service that they had received and more than 90 per cent of respondents said that they were likely or very likely to approach Allied Irish Bank (GB) for their future financial needs.

Furthermore, the Bank remains in the top quartile of suppliers, with a score of 83.4 per cent in the Satisfaction Index™ – a cross-industry benchmark of an organisation's ability to meet customer requirements. More than 68 per cent of customers reported Allied Irish Bank (GB) to be 'better' or 'the best' when compared to other business banks. Indeed, Allied Irish Bank (GB) has held the title of Britain's Best Business Bank in an independent survey by the Forum of Private Business Banking since 1994.

It is a testament to the Bank's long-standing commitment to staff development that since

Working with top-flight businesses throughout the country.

1825	1970s	1980s	1991	2001	2008
The Bank's first London office opens in Throgmorton Avenue.	AIB Group grows to create a strong branch network in Britain.	International success brings about Group investment in branches in the US.	In July, First Trust Bank is created from the merger of AIB Group's interests in Northern Ireland with those of TSB Northern Ireland.	AIB Group completes the merger of Wielkopolski Bank Kredytowy S.A. and Bank Zachodni S.A. in Poland. AIB Group has a 70.5 per cent shareholding in the new Bank Zachodni WBK S.A. (BZWBK).	Allied Irish Bank (GB)'s Private Banking and Corporate Banking teams move to new offices in Hanover Square, London.

Promotion

With a continued focus on growth and expansion, the Bank has taken an integrated approach to PR and advertising to create a strong presence in its local marketplace.

The Bank has also been advertising on one of the UK's largest poster sites since 1999. At just over a third of a kilometre in length and situated at Heathrow Airport Terminal 1, the advert is seen by more than four million passengers per year travelling to and from the Republic of Ireland.

Allied Irish Bank (GB) has a sound horseracing heritage and is a key provider to the racing industry – 27 of the 60 racecourses in the UK bank with it. A natural progression for the Bank was to become the first Founding Partner of Ascot Racecourse, an agreement that will see the Bank partner the racecourse until 2010.

1995, it has consistently achieved the recognition of the Investors in People (IiP) standard across its office network, exceeding 90 per cent of the measures set down by the new IiP national benchmark. Continuing investment in staff development has been the key to its success both in retaining employees and in providing high quality service for customers.

Product

In a fast-changing market, Allied Irish Bank (GB)'s commitment to tailoring products and services to meet a customer's specific needs underpins its offering. With resource and capabilities at every level, the Bank strives to provide continuity and ingenuity in adapting these products as business and market requirements change. All managers are decision-makers, developing long term relationships with their customers in providing day-to-day banking and are closely involved with their local business community.

Traditional banking continues to be at the core of Allied Irish Bank (GB)'s personalised Private Banking service, which provides comprehensive advice and has offices in Glasgow, Edinburgh, Manchester, Birmingham and London. Allied Irish Bank (GB) has

specialist Corporate Banking teams across Britain who work closely with branches to provide a seamless service in key sectors, supported by a solid understanding of the complexities of corporate and institutional business. The Bank's strategy is to deliver a first class service through business innovation, knowledgeable staff and short lines of communication, ensuring customers' business needs are met quickly and efficiently.

Recent Developments

In line with the Bank's mid-corporate business positioning, branches have been restyled to reflect the needs of modern day business banking for corporate customers, featuring meeting rooms and open office space. In June 2008, the Bank relocated its London Corporate and Private Banking offices to a prestigious new location, Hanover Square.

With 31 full service branches and five business development offices, the Bank has invested heavily in key business areas and more customer-friendly premises. This has allowed for greater access to teams of specialists who are available to inform on all areas of finance including Corporate Banking, Private Banking, Global Trade Services, Asset Finance and Independent Financial Advice.

Brand Values

The values of honesty, integrity and fairness are key to achieving an enduring business and personal relationships. The Bank, therefore, has a strong commitment to upholding its core brand values: dependable, engaging and pioneering. As part of AIB Group, the Code of Business Ethics for all employees reaffirms the general principles that govern how the Bank conducts its affairs. It recognises that maintaining the trust and confidence of customers, staff, shareholders and other stakeholders by acting with integrity and professionalism, as well as behaving with prudence and skill, is crucial to the continued growth and success of the Bank.

Allied Irish Bank (GB) has an active corporate social responsibility programme and currently supports a range of activities. It takes a responsible approach to its local environment and has committed to take action to actively reduce its impact on the global environment.

aibgb.co.uk

Things you didn't know about Allied Irish Bank (GB)

AIB Group, Ireland's leading banking and financial services organisation, operates principally in Ireland, Britain, Poland and the US, employing more than 24,000 people worldwide in over 750 offices.

Allied Irish Bank (GB) has been voted Britain's Best Business Bank on seven consecutive occasions since 1994.

Allied Irish Bank (GB) Private Banking has five offices (London, Manchester, Birmingham, Glasgow and Edinburgh) offering a full complement of private banking services.

American Express Company is a diversified worldwide travel, financial and network services company founded in 1850. It is a world leader in charge and credit cards, travellers' cheques, travel and business services. It provides the Corporate Card and other expense management services to companies, helps clients realise the greatest value from their investment in business travel, and acquires and maintains relationships with millions of merchants around the globe.

Global Consumer Group and the Global Business to Business (B2B) Group. The B2B Group has millions of corporate, merchant and bank partners across its global businesses: Commercial Card, Business Travel, Merchant Services (responsible for processing all transaction volumes on the American Express network), and Network Services (which works with partner banks issuing American Express cards).

Achievements

Offering products and services in more than 200 countries around the world, American Express has achieved the status of a truly global brand; it has made the top 15 in Interbrand's Best Global Brands list every year since 2002. In 2008 the Interbrand study valued the brand at more than US$21 billion, making American Express the most valuable financial services brand in the world.

American Express strives to be at the forefront of its industry through the provision of key products and services, responding to changing trends in order to best meet evolving customer and client needs. The Company prides itself on providing personalised customer service,

something which has seen employees personally delivering emergency replacement cards and travel documents to customers, as well as helping to locate and connect customers and their families in times of crisis.

It is an ethic that the Company extends to its employees. Recognising the importance of attracting and maintaining a leading workforce in order to successfully deliver its services, American Express has introduced initiatives such as flexible working arrangements, global exchange opportunities, leadership development programmes and community volunteering schemes. The Company has won 'employer of choice' awards around the world, including in the UK, India, Germany, the Netherlands, Spain, France, Italy, Argentina, Mexico and the US.

Product

American Express offers a range of products to help its business customers with their payments and travel needs.

The leading Corporate Card provider in the UK, American Express also provides expense management solutions that offer its customers the opportunity to simplify their day-to-day procedures, increase productivity and control when, where and how funds are spent. In addition, Cardmembers benefit from global acceptance and enhanced business and travel services.

American Express operates one of the world's largest travel agency networks, with more than 2,200 travel service locations in over 140 countries and territories worldwide.

Market

American Express has more than 90 million cards in circulation worldwide, and in 2007 US$647 billion was spent using American Express plastic. In 2007 the Company reported an income of US$4 billion, generated through its leading global payments and travel offering.

American Express is organised into two distinct, customer-focused groups – the

1850	1896	1958	1965	1976	1984
American Express is established in New York as an express mail company. It quickly becomes one of the era's most successful US businesses of its kind.	American Express opens its first London office. Mark Twain is among the first customers to visit the new office.	The American Express Card is first introduced. By year-end the Card is accepted at an estimated 30,000 establishments worldwide and is in use by 500,000 customers.	American Express becomes the first company in the industry to safeguard Cardmembers against fraud. The Corporate Card is introduced the following year.	American Express formally declares a privacy policy for its Cardmembers – a first for the industry.	The Platinum Card is introduced, followed in 1991 by the launch of the Membership Rewards programme.

American Express Business Travel is dedicated to helping its corporate clients realise the greatest possible value from their investment in travel through increased cost savings and greater spend control. Employing industry-leading booking technology, it provides travel management consulting expertise, strategic sourcing and supplier negotiation support, in addition to customer service around the world.

Merchants welcoming Cardmembers benefit from the relationship with American Express as well. As American Express' premium Charge Cards come with no pre-set spending limit, merchants can see bottom line benefits from the sale of high value goods and services. Those choosing to reward American Express Cardmembers with special offers through exclusive Cardmember websites also expose their businesses to a larger customer base. In addition, American Express generates industry and customer insight which can provide valuable information to help a business grow, such as identifying which special offers are most likely to resonate with high spending Cardmembers.

Recent Developments
In 2008, American Express launched the Corporate Platinum Card in the UK. The Platinum Card offers a wide range of business and travel benefits, including access to fast track security at airports and enhanced levels of travel insurance. Other special features, such as a concierge service, are designed to ease pressure on frequent business travellers – from assisting with impromptu meeting arrangements to sourcing an appropriate gift for a client.

American Express Business Travel also launched AXIOM, an online procurement platform, in the UK in 2008. By bringing together inventory from more than 160,000 suppliers globally, AXIOM goes beyond traditional air, hotel and car rental booking facilities, enabling closer control of additional business services such as dining, airport parking, ground transportation and parcel shipping.

In 2008 American Express' Global Network Services business and its partner Lloyds TSB launched a new offering – Lloyds TSB Duo Airmiles – which won Best New Credit Card Product at The Card Awards.

Promotion
As one of the world's most recognisable brands and financially successful companies, American Express offers exclusive activities and benefits to further enhance its brand, including Cardmember offers for merchant partners and relationship-building events for clients – such as American Express'

sponsorship of the UK premiere of Shine A Light, Martin Scorsese's Rolling Stones biopic.

In line with its status as an award-winning employer, American Express also lends its support to the Working Families organisation, sponsoring its 'Best Boss' competition which celebrates those who take practical steps to help their staff balance their work and home lives.

Brand Values
American Express is committed to delivering its brand promise of 'World-class service. Personal recognition' as a leading provider of travel and payments services worldwide: 'World-class service' denotes American Express as a premium, prestigious brand with global reach; 'Personal recognition' stands for treating each customer as an individual. The brand's values are further defined as providing extraordinary customer care, peace of mind worldwide, superior business intelligence and broad-based innovation.

americanexpress.com/uk

Things you didn't know about American Express

American Express started life in 1850 as an express mail company.

During World War I, American Express worked with the Red Cross to ship millions of parcels to prisoners-of-war.

The very first American Express Card was printed on purple paper; the embossed plastic cards were introduced in 1959.

American Express processes more than US$1 million of transactions every minute.

1997	1999	2006	2008
Global Network Services is created to work with banks issuing cards on the American Express network.	The Centurion Card is first launched in the UK.	The British Airways American Express Corporate Card is launched in the UK.	The American Express Card celebrates its 50th anniversary and the Corporate Platinum Card is launched in the UK.

The British Market Research Bureau (BMRB) has been providing high quality research solutions for 75 years. It offers a range of approaches including bespoke proprietary research and consultancy, syndicated data and cost-effective omnibus research. BMRB is one of the leading market research agencies in the UK and a key operating company within the Millward Brown Group.

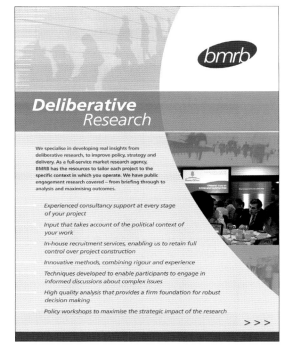

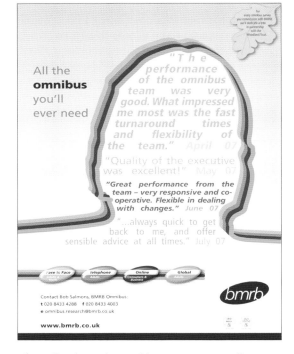

Market

Market research has seen a huge growth in demand in a number of key areas. The UK is the world's second largest market for market research and according to the Market Research Society (MRS), was worth an estimated £1.8 billion in 2007. As one of the largest market research agencies in the UK, BMRB has been at the forefront of this growth.

Achievements

BMRB's achievements run across all areas of the business and in its commitment to quality, its staff and its clients.

BMRB won two of the four BMRA Research Business Effectiveness Awards for 2005 – the awards for Best Agency and Quality &

Service Excellence. It was also short-listed for the People Management award. Indeed, BMRB was one of the first market research companies to have professionally recognised training programmes for both research and operations executives.

Very high standards of client satisfaction are consistently achieved. A survey in 2006 showed that 96 per cent of clients gave the company an overall performance rating of 'excellent', 'very good' or 'good'.

Product

BMRB offers market-leading research services: Brand owner insight – the Enlightenment service harnesses the power of in-house and other data sources and applies these to a range

of applications. It provides answers to all types of marketing questions, quickly and flexibly.

Employee and customer research – BMRB Stakeholder is a specialist unit dedicated to understanding customer loyalty and employee engagement. It helps organisations measure and respond to the needs of their customers, employees and other key stakeholders to improve their business performance.

Environmental and climate change research – BMRB offers a wealth of research resources and data on a wide range of issues relating to the environment. It conducts tailored qualitative and quantitative research among the general public, organisations and special interest groups.

1933	1934	1939	1969	1987	1997
The British Market Research Bureau is set up, making it the longest established research agency in Britain.	One of the earliest and largest studies on newspaper readership for the Daily Herald is carried out.	BMRB becomes one of the first agencies to conduct major surveys for Government, including a survey for the Ministry of Food to monitor wartime rationing.	BMRB develops the Target Group Index (TGI), which has since become a standard trading currency for the UK media sector.	BMRB joins WPP Group plc.	BMRB becomes the first in the industry to conduct Multi-Media Computer Aided Personal Interviewing (MM CAPI) nationally.

Media research – BMRB Media works with the leading media owners and advertising agencies. It offers research expertise across all media and regularly provides insight into work relating to mixed media. BMRB aims to provide creative solutions and excellent client service for media buyers, sellers, advertisers and regulators alike.

Omnibus surveys – fast, accurate and cost effective, BMRB Omnibus is a leader in face-to-face, telephone, online, mobile and global omnibus surveys. Its broad portfolio of services offers flexible schedules and methodologies to suit wide-ranging research requirements.

Over 50s research – BMRB offers a range of research solutions for marketers targeting the over 50s as a consumer group, for policy makers measuring the impact of the over 50s on public policy and expenditure, and for employers realising the potential of the over 50s workforce.

Social policy and public sector research – BMRB Social Research is one of the largest providers of public policy research in the UK with a team of more than 70 dedicated social researchers. Its reputation for quality, technical excellence and creative solutions is second to none. BMRB regularly conducts prestigious national projects such as the British Crime Survey.

Sports research – BMRB Sport offers effective research solutions for all sports sectors, from professional sports through to grassroots participation and active leisure. Its tools and techniques, designed to help the drive towards participation, are built around the principles of getting people to start, stay and succeed in sport. For the professional sport sector, BMRB offers research to identify and grow revenue streams from media and sponsorship rights, and from the fan base.

Syndicated marketing and media surveys – the Target Group Index (TGI) is the world's leading single source measurement of consumers' product and brand usage, media consumption and attitudes. Originally developed in Britain by BMRB, TGI now operates in more than 50 countries and is used by advertisers, media owners and agencies to provide worldwide consumer insight.

Recent Developments

BMRB was accredited ISO 20252 in April 2007. This new international standard sets a common level of quality for market research globally.

In the same year, BMRB and Henley Centre HeadlightVision (now The Futures Company) launched a joint initiative, the Institute for Insight in the Public Services (IIPS). The IIPS develops and promotes the use of citizen insight to support the transformation of public service delivery in the UK.

Promotion

BMRB uses a wide range of marketing communications tools to raise awareness and develop business for the products and services it specialises in.

BMRB's integrated marketing approach utilises advertising, PR, direct mail, online, email, delivering conference papers and sponsorship of industry events. In addition, it regularly publishes a wide range of newsletters, both printed and online, which focus on Social, TGI and Media research issues.

BMRB's findings and thinking are regularly published in the research and marketing trade press and in the national quality press. Coverage has been achieved in publications such as Research Magazine, Personnel Today, Human Resources, Marketing, Marketing Week, Brand Strategy, Campaign, The Times, the FT, the Guardian, The Independent, The Telegraph and BBC Online.

BMRB's Centre for Excellence seminar programme plays an active role in helping clients better understand all aspects of the research process. BMRB runs seminars and workshops for more than 100 clients a year.

Brand Values

By providing unimpeachable information, BMRB aims to empower clients to make better business decisions. An important contributory factor in maintaining BMRB's high standards is the quality of the company's staff training programmes – regarded as some of the best in the industry.

BMRB consciously avoids being a 'jack of all trades'. The company's established excellence in specific research sectors, reinforced by its comprehensive operational resources, enables it to be flexible and creative in meeting client needs.

BMRB's values can be summarised as: Principled – upholding the highest standards; Partners – to its clients and with other expert suppliers; Pioneering – in its use of new methods and technology; and Passionate – about its own work and that of its clients.

bmrb.co.uk

Things you didn't know about BMRB

When BMRB launched the Target Group Index (TGI) in 1969 it researched 25,000 respondents. By 2007 TGI had grown to more than 750,000 respondents annually, worldwide.

Over the last five years BMRB has conducted more than 150,000 interviews for the British Crime Survey.

From 1969 to 1983 BMRB, backed by the music industry and the BBC, produced the Record Charts (the 'Official Top 50').

Jay K, lead singer of the band Jamiroquai, once worked as a research interviewer in BMRB's telephone unit in Ealing.

Also in 1997, BMRB conducts its first web-based research project – a readership survey for The Lancet.

2005
BMRB wins two of the four BMRA Research Business Effectiveness Awards for 2005.

2007
BMRB and Henley Centre HeadlightVision launch the Institute for Insight in the Public Services (IIPS), to promote global best practice on how public sector bodies can better connect with citizens.

2008
BMRB celebrates its 75th anniversary.

British Gas Business has been supplying energy to businesses for the last 14 years and has more than one million UK customer supply points. It is the leading supplier of gas and electricity to business users in the UK and is dedicated to the needs of small and medium-sized enterprises through to large industrial and commercial businesses. It is the first energy company to offer account managers to all customers.

Save the worker
with British Gas Business

Market

British Gas Business operates in both the small and medium-sized enterprise (SME) and industrial and commercial (I&C) UK energy markets. The SME market has traditionally followed trends set by the domestic market although in recent years this pattern has reversed, with the SME sector heavily influencing the rest of the market. Currently SME customers are largely supplied by key domestic utility providers – including Scottish Power, Scottish and Southern, E.ON, npower and EDF – as well as smaller independents.

In contrast, the I&C market sees specialists taking a large part of the market share with brands such as Gaz de France, Shell Gas Direct, British Energy and Total Gas & Power having high profiles in the market. All contracts are given bespoke prices on

a fixed term basis, with switching websites having little influence on decision making.

Another key market for British Gas Business is the provision of related services for business, including insurance, energy management and energy efficiency products.

The energy market has been extremely volatile over the last three years, particularly in 2008. British Gas Business has maintained its footing, however, continuing to lead the small business market – traditionally the brand's heartland – with a 33 per cent share. In recent years, it has also increased its share in the middle and I&C markets.

Achievements

In 2007, British Gas and British Gas Business were able to offer the largest energy price

reductions among the six main suppliers. In 2008, British Gas followed this by achieving the lowest carbon intensity figures among the big six domestic suppliers, for the fourth consecutive year, with CO_2 emissions of 0.368kg/kWh – a further reduction on its 2007 figure.

A key factor in British Gas Business' success is its investment in its people, allowing and encouraging employees to grow and prosper within a supportive environment. This has been recognised by its placement in the 50 Best Workplaces in the UK 2008 index, published in the Financial Times, for the fourth year running.

In the same year British Gas Business won a Royal Society for the Prevention of Accidents (RoSPA) Silver Health & Safety Award and was

1948	1986	1994	1997	1999	2001
The Gas Act is introduced, creating a nationalised gas industry throughout England, Scotland and Wales – The Gas Board organisation is formed.	Competition opens up for large gas customers who use more than 25,000 therms of gas per year and then, six years later, for those using over 2,500 therms.	The Contract Trading division (later called Business Gas) is established in March after a British Gas restructure.	British Gas is separated into Centrica and BG plc. Business Gas transfers to Centrica within the British Gas Trading division.	In September, Business Gas enters the commercial electricity market.	B2B (trading as British Gas and Business Gas) acquires Enron Direct Limited for £96.4 million with a portfolio of 160,000 commercial electricity customers.

a finalist for the Health and Wellbeing Award at the HR Excellence Awards. It was also a regional finalist in the Yakult Healthy Workplace Awards in 2007. Furthermore, British Gas Business was short-listed in three categories at The National Sales Awards 2009 and was nominated for B2B Marketing's 2008 Best Internal Campaign award – building on the success of its corporate marketing manager who scooped Marketer of the Year in 2007.

Product

British Gas Business has been supplying gas to businesses for generations, but now also supplies electricity to more than half a million business customer supply points. The company has a workforce of more than 2,000 people, all dedicated to providing business customers with the energy products and service they need – from arranging new connections through to offering account-managed, day-to-day energy support.

In response to a growing frustration among Britain's SMEs at the lack of flexible insurance solutions, British Gas Business has launched the first dedicated online business insurance comparison service for small firms: Insurance-for-Business. Research revealed that while more than half of all SMEs want to purchase their business insurance over the internet, the absence of a bespoke service has seen only 15 per cent buy online (Source: Finaccord 2006). British Gas Business' service changes this situation by providing a fast, easy route to a wide choice of business insurance from some of the UK's most trusted insurers.

Recent Developments

As a result of customer research, during 2007/08 British Gas Business extended its account management service to provide dedicated and personalised support for all SME customers as well as its I&C customers – the only business supplier to do so.

The company also responded to customer concerns regarding inaccurate meter readings and is now the leading provider of Smart Meters to its business customers. By sending automated readings and helping to monitor and track usage, Smart Meters are especially useful for larger I&C customers who can then identify ways to save energy.

The acquisition of BMSi in October 2008 strengthened British Gas Business' capabilities in energy management. It is extending the portfolio of products and services it offers to customers, helping them to control and reduce their energy use. The Energy360 product offering will include a range of energy efficient and green technology products, energy monitoring and control products, as well as energy auditing software.

Promotion

The TV advertising for the British Gas brand impacts business and domestic customers alike. A more tailored approach is taken for communications to business customers, reflecting the specific messages for this audience. Targeted and timely campaigns inform SME customers about energy issues and ways to save energy, prompted through online and direct marketing channels.

The I&C energy market requires a different approach; getting to the key decision maker is a tougher task with gate-keepers, boardrooms and complex business structures to contend with. Accurate data and stand-out

communications are essential to secure success, remaining in the purchaser's mind for a long time, ready to be recalled when fixed term contracts come up for renewal.

Developing relationships with key partners such as the Federation of Small Businesses (FSB) and EEF, providing engineering and manufacturing support and advice for businesses, helps British Gas Business to reach key customers, as does attendance at events such as Business Startup and The Restaurant Show as well as sponsorship of the Southern Football League.

Brand Values

British Gas Business places its people at the heart of its brand promise – 'Energy experts powering British business'. It aims to be approachable and attentive to the needs of its customers, committed to getting things right first time and to providing enterprising services that make real improvements; allowing its customers to get on with running their own businesses.

britishgas.co.uk/business

Things you didn't know about British Gas Business

British Gas Business' biggest customer uses enough gas per year to supply the whole of Oxford with domestic gas.

British Gas Business supplies electricity to more than half a million business customer supply points.

In 2008, British Gas had the lowest carbon intensity figures among the six main domestic suppliers.

In November 2008, British Gas Business was presented with a Green Apple Award for its successful work in environmental best practice, having reduced the energy consumption of its offices by 10 per cent.

2002
Electricity Direct is acquired for £63 million with a portfolio of 97,000 commercial electricity customers.

2007
The British Gas Business brand is revitalised and all business customers are given their own account manager. Insurance-for-Business is also launched.

2008
British Gas Business is named as one of the FT's 50 Best Workplaces in the UK, for the fourth consecutive year.

Also in 2008, British Gas Business acquires BMSi, is appointed as supplier to the customers of E4B and purchases the customer contracts of BizzEnergy.

British Gypsum is a major authority in the UK construction industry and the country's leading manufacturer and supplier of gypsum-based plastering and drylining solutions. With a long history of providing innovative, cost-effective and reliable products that meet the demands of the construction industry, the company is renowned for its pioneering work in training and product development as well as its forward-thinking strategy on sustainable development.

Market

British Gypsum is the market leader in the supply of interior building solutions for the residential, commercial and RMI (refurbishment, maintenance and improvement) sectors of the construction industry and has used its substantial expertise to develop the UK's leading range of wall, wall lining, floor, ceiling and encasement systems.

Five major manufacturing plants in Barrow-upon-Soar (Leicestershire), East Leake (Leicestershire), Kirkby Thore (Cumbria), Robertsbridge (East Sussex) and Sherburn-in-Elmet (North Yorkshire) provide nationwide manufacturing and distribution capabilities, serving the needs of a diverse customer base from specifiers, architects, contractors and housebuilders to specialist distributors, builders' merchants and DIY outlets.

Achievements

In 2006, British Gypsum was named Best Overall Supplier by Travis Perkins and Sustainability Supplier of the Year by AMEC. In presenting the AMEC award for the company's work on Gateshead's Queen Elizabeth Hospital, AMEC's managing director said the project "demonstrated the kind of environmental results that can be achieved through good design, careful specification of products and British Gypsum's innovative Plasterboard Recycling Service".

This strong reputation stems from the company's determination to bring innovative, sustainable products to the country's building projects. British Gypsum pioneered the introduction of lightweight, fast-track building solutions in the UK and has had a significant impact on the residential and commercial built environment. Prestigious projects include The O2 arena, Emirates Stadium, St Pancras International and Putney Wharf.

The company's training and testing facilities reflect its market-leading status. Its Drywall Academy is a centre of excellence for training, with NVQ accreditation and Construction Industry Training Board recognition. Around 6,000 people pass through its three purpose-built training centres each year, gaining specialist knowledge in all aspects of drylining. As well as equipping contractors, organisations and its own employees with the latest industry skills, British Gypsum has been pioneering merchant training for more than 30 years.

In addition, British Gypsum's UKAS-approved testing laboratories are the best-equipped and most advanced drywall testing facilities in Europe. As a result, more than 10,000 tests and substantiation reports underpin the performance of drylining products and systems across the industry.

1917	1964	1967	1972	1975	1978
The British Plaster Board company is founded.	Gypsum interests are amalgamated to form British Gypsum.	British Gypsum opens its first dedicated training facility.	The White Book is first published.	British Gypsum launches the first performance plasterboard.	British Gypsum introduces metal framing into drylining systems.

hailed as a world-class example of best practice in business planning.

Product

British Gypsum offers a range of more than 700 products including Gyproc plasterboard, Thistle plaster, Gypframe metal, specialist board products and ceiling products. In each area, the company is constantly reviewing, improving and adding to its products to ensure it has the most comprehensive and innovative offering available.

Customers benefit from a complete package of goods and services that includes on-site technical supervision and the SpecSure lifetime system warranty. Designed to deliver peace of mind, SpecSure guarantees systems are built from the highest-quality components, rigorously tested to provide guaranteed acoustic, fire, impact and thermal performance to meet even the most demanding of building requirements.

Supported by its Drywall Academy, British Gypsum provides the most comprehensive technical and training support package in the industry. From initial project design and planning through to site installation and beyond, specialist teams of technical experts deliver quality technical advice every day.

The company's service even extends to waste collection and recycling. In 2001, it invested heavily in launching its Plasterboard Recycling Service, marking a major innovation for an industry faced with escalating waste costs. Now an established commercial venture, the scheme collects waste from construction sites and delivers it to one of two dedicated, cutting-edge recycling plants. Here, raw materials are extracted that can be fed back into the manufacturing process without affecting quality.

Recent Developments

Sustainability and environmental considerations are given real emphasis in British Gypsum's extensive Corporate Social Responsibility (CSR) programme; the company is committed to minimising its impact on natural resources and promoting sustainable development. The programme has earned British Gypsum the prestigious Taylor Woodrow Sustainability Award 2007 and was short-listed in the 2007 Building Commitment to the Environment Awards. In 2008 the company also achieved runner-up in the Shepherd Construction Supplier of the Year Awards.

British Gypsum's products and systems are continually evolving. Recent launches include Glasroc Rigidur super-impact-resistant board, part of the Gypwall EXTREME system for high-traffic public areas; Gyproc SoundCoat, an innovative sealer providing superior acoustic performance; and Thistle Durafinish, a revolutionary new super-hardwearing finish plaster which greatly improves resistance to all common types of day-to-day impact.

Reinforcing the company's policy of continuous improvement, November 2008 saw it become the first plaster and plasterboard manufacturer to achieve ISO 14001:2002 environmental management systems certification across all manufacturing and mining sites in the UK.

Major investments have also been made in the company's manufacturing plants at East Leake and Sherburn-in-Elmet. In June 2007, £120 million was spent on significantly increasing capacity for both plaster and plasterboard products, ensuring it will continue to stay on top of rising demand. The two plants are recognised as among the most advanced in the world and the investment has been

Promotion

The strength of British Gypsum's brand lies in the close partnerships the company establishes with clients, building owners, designers, merchants and contractors. An important part of this is its commitment to making comprehensive, practical information readily available to the construction industry.

The company's website alone receives 50,000 visits per month, with all brochures, product data sheets and even the company's renowned White Book and Site Book available to download. The White Book is seen as the industry's leading publication on drylining, while the Site Book gives valuable guidance on site use and installation. An in-house design team also produces technical guides tailored to specific construction sectors.

Continuing its CSR strategy, British Gypsum sponsors CRASH, the construction industry's charity for the homeless. The company donates funds, provides materials to build shelters and encourages employees to take part in local projects.

Brand Values

British Gypsum's success is grounded in a set of clearly defined guidelines: professional commitment, respect for others, integrity, loyalty and solidarity.

british-gypsum.com

Things you didn't know about British Gypsum

It would take the water from four Olympic-size swimming pools to mix the amount of plaster delivered by British Gypsum every week.

Every day, British Gypsum delivers enough bagged plaster to make a pile 35 times the height of Canary Wharf Tower.

British Gypsum is part of Saint-Gobain, the world's largest manufacturer of plasterboard and plaster.

The Drywall Academy advice line receives more than 10,000 enquiries every month.

1991
The UK's largest plaster mining and manufacturing facility is built at Barrow-upon-Soar, Leicestershire.

2001
British Gypsum introduces a Plasterboard Recycling Service for its customers.

2008
British Gypsum gains full ISO 14001:2004 certification for environmental management systems across its mine and manufacturing sites in the UK.

BSI Group is a global independent business services organisation that inspires confidence and delivers assurance to customers with standards-based solutions. The Group's key offerings are: the development and sale of private, national and international standards; management systems assessment and certification; testing and certification of products and services; performance management software solutions; and training services.

Market

BSI works with clients operating in a myriad of sectors including communications, construction, engineering, electronics, food and drink, agriculture, consumer goods, banking and public sector. In order to compete and inspire their customers' trust, BSI's clients – which include 75 per cent of FTSE 100 companies, 42 per cent of Fortune 500 companies and 42 per cent of companies listed on the Hang Seng – rely on industry benchmarking and quality assurance, and the BSI Kitemark® is seen as one of the most trustworthy marks to be gained. BSI is one of the world's leading providers of standards-based solutions, covering every aspect of the modern economy.

Achievements

Founded in 1901, BSI Group today employs more than 2,300 staff and generated a turnover of £179 million in 2007. It services clients in 120 countries and assists nations such as Albania, Russia, Serbia and Sierra Leone in developing and improving their emerging standardisation infrastructures.

The organisation produces an average of 2,000 standards per year and has recently published the world's first standard for risk management, BS 31100, and business continuity management, BS 25999.

BSI has won a number of recent awards including, in 2008, a Continuity, Insurance & Risk (CIR) Award for Industry Advancement for its work in developing BS 25999 and the title of Best Safety Initiative

at the Fleet News Awards for the Thatcham BSI Kitemark® scheme for vehicle body repair. In 2009, BSI's Kitemark® has also been recognised as a Business Superbrand in its own right, for the second consecutive year.

The ISO 9000 quality series was developed from British Standard BS 5750, first published in 1979 and is recognised as the world's most successful standard; adopted by more than 950,000 organisations in 175 countries. Furthermore, the most widely accepted environmental management systems standard, ISO 14001, was derived from BS 7750 and has been implemented in 148 countries.

Product

BSI operates globally through three divisions: BSI British Standards, BSI Management Systems and BSI Product Services.

BSI British Standards develops standardisation solutions to meet the needs of UK business. It works with businesses, consumers and the Government to represent UK interests and to make sure that British, European and international standards are useful, relevant and authoritative. BSI British Standards' products and services help organisations to successfully implement best practice, manage business-critical decisions and achieve operational excellence.

BSI Management Systems is one of the world's largest certification bodies: over 64,000 certified locations, clients in more than 120 countries and market leader in the UK and North America. The division provides assessment, certification, verification and training services in management disciplines including business continuity,

1901	1903	1929	1953	1979	1992
BSI Group is founded as the Engineering Standards Committee (ESC). One of the first standards to be published is to reduce the number of sizes of tramway rails.	The Kitemark® is first registered as a trademark.	The ESC is awarded a Royal Charter and in 1931, the name British Standards Institution (BSI) is adopted.	In the post-war era, more demand for consumer standardisation work leads to the introduction of the Kitemark® for domestic products.	BS 5750, now known as ISO 9001, is introduced to help companies build quality and safety into the way they work. The Certification mark is also introduced.	BSI publishes the world's first environmental management systems standard, BS 7750 – now known as ISO 14001.

environment, food safety, health and safety, information security, integrated management, quality and social responsibility. Its award-winning Entropy Software™ provides auditable solutions to improve environmental, social and economic performance.

BSI Product Services is best known for the Kitemark® which is the UK's oldest and most trusted product quality mark. The division provides product and services testing and certification to ensure that vital safety and performance requirements are met. BSI Product Services provides CE marking under 17 European Directives for companies wishing to trade in the EU.

Recent Developments

BSI Group's website was relaunched in 2007 with full ecommerce capabilities, including all 40,000 standards and publications available to purchase online for the first time.

In 2007 BSI and Thatcham developed PAS 125, a specification for vehicle bodywork repair, with the ensuing Thatcham BSI Kitemark® scheme providing independent certification that a bodyshop is competent to safely repair vehicles in accordance with the standard. Another automotive sector development is the Kitemark® scheme for Garage Services

which ensures that the standards of PAS 80 are met and maintained for the servicing and repair of vehicles.

The same year saw the introduction of the world's first standard for sustainable event management, BS 8901. The following year the standard was used as the basis for the GetGreenGo™ initiative, BSI's sustainable events challenge for UK schools.

In 2008, BSI became one of the first organisations to receive global accreditation to deliver certification against the business continuity management standard BS 25999; it went on to be the first in the world to issue a BS 25999 certificate. It was also awarded global accreditation to deliver certification against ISO/IEC 20000 for IT service management.

In April, PAS 74 was published in conjunction with BSI's Kitemark® for Child Safety Online. The Kitemark® scheme was developed by BSI in partnership with the Home Office and Ofcom and aims to provide parents and carers with the ability to identify the most effective internet filtering products currently on the market.

A significant development for BSI is its recent partnership with the Carbon Trust and Defra, working together to develop a standard methodology for the measurement of the embodied greenhouse gases in products and services. The draft standard (PAS 2050) was piloted by nine companies, including Coca-Coca and Cadbury Schweppes and was published following extensive consultation in October 2008.

Promotion

Few organisations have a stronger claim than BSI Group to the assertion that it raises standards worldwide; for this reason it has

chosen 'raising standards worldwide™' as its strapline, which was deployed in 2006.

In July 2002 a single BSI brand was created and the organisation now has a consistent and clear visual identity, with all BSI staff working to maintain the standard. To reinforce the brand internally, BSI's brand identity website – rebuilt in 2008 – is a crucial tool, making the corporate guidelines easily accessible to staff and suppliers.

BSI's external marketing focuses on achieving the long term goal of a coherent global brand identity. Public relations plays a key role, as does BSI's business magazine, Business Standards, with a readership of 101,000 reaching into the business community.

Brand Values

BSI Group's core brand values are integrity, innovation and independence. They are the foundation of the BSI brand, supporting the organisation as it works towards its vision of inspiring confidence and delivering assurance to all customers through standards-based solutions.

BSI continually strives to deliver its brand values, with the aim of building a powerful, globally recognised brand, satisfying the needs of all stakeholders.

bsigroup.com

Things you didn't know about BSI

According to a YouGov survey in August 2008, 49 per cent of UK adults look for a Kitemark® when choosing products or services to buy.

The original BSI committee met for the first time on the day Queen Victoria died – 22nd January 1901.

BSI Management Systems UK is the world's first carbon neutral certification body.

2002	2006	2007	2008
KPMG's ISO registration business in North America is acquired, making BSI Group the largest certification body in the region.	BSI acquires German certification company NIS ZERT, UK and Canadian-based software solutions company Entropy International Ltd and Australia's Benchmark Certification Pty Ltd.	BSI publishes the world's first standard for business continuity management certification, BS 25999-2, and BS 8901 for sustainable event management.	BSI publishes the world's first standard for assessing the life cycle greenhouse gas (GHG) emissions of goods and services: PAS 2050.

Operating in 176 countries around the globe, BT is one of the world's leading providers of communications solutions and services. The company's principal activities include networked IT services, local, national and international telecommunications services, and higher-value broadband and internet products and services. BT consists primarily of four lines of business: BT Global Services, Openreach, BT Retail and BT Wholesale.

Market

BT operates in a thriving, multi-trillion pound industry that spans the whole world. In recent years the global communications market has been focused on convergence, whereby the boundaries between telcos, IT companies, software businesses, hardware manufacturers and broadcasters have become intertwined to create a new communications industry – an industry driven by the relentless evolution of technology and insatiable customer demand for innovative communications solutions.

Achievements

BT has successfully transformed itself in recent times. It has evolved from being a supplier of telephony services to become a leading provider of innovative communications products, services and solutions. Its business customers range from multinational, multi-site corporations to SMEs and start-ups.

More than 80 per cent of the FTSE 100 and 40 per cent of the largest Fortune Top 50 companies rely on BT for networking, applications and system integration. The National Health Service (NHS), the Post Office, T-Mobile, 3, Nestlé, Fiat, Microsoft, Philips, Unilever and the Bavarian National Government are just some of the organisations working with BT to maximise the power of networked IT and communications services.

BT has been a driving force behind the success of 'Broadband Britain'. Thanks to the company's investment, nearly every home in Britain now has access to broadband. In July 2008,

BT announced plans for the UK's largest ever investment in fibre-based, super-fast broadband. The £1.5 billion programme will deliver a range of services for customers giving them top speeds of up to 100 Mb/s with the potential for speeds of more than 1,000 Mb/s in the future.

In September 2008, BT was recognised – for the eighth year running – as the world's top telecommunications company in the Dow Jones Sustainability Index (DJSI). In addition, BT has been granted a Royal Warrant to supply communications, broadband and network services for Her Majesty The Queen. This

let's make a **better** world

took effect in January 2007 and is approved for use for the next five years.

Product

BT provides a wide range of world-class communications solutions for all types of business organisation – from sole trader start-ups to multi-site global enterprises. The company's vision is to be dedicated to helping customers thrive in a changing world, through easy-to-use products and services that are tailored to their needs.

For business customers, traditional products such as calls, analogue/digital lines and private circuits are combined with products and services such as networking and network

1984	1991	2003	2005	2006	2008
BT is privatised making it the only state-owned telecommunications company to be privatised in Europe.	British Telecom is restructured and relaunches as BT.	BT unveils its current corporate identity and brand values, reflecting the aspirations of a technologically innovative future.	Following the Telecommunications Strategic Review (TSR), BT signs legally-binding undertakings with Ofcom to help create a better regulatory framework.	Openreach launches and is responsible for managing the UK access network on behalf of the telecommunications industry.	BT becomes the Official Communications Services Partner and a Sustainability Partner for The London 2012 Olympic and Paralympic Games.

management, broadband, mobility, CRM, applications management and hosting as well as desktop services. Smaller businesses benefit from BT's IT Manager service and the social networking site, BT Tradespace, which is designed to help businesses interact with customers as well as each other.

BT Business Total Broadband allows UK businesses of all sizes to turn their BT Business Hub into a BT Openzone wireless hotspot at no extra cost. This will allow anyone visiting their premises – be it an office, shop, restaurant or depot – to access the internet over a secure channel.

For larger and global organisations, BT Global Services provides a range of specialist network-centric propositions and practices spanning high performance networking, applications management, outsourcing and managed services, and business transformation. BT Global Services serves corporate and government customers worldwide, and wholesale customers outside the UK.

Recent Developments
In recent years, BT has transformed itself from a narrowband company into a broadband one. It has now embarked on the next stage of its transformation – one that is just as important and equally radical – moving from being a hardware-based business to becoming a software-driven company. This means instantly delivering new software services for customers at the push of a button rather than through a process of screwdrivers, rewiring and customer visits. This will dramatically increase the speed at which BT can design new services and deliver them to its customers.

BT is also currently rolling out its 21st Century Network (21CN), the world's most advanced next generation network.

Promotion
BT is the Official Communications Services Partner and a Sustainability Partner for The London 2012 Olympic and Paralympic Games. This puts BT at the heart of the biggest event Britain will stage in the next decade. BT will be integral in helping London to stage a 'Digital Games', responsible for providing key communications services to the operational workforce and at Games venues. In addition, BT will receive exclusive marketing rights to use the London 2012 brand within its category.

In April 2008, BT launched a new campaign aimed at businesses and featuring Peter Jones of Dragons' Den fame alongside the 1980s anti-heroes, The Gremlins. The TV advert

showed Jones struggling with IT problems while working late in the office and announced BT's 24-hour IT and communications support offering, which is available to all BT Business customers. The campaign ran across TV, print, posters and online.

In sponsorship, BT is title sponsor of 'BT Team Ellen' – the sailing team headed up by renowned sailor Ellen MacArthur. The sponsorship agreement means that Ellen is the ambassador for BT's worldwide corporate social responsibility programme.

BT Global Services' Bigger Thinking campaign positions BT as the thought leader and the partner of choice for networked IT services across the globe. It demonstrates to a senior executive audience that BT understands the big issues that are of concern to them in their business. The campaign is centred on biggerthinking.com and incorporates television, print and posters across Europe, the US, India and China.

Brand Values
BT's corporate identity defines the kind of company it is today – and the one it needs to be in the future. Central to that identity is a commitment to create ways to help customers thrive in a changing world. To do this, BT focuses on 'living' its brand values

which are as follows: Trustworthy – doing what it says it will; Helpful – working as one team; Inspiring – creating new possibilities; Straightforward – making things clear; Heart – believing in what it does.

The BT strapline – 'Bringing it all together' – aims to convey leadership in the way in which BT enables global business customers to profit from convergence.

bt.com

CBRE
CB RICHARD ELLIS

CB Richard Ellis is the global leader in commercial real estate services. The company advises property owners, investors and occupiers on every aspect of their real estate strategies, assisting them in the development, buying, selling, financing, leasing, valuing and managing of assets and providing a broad range of consultancy services across every major market in the world.

HOW TO OPEN DOORS ALL OVER THE WORLD

Property advice with a truly global reach.
cbre.co.uk

Market

Over the last few decades, the increasing attractiveness of property as a robust, low-risk return asset class has led to a sharp increase in investor demand for commercial real estate across the world. Trophy buildings such as General Motors' landmark office in New York, HSBC's Canary Wharf Tower in London and the Bank of Santander's Madrid headquarters have commanded global interest and record prices. With unrivalled access to the global investment market, CB Richard Ellis has successfully helped its clients to capitalise on this rapid growth, transacting more deals than any other advisor – US$264 billion transacted worldwide in 2007.

Inevitably, over more recent months, global economic and financial turmoil and the

NO ONE KNOWS LONDON QUITE LIKE CBRE

associated reappraisal of risk have curtailed the pace of growth and led to repricing across the property sector. Commercial real estate, however, remains attractive relative to other, more volatile asset classes and investors will continue to look to property for stable returns in the longer term.

Beyond the investment markets, globalisation and consolidation have also had a significant impact on the way that corporates approach their real estate strategies. The world's largest organisations are increasingly choosing to centralise and outsource their international property management requirements to service providers like CB Richard Ellis to improve efficiency and lower costs. Today the company manages in excess of two billion sq ft of building space around the world and more than 70 per cent of corporates in the FTSE 100 have turned to CB Richard Ellis for real estate consulting advice.

Achievements

In 2008 CB Richard Ellis made history by becoming the first property services company to enter the Fortune 500, debuting at number 404. Other recent accolades include being named one of the 50 'best in class' companies by BusinessWeek (for the second consecutive year) and the company's ranking as the top

global commercial real estate services provider in the Euromoney Liquid Real Estate Awards 2008. In addition to its client service delivery, the company is also recognised for its team spirit and internal culture and was named the Best Company to Work for in Ireland in 2008 (100-250 employees category) and one of the top 10 Best Workplaces in France by the Great Place to Work® Institute.

CB Richard Ellis is also the first commercial real estate services company to join The Climate Group and is currently helping corporate occupiers, investors and developers across the world to improve their energy performance and meet government policy and environmental legislation. In parallel, the company is working towards its own goal of becoming carbon neutral by 2010.

Product

CB Richard Ellis advises on all aspects of real estate in every major market in the world, providing a full suite of transaction-based and consulting services. These include strategic advice and execution for property sales and leasing; corporate services; property facilities and project management; mortgage banking; appraisal and valuation; development services; investment management; and

1773	1960s	1998	2003	2004	2006
Richard Ellis is founded at 126 Fenchurch Street, London.	International expansion begins for London's Richard Ellis with the opening of offices in Paris, Brussels, Australia, Canada and South Africa.	US commercial real estate services leader, CB Commercial, acquires Richard Ellis and the business subsequently changes its name to CB Richard Ellis.	CB Richard Ellis merges with US leader Insignia/ESG to become one of the world's leading commercial real estate services firms.	CB Richard Ellis Group completes IPO and begins trading on the New York Stock Exchange.	CB Richard Ellis debuts on the Forbes Global 2000, the only commercial real estate services firm on the list.

research and consulting. This breadth of service is matched by unrivalled market analysis and intelligence, a pool of talented and diverse people and a proven track record in all major business sectors including retail, industrial and logistics, financial services, automotive, airports and aviation, hotels, life sciences, media and more.

Recent Developments

Continuous investment in new services, new markets and new people defines CB Richard Ellis. Despite being founded more than 230 years ago, the company is still celebrated for being innovative today.

Over recent years, the firm has focused on strengthening its service offering across geographic borders and service lines to meet growing client needs for a truly international, integrated real estate solution. Since 2005, the firm has acquired 52 businesses and opened many new offices worldwide in both traditional and emerging markets, most recently adding to its presence in Italy, Romania, Australia, Bahrain and Canada.

Geographic expansion has been matched by a raft of new services designed to help clients adapt to changing market conditions. More recently these have included the creation of a dedicated Insolvency and Corporate Recovery team – to advise banks and other investors on how to extract returns from struggling real estate investments – and a Debt Advisory Service incorporating more than 120 dedicated finance professionals in over 35 markets. For those clients wanting to invest in property without wanting to own the actual asset, CB Richard Ellis has also established a joint venture with GFI to develop the first property derivatives market in Europe.

Promotion

All CB Richard Ellis marketing and advertising campaigns endorse the company's belief in 'going beyond' – one of its key brand values – while also reinforcing its commitment to continuous improvement. As one of the world's leading property advisers, consistency in communication is essential; CB Richard Ellis has invested heavily in aligning all internal and external communications to the company strategy and in making advertising campaigns relevant to the brand's target audience. Adverts for a 2008 campaign in The Times, for example, focused on sustainability and energy – issues that are increasingly important to its clients.

Another key advertising campaign in 2008 recognised the increasing globalisation of clients and their changing buying strategies. It therefore centred on highlighting the brand's

extensive global network: 'Two thirds of the world is covered by water, the other third by us.' The campaign featured posters in secondary city airport locations where clients may not necessarily expect the company to have offices.

Brand Values

CB Richard Ellis is built around the core idea of continuous improvement. This fundamental value has become ingrained in the company's DNA, providing the founding philosophy on which everything else is built. Continuous improvement is a company ethos that drives its pursuit of creating value through new opportunities, new ideas and new solutions to customers. CB Richard Ellis aims to always put its customer at the heart of everything it sets out to achieve; to make good its corporate promise to deliver exceptional service and value for money.

cbre.eu

Things you didn't know about CB Richard Ellis

CB Richard Ellis manages in excess of two billion sq ft of building space around the world.

In 2008 CB Richard Ellis advised the US$2.9 billion sale of New York's landmark General Motors building – the largest single-building sale of all time.

Eighty-five per cent of the world's top corporations choose to work with CB Richard Ellis.

In 2008 CB Richard Ellis made history when it became the first property services company to enter the Fortune 500, debuting at number 404.

2007
CB Richard Ellis announces its commitment to becoming carbon neutral by 2010.

2008
The company is named one of the BusinessWeek 50 'best in class' companies for the second year running, sitting in 11th place.

Also in 2008, CB Richard Ellis becomes the first property services company to enter the Fortune 500, debuting at number 404.

A UTC Fire & Security Company

One hundred and ninety years of history and innovation have made Chubb into a global leader in security and fire protection. It supplies systems and services to most of the FTSE 100 companies as well as the highest levels of Government, defence, banking and industrial companies. Each year Chubb performs 150,000 security systems site inspections, services over four million fire extinguishers and provides more than 12 million personnel hours of security.

Market

Chubb is one of the most respected brand names in the fire safety and security solutions market, which is highly fragmented and fiercely competitive. The company's strengths are underpinned by a global infrastructure, a highly skilled and experienced workforce, a diverse range of quality products and services and a reputation for service excellence. Chubb protects premises, property and assets throughout the UK and worldwide, operating across four continents.

Achievements

From inventing the Detector Lock in 1818, to launching one of the first dedicated CCTV monitoring centres in 1999, Chubb's rich history of innovation continues today. For instance, Chubb was one of the first national security installers to adopt EN Standards for the installation of monitored intruder and holdup alarm systems when British Standards were phased out in 2005. Furthermore, in 2007 Chubb was presented with a Business Commitment to the Environment Award for

its groundbreaking extinguisher recycling programme, which processes more than 500,000 units every year.

As well as protecting day-to-day services and structures, Chubb is also responsible for securing some of the world's most treasured and prestigious locations. In the UK, Chubb is entrusted with protecting national icons such as Westminster Abbey, the British Museum, Alnwick Castle (the filming location of Harry Potter's school, Hogwarts) and Diamond Synchrotron (the largest scientific facility in the UK).

Product

Formerly associated with locks and safes, and a household name since the 1840s, Chubb now provides electronic security and fire protection services to businesses of all sizes, worldwide.

Chubb's main product offerings include electronic security, monitoring and response services, fire protection, fire detection and fire suppression systems. Chubb's ability to integrate its products and services into tailored, comprehensive solutions, makes it uniquely positioned to meet a broad range of customer requirements.

Chubb invests extensively in service innovation and technical development. By combining in-house design expertise with components sourced from some of the world's leading technology suppliers, Chubb is able to remain at the cutting-edge of system design and service improvement. In recent years Chubb has introduced customers to a number of

1818	1835	1870s	1945	1997	2000
Charles and Jeremiah Chubb respond to the increasing demand for greater security by inventing the original secure lock mechanism, patented as the Detector Lock.	The Chubb brothers patent the burglar-resistant safe.	A Time Lock mechanism is developed for protecting vault and safe doors. Although the designs have since been refined, the basic principles of security and quality have remained the same.	Chubb expands its operations overseas and extends its product range into fire protection.	Chubb is sold to Williams plc.	In August, Chubb's Lock Security Group is acquired by Assa Abloy and in November, Chubb de-merges from Williams plc to become Chubb plc.

advancements, such as new wireless technologies, Remote Video Response (RVR) and the trend towards Integrated Security Management (ISM).

Recent Developments

Chubb's RVR service is at the forefront of remote CCTV monitoring. The service remotely monitors CCTV video images from sites over IP networks and provides specialist security protection for large, open and vulnerable sites.

With the advent of Chubb's AFx system, integrated security is no longer only specified for large public sector organisations, such as the Ministry of Defence. More and more Chubb customers are choosing to integrate their security requirements onto a single platform in order to benefit from improved cost efficiencies, greater control and increased flexibility.

The Chubb ControlMaster1000 fire detection system, launched in 2007, has the potential to integrate with building systems and CCTV and is showcased at the Schools for the Future project at the Building Research Establishment. The system design was based on the Chubb Resonance fire detection system, which protects the Eiffel Tower. Chubb provides a total fire risk assessment solution, with a national network of consultants and fire safety training complementing its traditional range of fire protection and fire detection services.

Promotion

Chubb is positioned as the UK's leading brand for security and fire protection. Chubb not only provides bespoke solutions for businesses of all types and sizes, but also commits to keeping customers informed of any legislative changes that could affect the security or fire systems they are operating. This includes running educational seminars and publishing informative guides to support communities across the UK. In addition, since 2003 Chubb has sponsored the Scouts' Fire Safety Badge to help educate children about fire safety issues.

Brand Values

The Chubb brand is one of the most recognised security and fire brands in the world. Throughout its history, the company has demonstrated an ability to perform in new sectors and to incorporate new technologies in order to provide the most advanced and cost effective solutions.

Trust, integrity and strength are Chubb's core brand values. With the backing of its parent company, United Technologies Corporation (UTC), the Chubb brand is set to get even stronger with further investment in local service delivery, product innovation and people development.

Chubb is a national name – delivering at a local level – committed to service excellence.

chubb.co.uk

Things you didn't know about Chubb

In UK prisons, the phrase, 'Chubbing-up for the night' is a commonly used euphemism for 'locking-up for the night'.

The reputation of the Chubb brand has led to it being used as the generic term for security mortice locks, regardless of who the actual manufacturer is.

More than 60,000 Scouts have passed their Fire Safety Badge since 2003.

Chubb is the only national security company able to offer customers the complete security service, including installation, maintenance, monitoring and response services.

Chubb's Keyholding Service responds to more than 300,000 alarm activations each year.

The Chubb logo was originally designed to represent the front of a mortice lock.

2003	2005	2007	2009
In July, Chubb plc is acquired by United Technologies Corporation (UTC).	In April, UTC acquires Kidde plc, forming UTC Fire & Security, the number two global player in the fire safety industry.	In July, UTC increases its share of the UK fire and security market by purchasing Initial Fire and Security, integrating it into Chubb's UK business.	UTC Fire & Security employs more than 43,000 people in 30 countries, with a family of leading global brands including Kidde, Lenel and Chubb.

Chartered Institute of Management Accountants

CIMA is the world's leading and largest professional body of Management Accountants. In 2009, CIMA celebrates 90 years of shaping the future and promoting the science of management accounting. CIMA sponsors leading-edge research and constantly updates its qualification, professional experience requirements and continuing professional development to ensure it remains the most relevant international accounting qualification for business.

Market

CIMA's vision is to have its members driving the world's successful organisations. With 164,000 members and students operating in 161 countries, the qualification produces versatile professionals who have been assessed in a practical business setting and can operate in all areas of organisations, able to use finance skills to provide meaningful analysis, decision support and risk management. An in-depth understanding of the businesses in which they operate ensures an ability to pre-empt and adapt to their changing needs. The strong threads of business governance, ethics and management which run through the CIMA syllabus put members in a position where they are a highly attractive proposition for companies, not-for-profit and public sector organisations alike.

Achievements

CIMA's reputation as a guardian of accounting excellence continues to grow. The institute provides support to some of the world's leading employers. Proof of the institute's success can be found in the quality of employment its members achieve across the world; 33 per cent of CIMA members are currently in senior management positions, 14 per cent are financial controllers and a further 10 per cent are finance directors. Approximately seven per cent have risen to the position of chief executive officer, managing director or another kind of directorship (Source: CIMA member survey 2008). This means that the majority of its members are already in positions where they can make a significant impact on the business world.

Product

When CIMA students begin their studies, they are embarking on a partnership that often continues throughout their working lives. The syllabus covers a wide range of topics including financial and non-financial analysis, risk management, information management, project management and the development of business strategy. This knowledge, combined with the working experience they are required to attain before they fully qualify, provides them with all the key links to career success.

Once CIMA students have shown that they have the appropriate business experience to become fully qualified members of the institute, their journey continues. Under CPD requirements, all members must ensure that they keep up-to-speed with relevant developments in the business world. They must also comply with the institute's code of ethics.

CIMA offers students and members an extensive range of learning resources to promote career success. Management accounting books, brochures, reports, seminars, guides and webcasts are tailored to every stage of professional development.

Recent Developments

CIMA is the only professional accounting qualification to launch a new syllabus

1919	1975	1986	1995	2002	2009
The Institute of Cost and Works Accountants is founded, its objective being to provide the range of information needed to plan and manage modern business.	The institute is granted a Royal Charter.	The institute changes its name to the Chartered Institute of Management Accountants, recognising the importance and commercial relevance of management accountants.	CIMA's members are given the right to use the title, 'Chartered Management Accountant'.	Because of its growth, the institute relocates to its current global headquarters in central London.	CIMA celebrates its 90th anniversary.

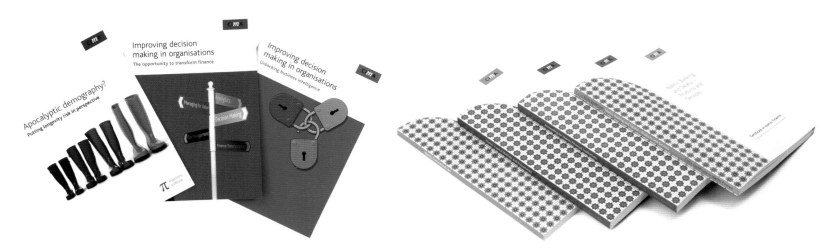

every four years to ensure it remains the most relevant qualification for financially qualified business leaders. Its latest syllabus, launched in December 2008 with the first examinations to be held in 2010, has already received praise from business professionals and academics alike.

2008 also saw the launch of CIMAstudy.com, benefiting CIMA students around the world. A joint venture between CIMA and Elsevier, it provides online, interactive and on-demand training at managerial and strategic levels of the CIMA qualification. Since its launch, students from more than 20 countries have made use of the online tools.

The introduction of a global qualification in Islamic Finance saw CIMA become the first chartered accountancy body to address the demand from the global business community to develop the knowledge and skills required to service this increasingly important market.

In keeping with its global reach, CIMA joined forces with the Institute of Business Ethics to release a global survey on the importance of business ethics within the business world. It was supported by a high profile Global Ethics Debate with internationally renowned ethics expert Dr Noreena Hertz.

With the economy in recession, a CIMA report explains the difference a management accountant can make to effective decision-making and risk management in public sector organisations. 'Doing the Business: Managing

Performance in the Public Sector' explores performance management strategies in the public sector to provide best practice advice.

CIMA's Innovation and Development programme has produced several high level reports to influence the boardroom agenda. These include 'Apocalyptic demography? Putting longevity risk in perspective', published in association with the Pensions Institute at Cass Business School and 'The Financial Reporting Supply Chain'. This report, calling for less complexity in corporate reporting, arms finance directors around the world with a snapshot of their peers' opinions on how financial reporting needs to move forward.

Promotion

CIMA continues to reassert its role as the finance qualification for business through its global corporate advertising campaign. The institute has collaborated with some of the world's most influential organisations to highlight how CIMA works with them to provide the skills to help drive success in their organisation.

The CIMA professional qualification was recognised in 2008 as equivalent to a master's degree, according to the independent UK agency responsible for government scoring of immigrants' qualifications. This has enabled CIMA to further promote its qualification around the world to prospective students. Meanwhile, promotion of the range of support available to CIMA students was given a boost by the launch of an e-magazine, Velocity.

The CIMA Economic Survey, launched in 2008, has helped to raise the profile of the CIMA brand itself. This regular survey garners the opinions of 200 CIMA finance directors across the UK, working in manufacturing, retail, financial services and the public sector.

Brand Values

CIMA is positioned as the qualification for business with a management accounting focus. It is driven by five core values: customer-focused, professional, open, accountable and innovative. These values aim to ensure a consistent company culture that is supported by all CIMA employees.

CIMA has also identified a purpose, vision and mission to enhance its sense of direction. The institute's purpose is to strive for the ever greater employability of its members. Its vision is to see CIMA members driving the world's most successful companies and its mission is to be the first choice for employers in the qualification and development of professional accountants in business.

cimaglobal.com

Things you didn't know about CIMA

The first president of CIMA was Lord Leverhulme, the grandson of William Hesketh Lever, founder of Lever Bros (now Unilever).

Derek du Pré, father of world famous cellist Jacqueline du Pré, was the secretary of the institute between 1958 and 1964. Jacqueline practised at 63 Portland Place, CIMA's then headquarters, prior to her debut in 1961 at Wigmore Hall.

Leading CIMA members include Andrew Higginson, Tesco's finance director; Douglas Flint, chief financial officer at HSBC; and Hanif Lalani, CEO of BT Group plc's Global Services division.

In 2008 CIMA qualified its 75,000th member.

CNN is the world's leading global 24-hour news network, delivered across a range of multimedia platforms including television, mobile phones and the internet. Launched in 1985, the channel's output comprises its trademark breaking news, business news, sports news, current affairs and analysis, documentaries and feature programming. CNN viewers are global citizens; mostly business decision makers and opinion leaders, educated, well travelled and with high personal income.

Market

Since CNN pioneered the genre of 24-hour news, the pan-regional news market has expanded to include more than 100 news channels worldwide. CNN has remained at the forefront of this increasingly competitive market, warding off competition from domestic and pan-regional news services with its growing international newsgathering operation and intricate network of regionalised services and affiliates.

According to the European Media and Marketing Survey (EMS) 2008, CNN International continues to be the international news channel of choice for reaching the European elite, leading all international news channels in monthly reach (EMS Select 2008) and is also market leader for combined TV and online monthly reach, confirming its top positioning for connecting with audiences in today's digital world.

CNN continues to attract a range of high profile advertisers with its cross-platform advert sales offering, one of the most comprehensive and innovative in the industry.

Online is currently the fastest-growing driver of the advert sales business, drawing major clients such as ARTOC, Philips, Zenith Bank and Ericsson, while TV remains strong.

In 2008, CNN's Tourism Advertising Solutions & Knowledge (TASK) Group continued to deliver 'best of breed' advice, information and intelligence for clients to enhance their brand building efforts.

Achievements

In 1980, CNN launched as a single US network available to 1.7 million homes. Twenty-seven years later, CNN's 22 branded networks and services are available to more than two billion people in over 200 countries and territories worldwide, distributed across a range of platforms including mobile and IPTV, over and above the landmark television service and international website, CNN.com.

CNN has become synonymous with breaking news, acting as a visual history book for the world. As stories from across the globe have hit the headlines, CNN has been there: Tiananmen Square, the 11th September terrorist attacks in the US and the ensuing war against terror in Afghanistan, the July 2005 London bombings, Saddam Hussein's trial and

1980	**1985**	**1989**	**1995**	**1997**	**1999**
CNN launches on 1st June as a single US network; the brainchild of media entrepreneur Ted Turner, it becomes the first round-the-clock news channel.	CNN International launches, along with live 24-hour transmission to Europe.	CNN becomes available worldwide, 24 hours a day, with transmission via a Soviet satellite to Africa, the Middle East, the Indian subcontinent and South East Asia.	CNN.com, the world's first major news website, is launched. This is followed by the all-encompassing international edition.	CNN launches a regionalisation strategy with the guiding philosophy, 'Global reach, local touch'.	CNN Mobile launches, the first mobile telephone news and information service available globally with targeted regional content.

Breaking U.S. Geological Survey: quake struck 10km below surface

2006 execution, and in 2008, the US presidential elections, the Myanmar cyclone, the Russia/Georgia conflict and the terror attacks in Mumbai, to name a few.

With an eye on changing consumer trends, CNN embraces the range of emerging, non-linear distribution outlets to maximise its presence across all platforms. Recent years have seen CNN content and archive footage completely reformatted for use across new platforms and devices – short-form video content is now an integral feature of CNN.com and CNN Mobile, as well as being available on third party IPTV and video-on-demand outlets.

CNN's user-generated content initiative, iReport, has garnered hundreds of thousands of submissions from nearly 200 countries and territories around the world since its 2006 launch. Images, video and text-based eyewitness accounts from a network of 'citizen journalists' add a deeper, more personal perspective to many of the stories unfolding on CNN. Defining moments have included the 2006 coup in Thailand and 2007's unrest in Myanmar. When national media and internet outlets were shut down, iReport ensured that images and developments from those countries continued to reach the rest of the world. In 2008, CNN put viewer comment at the centre of its US presidential elections coverage with its 'World View' initiative, giving voice to thousands of students worldwide through self-authored video footage.

Product
CNN's global news group currently consists of nine international networks and services, five international partnerships and joint ventures as well as eight US-based services. Available in six languages, the channel's joint ventures include CNN-IBN, CNN Turk, CNN+ in Spain and Japan's CNNj, as well as a number of websites including CNN.co.jp in Japan and CNNenEspanol.com.

While breaking news remains the CNN trademark, its feature programming line-up

caters to a wide range of audiences covering business, sport, lifestyle and entertainment, compelling documentaries and special landmark programming. Throughout the year, CNN's best known faces, including Richard Quest, front regular shows such as CNN Business Traveller. Special documentaries in 2008 included 'Scream Bloody Murder', presented by CNN's chief international correspondent, Christiane Amanpour, 'Through Their Eyes', presented by CNN's Baghdad-based international correspondent Arwa Damon and 'Planet in Peril: Battlelines', presented by Anderson Cooper, Dr Sanjay Gupta and Lisa Ling.

Recent Developments
The network has continued to consolidate its position as a market leader by integrating its content across a range of platforms. 2008 saw the channel launch a new mobile Java application offering users an enriched, personalised service. On mobile, CNN International also offered free, bespoke Euro 2008 and Beijing Olympics content to consumers. In addition, the company launched iReport.com, the network's first uncensored, unfiltered, unedited user-generated community website and became the first international news broadcaster to launch a standalone Google gadget.

Internationally, CNN has made a robust investment in its newsgathering operations, opening seven new bureaux in the past year. Expansion plans continue and include the fulfilment of a recently announced regional news gathering hub in the United Arab Emirates and investment in its in-house wire operations.

Promotion
Since launch, the CNN logo has been one of the world's most instantly recognised brands and is promoted via select marketing opportunities and partnerships.

CNN is the leading television news provider for 'global citizens'. These include world and

opinion leaders and business decision makers; often hugely successful, affluent, challenge-seekers who are well travelled and independent thinkers.

Brand Values
For more than 28 years CNN has stood by the news values of accuracy, intelligence, transparency and diversity. The network's commitment to digital integration also ensures that its audiences get access to CNN 'whenever, wherever and however'.

Core brand values are reflected in the network positioning messages: Be the first to know; Live from anywhere; Quoted everywhere; Essential for business.

cnn.com/international

2006 CNN launches its citizen journalism initiative, iReport.

2007 CNN launches across major IPTV and VOD outlets including YouTube, and CNN.com is redesigned to incorporate video, text and images within the storytelling page.

2008 iReport.com is born – an online incarnation of iReport, it is the company's first unfiltered, uncensored user-generated content website.

Also in 2008, CNN appoints 12 new correspondents and increases its newsgathering operations to 46.

conqueror

Now in its 121st year, Conqueror is recognised worldwide as a symbol of quality in external business communications and as the gold standard for business stationery. With brand values built on constant innovation and unparalleled quality, Conqueror boasts industry-leading green credentials, making it the ideal choice for image- and environmentally-conscious companies across 120 countries worldwide.

Recent achievements include the development of a new set of environmental credentials, which mean that Conqueror now boasts a comprehensive green offering. As well as becoming Europe's first CarbonNeutral® fine paper brand, Conqueror has achieved full FSC certification and is launching a new range of premium 100 per cent recycled papers in 2009.

Conqueror also continues to achieve best-in-category performance, cementing its status as one of the most well-known and favoured paper brands; in blind and branded tests Conqueror is consistently chosen as the best quality and overall preferred sheet available.

Product
Conqueror products are designed to help a range of users to achieve standout in the ever crowded marketplace – whether printers, designers or end-users. The paper offers a solution for a spectrum of needs, with multi-functional, sustainable products that guarantee performance across the latest print processes. Constant monitoring of fashion trends means that Conqueror also offers creativity and quality for materials requiring an eye-catching finish, such as brochures, annual reports, promotional materials or packaging.

The range is extensive, grouped into five sub brands all with full FSC certification and CarbonNeutral® accreditation: Conqueror Smooth/Satin, for a 'fresh and contemporary' look; Conqueror Concept/Effects, a 'futuristic and trend setting' stock; Conqueror Digital for high performance digital printing; Conqueror Connoisseur, 'luxurious and classic'; and Conqueror Texture for producing tactile images.

their carbon footprint and as a result, end-users now actively choose products that can support this. The Conqueror range is constantly adapted to meet these changing market demands, resulting in distinctive products that boast the highest environmental credentials.

Achievements
With a constant focus on product development to meet new market demands, Conqueror has embraced change. From traditional beginnings during the era of pen and ink, through to the modern multiple print and digital communication technologies, Conqueror delivers high quality results across a variety of applications. With brand awareness levels at over 70 per cent in the UK in 2008 (Source: ICM Research), Conqueror is one of the few paper brands requested by name and remains synonymous with quality business stationery.

Market
In today's digital age, paper continues to be used as a key communications tool that can help companies to promote a positive business image. Conqueror is a long-established mark of quality and provides cut through in the busy commercial environment where new and existing businesses compete for brand recognition.

As companies face increasing environmental pressures, many are looking for ways to reduce

1888	1945	1960s	1990s		2001
Conqueror paper first rolls off the paper machine at Wiggins Teape. Conqueror Laid is born.	Changes in the production of Conqueror are introduced and quality control and specialised colour matching are developed.	Conqueror continues to develop and grow its export business.	The Arjowiggins Appleton group is formed from the merger of Wiggins Teape with the French paper manufacturer Arjomari and the US manufacturer, Appleton Papers.	Conqueror also launches its first recycled range and the revolutionary CX22 finish.	A new, contemporary, stylised logo and identity based on the Conqueror name is launched. Innovative iridescent papers are added into the Conqueror Concept/Effects range.

co₂nqueror
NEUTRAL

Your choice of environmentally friendly business stationery says a lot about you.

It says who you are.

www.conqueror.com/green

ARJOWIGGINS

Within the range, a selection of contemporary colours, finishes, textures and watermarks are available, as well as co-ordinated boards and envelopes. Through the combination of quality and versatility, Conqueror aims to guarantee a look and feel of effortless style and professionalism, bolstered by impeccable environmental credentials.

Recent Developments

Conqueror has remained at the cutting-edge of the paper industry by continuing to drive forward new product innovation. In 2007, Conqueror became the first CarbonNeutral® fine paper brand in Europe, with full FSC certification across the range. The 2009 addition of premium 100 per cent recycled papers, which offer unmatched levels of whiteness and brightness, allows companies with stringent corporate social responsibility (CSR) policies to communicate their environmental commitment without compromising on quality.

Promotion

A 'push-pull' marketing strategy has been developed successfully for Conqueror, focusing on distribution partners, printers, designers and end-users. A strong emphasis is put on brand awareness and brand building, with the wide range of applications at the heart

of any campaign. Promotion of the brand is underpinned by a global communications strategy which delivers a consistent image and clear, targeted messages that are tailored to key audiences.

Direct mail was the main driver in the 2007 'Blank Sheet Project', along with online and press advertising. Developed to promote Conqueror's CarbonNeutral® status and FSC certification, the campaign was aimed at SMEs, CEOs, CSR directors, existing customers and printers, encouraging businesses to share ideas about easily achievable steps that can be taken to help reduce carbon emissions.

Most recently, Conqueror has been supported by an extensive national press and online advertising campaign, incorporating a refreshed Conqueror CarbonNeutral® logo and a newly created strap line: 'It says who you are.' The campaign was designed to reflect the high quality of the range and to demonstrate how small steps, such as using an environmentally-friendly paper for business communications, can be used to send a positive message to stakeholders.

The campaign was underpinned by end-user activity including Conqueror notebooks being

placed at a number of high profile events with the Institute of Directors and educational environmental seminars hosted for end-users, designers and printers.

Brand Values

Conqueror has a rich heritage in providing high quality, distinctive papers. It is renowned for reliability in both professional and creative communications and is committed to delivering the ultimate impact for image-conscious businesses. Indeed, recent customer research commissioned for Conqueror and carried out by ICM revealed the brand has the highest awareness and current usage levels among its competitive set. The same research also found that Conqueror paper is perceived as a trusted, high value brand that can enhance a company's image.

Through ongoing investment in research and development, Conqueror aims to remain at the forefront of the paper industry, meeting increasing demand for exceptional performance while maintaining its relevancy in today's market.

conqueror.com

2003	2004	2007	2009
Conqueror launches a specific collection of products into the Office and Retail channel, focusing on the home-based and small and medium-sized businesses.	Conqueror Digital Multi Technology is introduced as the only fine paper that is printable on offset and digital presses.	Conqueror becomes the first CarbonNeutral® fine paper brand in Europe while also only using pulp from FSC certified sources across the entire range.	Conqueror launches a premium 100 per cent recycled offering in response to market demand for sustainable papers which deliver the highest possible quality.

Costain is an international engineering and construction group with a reputation for technical excellence founded on more than 140 years of experience. One of the UK's leading construction companies, Costain is playing a key role in building a successful infrastructure for the nation's future. Its well-defined culture, strong values and core strategy – 'Being Number One' – are designed to ensure its ongoing success.

£900 million of new work was secured during a six-month period alone (ending June 2008) including the extension of the Southern Water AMP4 contract to 2015, the A14 highway development in Cambridgeshire and the Bell Common Tunnel Project on the M25.

Market

Costain is at the forefront of the construction industry's effort to meet the challenges faced by the UK today. With a rapidly increasing and ageing population, Britain's frontline services, energy and transport infrastructure are being overhauled to provide the necessary capacity for future generations. The ongoing successful delivery of numerous high-profile projects, from St Pancras International in rail to the A2/A282 project in highways, to time and budget, continues to strengthen Costain's brand and market position within this highly competitive sector.

Despite the current economic environment, Costain believes its blue-chip customers, in particular those in the public sector, will continue with their investment programmes. This places Costain, with its strong cash balance and record order book, in a good position to deliver growth in line with expectations.

Achievements

A landmark set of results for 2007 saw the Costain Group deliver a £19.8 million pre-tax profit and a return to shareholder dividend for the first time in 15 years. Approximately

As contractors' ethical and environmental credentials come under increasing scrutiny, Costain's focus on corporate responsibility (CR) stands firm. Two years ago it formed its own CR committee and joined Business in the Community (BITC), a charitable organisation that helps FTSE 250 companies define their CR policies and benchmark progress. In 2008 Costain achieved a Silver rating in BITC's CR Index with a score five per cent above the construction sector average. In the same year, its environmental performance while constructing a new plant for Bristol Water, at Axbridge Raw Water Treatment Works

1865	1933	1939-1945	1951	1971	2008
Richard Costain, a 26 year-old jobbing builder from the Isle of Man, sets up a construction business in Liverpool.	Costain floats as a public company, with a share capital of £600,000.	The company plays an active part in the war effort, including constructing 26 aerodromes, part of the Mulberry Harbours, munitions factories and 15,000 post-war prefabricated Airey houses.	Costain builds the Skylon and Dome of Discovery for the Festival of Britain.	Costain becomes the first contractor to win the Queen's Award for Export Achievement.	Costain pays a dividend to shareholders for the first time since 1991.

in Somerset, earned it a CEEQUAL (Civil Engineering Environmental Quality Assessment and Award Scheme) 'excellent' award, reflecting the brand's ongoing commitment to environmental matters.

Product

Costain's primary markets are health, water, education, highways, rail, oil and gas, nuclear, marine, retail, waste management and airports. The rail market is substantial and following its recent success at London's St Pancras International, Costain is becoming a noteworthy player, establishing partnerships with principal customer bases – Network Rail, Transport for London and metro systems such as Crossrail.

Across all sectors the Costain product is defined by excellent design and the quality of its workmanship. Innovation keeps the company ahead in a competitive marketplace. Costain succeeds in delivering challenging projects through an uncompromising adherence to specification and procedure and by utilising its experiences and extensive knowledge at all stages of the project, with a view to becoming 'the construction brand'.

Recent Developments

Costain was recently refocused around its 'Being Number One' strategy to develop market leading positions in its primary sectors. However, the Group is also turning its expertise to emerging markets such as waste management and airports and was recently appointed the preferred contractor for the Greater Manchester Waste Disposal Authority's PFI contract. The £370 million plus

capital works programme – the largest PFI waste management deal in Europe – involves constructing 45 facilities on 28 sites for completion in 2011.

Airports, another key emerging market, provides Costain with significant infrastructure opportunities and enables it to apply its 'One Costain' cross-sector approach. The recent appointment to BAA's Complex Building Framework, worth some £6.6 billion over 10 years, is a leading example.

Costain also recently built west London's Wood Lane Station, the first new London Underground station on an existing line in 70 years. The Hammersmith & City Line station opened in October 2008 providing key access to the new retail development in White City.

Promotion

Costain promotes itself through a variety of communication channels including using national and international trade fairs, advertising in key technical titles and business-focused papers such as the Financial Times and through its news magazine Blueprint.

Throughout 2008 Costain unveiled a wide-ranging brand awareness programme to ensure that every site and employee conveyed a consistent brand image, including a book and supporting website called 'Representing Costain'. As part of the programme it also produced two additional branding books, one for customers and one for employees, both focusing on company values and major projects.

The Costain website is also used as a platform through which to underline brand values. With the steady increase in online traffic these sites have become an important medium through which to promote the high standards that have become synonymous with the brand.

Brand Values

Costain's brand and reputation are built around the Group's ability to meet customer expectations. Its seven key brand values – Customer focused; Open and honest; Safe and environmentally aware; Team players; Accountable; Improving continuously and therefore the Natural choice – encapsulate this ethos and drive its vision to become overall market leader, as set out by its 'Being Number One' strategy.

costain.com

Things you didn't know about Costain

The Costain Group was named 2008's Major Contractor of the Year by New Civil Engineer magazine. Judges considered factors including order book and overall strength.

London's St Pancras International, a Costain joint venture project, received the Major Project Award at the 2008 British Construction Industry Awards.

In 2008, Costain's Castleford Footbridge project received national television coverage on Channel 4 and wide acclaim for its promotion of community awareness.

One million vehicles travel through Costain highway works every day.

St Martin-in-the-Fields, in London's Trafalgar Square, was the subject of a major renovation and restoration project which was carried out by Costain and finished in 2008. To commemorate the completion, HRH The Prince of Wales and other dignitaries including the Archbishop of Canterbury attended a special thanksgiving service.

design WEEK

Since its conception Design Week has provided its readers with a key source of exclusive news, sharp commentary and top design jobs. For 22 years it has been reporting on all aspects of the design industry, breaking news and showcasing design talent from across the globe – making it the discerning choice for design professionals.

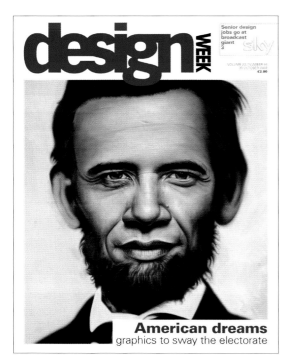

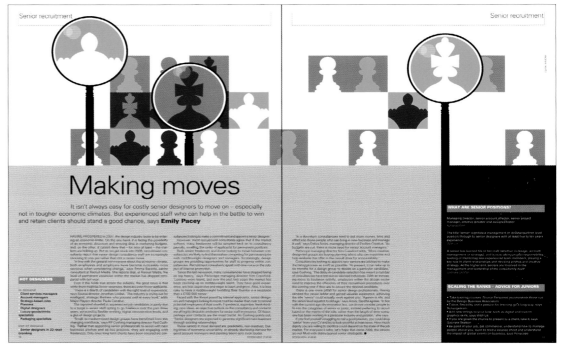

Market

Design Week is the leading market title within the UK's design community. Every week nearly 10,000 designers and clients pay to receive the magazine, making it the highest 'paid-for' circulation of any UK design magazine and one of the few B2B magazines with an entirely paid-for circulation. Seventy-two per cent of copies are sold through subscription, the remainder through newsagents, creating a dedicated reader base; with a pass-on readership of 2.5 per cent the magazine is currently seen by around 35,000 design professionals each week.

While its core readership, comprising mainly designers and design consultancies, remains UK-based, Design Week is attracting more international readers, particularly to its website which has registered 535,773 page views and 61,116 visitors per month, of which approximately 20 per cent come from outside the UK (Source: HBX Analytics October 2008).

Achievements

The Design Week Awards, developed to reward excellence and innovation and now in their 21st year, have become one of the brand's most notable achievements. The annual event, highly regarded by designers both in the UK and abroad, has more than 1,000 entries evaluated by a panel of eminent judges from across the design industry. The 20th anniversary year event marked the debut of a Hall of Fame honouring six leading companies for their outstanding contribution to the design industry over the years.

The younger Benchmarks Awards, launched in 2005 to set a standard in the recognition of excellence in brand communications, are also establishing their industry credentials with entry levels increasing from 161 in the launch year, to more than 200 in 2007 and 2008. They now include a Client of the Year category, honouring the partnership between client and designer.

Design Week is widely acknowledged for the quality of its surveys such as the Top 100, an annual list which ranks design consultancies by profitability, and the Creative Survey that ranks design consultancies and in-house design teams by their success in winning global awards over the previous three years.

1986	1987	1989	2004	2005	2006
Design Week launches in September as a weekly subscription magazine aimed at the design community.	The Top 100 is launched – an annual list of design consultancies ranked by profitability.	The Design Week Awards are developed, celebrating creative excellence and innovation across 22 specialisations.	An online version of the Books series, newdesignpartners.com is introduced providing an opportunity for agencies to showcase their work to a targeted audience.	The Benchmarks Awards are launched, establishing an industry standard in the recognition of excellence in brand communications.	Launching in November, Designweek.co.uk provides the latest breaking design news across a range of commercial design disciplines.

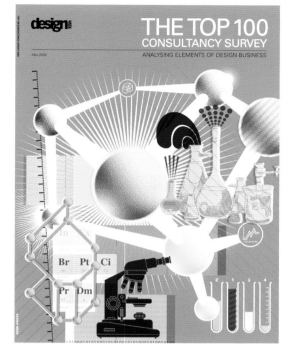

Character count
30 years of Lego stars

Drinking in praise
London on Tap's winning carafes

In addition, the annual Hot 50 listing charts the people, movements and organisations that have had the most impact on design in the previous 12 months. Her Majesty The Queen, Banksy and Sir Christopher Frayling are among those to have featured.

Product
Over the coming 12 months, Design Week will publish more than 1,200 pages of news, features and surveys about the latest developments in the UK design industry – the most editorial pages delivered by a design title and offering informed reporting on events, trends and developments that affect the day-to-day work of designers.

Design Week also acts as a conduit, putting designers in front of potential clients via its Books series. Originally created in the early 1990s as a directory of design consultancies showcasing work to the Marketing Week circulation, it was collectively relaunched as the Brand Communications Books, to better reflect the multi-disciplinary nature of today's design. The series has sparked debate on brands and branding for more than a decade with each issue featuring comment, opinion and analysis.

From breaking news alerts to generating 10,000 plus job applications each month, Design Week's website, launched in November 2006, draws together the latest views, opinion, features and design news, making it a valuable resource for creative communities. The

website now generates over half a million page impressions per month with more than 60,000 unique visitors per month.

Recent Developments
A recently launched weekly newsletter – In Depth – focusing on analysis, features and opinion has increased the brand's online traffic. It was introduced following a successful trial during which feature stories were added to the website's news alerts; throughout the week of the Oscars, for example, an item ran requesting suggested entries for an imaginary Film Title Design category – this was picked up by a number of blogs and generated more than 4,000 page impressions.

In February 2009, an exclusive Design Week supplement was published following the completion of a research project in association with YouGov. The supplement details the findings of the research, which set out to examine the skills shortages in the design industry, both from the view of designers and their clients.

Promotion
In keeping with its creative bent, brand promotion veers towards the unconventional. 'Free the Mac Monkey', launched in the summer of 2008 as a joint collaboration with Creative Review, was aimed at increasing subscriptions for both titles. The quirky online strategy featured a 'monkey cam' directing users to a website to follow the antics of Martin the Mac Monkey – representing Mac operators who had yet to experience Design Week and Creative Review. New subscribers received a limited edition t-shirt and a donation from every subscription was made to the monkey sanctuary in Bournemouth.

Design Week's New Design Partners website is a directory offering design consultancies a platform through which to showcase work to targeted businesses. Aimed specifically at readers of leading marketing titles such as Marketing Week and Brand Strategy (both published by Design Week's parent company

Centaur Media), many of whom have a guaranteed annual design budget in excess of £100,000, newdesignpartners.com has a distinct advantage over competing directories.

Brand Values
Design Week's brand values are built around integrity, accuracy and balance in content. Whether in print or online, it aims to provide a hub for the creative community – a forum for ideas and a networking vehicle that marks it out as the 'village voice' of the UK design industry.

designweek.co.uk

Things you didn't know about Design Week

Design Week's editor Lynda Relph-Knight has been awarded an honorary MA in design by the former Surrey Institute of Art & Design and a fellowship at the Royal College of Art.

Design Week has been represented at Downing Street, when the then Prime Minister Tony Blair hosted design industry dignitaries as part of his 'Cool Britannia' campaign, and twice at Buckingham Palace – at a reception for some 700 guests in the creative industries and at a Royal garden party celebrating 250 years of the Royal Society of Arts.

In the late 1990s a Design Week cover was included in the respected D&AD Annual, which has set design industry standards since 1962.

In 2005, shortly after its redesign, Design Week was ranked 13th in a Guardian Media poll of magazines judged on their excellence and relevance to their readership.

A Passion to Perform.

Deutsche Bank

Deutsche Bank is a leading global investment bank with a strong and profitable private clients franchise, providing the full range of financial services to corporate, institutional, high net worth and retail clients. Deutsche Bank is one of the most diverse global platforms in the financial services industry with a major presence in Europe, the Americas, Asia Pacific and the emerging markets.

Women in European Business Conference 2008.
"Finding Your Voice"

A Passion to Perform.   Deutsche Bank

Deutsche means Diversity.

A Passion to Perform.   Deutsche Bank

Market

Against a background of global financial crisis, Deutsche Bank's universal banking model has enabled it to navigate the turmoil relatively successfully and it has remained open for business, providing clients with advice, products and services to help them negotiate a period of financial uncertainty. The Bank has maintained its strong commitment to risk management while strengthening businesses with stable earnings streams.

The Bank remains one of the leaders in investment banking, with one of the world's most powerful sales and trading franchises. Moreover, Deutsche Bank continues to grow its global corporate finance platform with a strong European presence and a growing platform in the Americas and Asia.

Deutsche Bank is also one of the world's leading asset managers with significant positions in both institutional and retail asset management and is a leading mutual fund provider in the US and Europe. The Bank's retail business has been strengthened through a series of acquisitions including a minority stake in Postbank in 2008.

Achievements

Deutsche continues to win accolades for its performance across all product disciplines and regions. In the Euromoney Awards for Excellence 2008, Deutsche Bank won 21 prizes, including Best Risk Management House and Best Foreign Exchange House. As well as M&A, debt and equity awards, Deutsche Bank was also named Best Cash Management House in the Americas.

Deutsche Bank achieved further success in Global Finance magazine's awards and was named Best Investment Bank in Western Europe and Best Bank in Germany.

Product

The Private Clients and Asset Management Division (PCAM) comprises three areas: Private and Business Clients, providing private clients with an all-round service encompassing daily banking, investment advisory and tailored financial solutions; Private Wealth Management, catering for high net worth clients, their families and select institutions worldwide; and Asset Management, combining asset management for institutions and private investors.

The Corporate and Investment Bank (CIB) comprises Global Markets and Global Banking. Global Markets handles all origination, trading, sales and research in cash equities, derivatives, foreign exchange, bonds, structured products and securitisations and occupies a leading position in foreign exchange, fixed-income and equities trading and derivatives. Global Banking comprises Global Cash Management, Global Trade Finance and Trust & Securities Services and handles all aspects of corporate finance,

1870	1872	1917	1926	1970s	2008
Deutsche Bank is founded in Berlin to support the internationalisation of business and to facilitate trade relations between Germany, other European countries and overseas markets.	The first international branches open, in Yokohama and Shanghai, and trade relations begin with the Americas. The following year the first London branch opens.	Deutsche Bank M&A transactions begin.	Deutsche Bank arranges the merger of Daimler and Benz, takes on advisory roles for BP in a major UK deal, and advises on and finances the £2.6 billion London Underground Financing.	Deutsche Bank pushes ahead with the globalisation of its business: Deutsche Bank Luxembourg S.A. is founded and offices open in Moscow, Tokyo, Paris and New York.	The Bank now offers financial services in 75 countries throughout the world and has more than 80,000 employees.

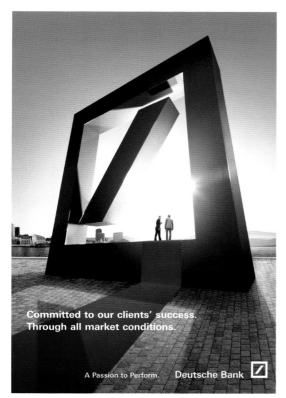

Committed to our clients' success.
Through all market conditions.

A Passion to Perform. Deutsche Bank

autobahn®. A driving force in electronic markets.
Engineered by Deutsche Bank for your success.

A Passion to Perform. Deutsche Bank

An international
showcase for talent.

A Passion to Perform. Deutsche Bank

including advising corporations on M&A and divestments, and support with IPOs and capital market transactions.

Recent Developments
In line with all of the world's major banks, Deutsche Bank has embarked on a de-risking and de-leveraging programme to strengthen its capital base. During 2008, the Bank reduced its reliance on the troubled wholesale funding and maintained a diverse funding base.

The financial crisis naturally overshadowed the existing management agenda: leveraging the global platform for accelerated growth. This involves maintaining cost, risk, capital and regulatory discipline; further growth of stable businesses; continued organic growth with selected acquisitions; and the build up of the Bank's competitive edge in its Corporate and Investment Bank. Deutsche Bank remains well placed to seize opportunities once markets recover.

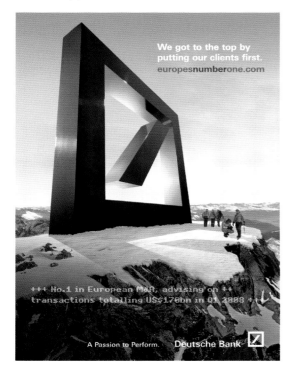

We got to the top by
putting our clients first.
europesnumberone.com

+++ No.1 in European M&A, advising on ++ transactions totalling US$176bn in Q1 2008 ++

A Passion to Perform. Deutsche Bank

Promotion
Deutsche Bank's communication initiatives leverage its renowned brand icon, the symbol for growth in a stable environment, designed by the graphic artist Anton Stankowski and introduced in 1974.

The global brand communications concept places the Deutsche Bank brand icon centre stage in conveying the corporate messages. Introduced in March 2005, the 'Winning with the Logo' concept gives the logo a physical presence, becoming Deutsche Bank's tangible face for globally aligned communication of its winning corporate story. The campaign conveys Deutsche Bank's enhanced brand image, depicting leadership, global performance and client-orientated delivery. Each manifestation reflects a different interpretation of the Deutsche Bank logo to a specific market.

The communication is aimed at people with a contemporary mindset, a can-do, achievement-oriented attitude. To ensure impact and brand alignment of its communications initiatives, Deutsche Bank regularly monitors progress of brand-related key performance indicators.

Deutsche Bank actively embraces its role as a corporate citizen. It regards corporate social responsibility (CSR) not as charity, but as an investment in society and in its own future. Deutsche Bank's goal as a responsible corporate citizen is to create social capital. The Bank leverages its core competencies in five areas of activity: with its social investments it creates opportunities; with its involvement in art it fosters creativity; and via its educational programme it enables talent. A commitment to sustainability ensures long term viability, and the Bank's employees regularly commit themselves as Corporate Volunteers in their local community.

The Bank's foundations and charitable institutions play a key role, firmly anchoring its

CSR activities around the world. From a global CSR budget of 82.2 million euros in 2007, 6.8 million euros were dedicated to the UK. Projects have included numerous employee volunteer programmes in disadvantaged areas of London, working closely with more than 65 non-profit partner organisations.

Brand Values
Deutsche Bank is a European global powerhouse dedicated to excellence, constantly challenging the status quo to deliver superior solutions to demanding clients and superior value to its shareholders and people. 'A Passion to Perform.' applies not only to the Bank's relationships with its clients, but to every aspect of life at Deutsche Bank – it is the way Deutsche Bank does business.

db.com

Things you didn't know about Deutsche Bank

Deutsche Bank first listed its shares on the New York Stock Exchange on 3rd October 2001.

Deutsche Bank's 'diagonal in the square' logo was first introduced in 1974, created by painter and graphic artist Anton Stankowski.

Deutsche Bank is truly multicultural; its employees come from more than 145 nations and it generates 71 per cent of its earnings outside of the home market.

Deutsche Bank employs around 7,800 people in London and is one of the largest employers and occupiers of space in the Square Mile.

Eddie Stobart

Eddie Stobart forms the road haulage element of the Stobart Group, a fast developing public limited company with wide-ranging multimodal transport interests. As it approaches its 40th year, the UK's best known logistics brand today employs over 5,000 people at more than 30 sites, operates around six million sq ft of premium warehousing capacity and has a fleet approaching 2,000 trucks.

Market
In the notoriously hard-pressed road haulage sector, the iconic 'Eddie Stobart' name is one of the brand's greatest strengths. Highly competitive pricing and renowned levels of customer service and efficiency, combined with 95 per cent brand recognition throughout the UK, have ensured that Eddie Stobart is not only surviving but is expanding and increasing in profitability.

Achievements
In an ever-more environmentally conscious world, road transport is an increasingly contentious issue due to its CO_2 emissions. Eddie Stobart has been at the forefront of the sector's responses to environmental considerations; Stobart Group was one of the first businesses to train drivers in the Safe and Fuel Efficient Driving (SAFED) techniques which can reduce fuel consumption by as much as 10 per cent.

A proactive approach has also been taken to address the traditional haulage problem of 'empty miles'; Eddie Stobart now has the best fleet utilisation figures in the industry. Through incisive planning, shared capacity solutions and more strategic developments, Stobart Group is committed to developing efficiency even further. Indeed, it is in the midst of high level negotiations to introduce a new environmental trailer design that could cut the number of trucks on Britain's roads by as much as 13 per cent.

Product
Part of the larger Stobart Group, Eddie Stobart itself is split into five operational divisions centred on road transport.

Stobart General Distribution represents ambient haulage services. The extensive general fleet is controlled using in-cab GPS systems and advanced planning software; leading-edge IT that has played a key role in achieving exceptional load efficiency on behalf of many of its blue-chip clients.

1950s	1960s	1980	1988	1992	2001
Eddie Stobart establishes an agricultural contracting business in the Cumbrian village of Hesket Newmarket.	The company incorporates to form Eddie Stobart Limited in order to fully develop its transport and distribution interests.	The business relocates to Carlisle. The fleet, numbering just eight vehicles, consists mainly of tippers but rapidly develops to include the more versatile artics.	A second depot is opened at Burton-upon-Trent, with 450,000 sq ft of warehousing and 50 vehicles.	Eddie Stobart is voted Haulier of the Year by the Motor Transport Industry, testimony to its dedication and hard work in revolutionising the sector.	Rapid, sustained growth results in a fleet of 900 vehicles and 2,000 staff operating from 27 sites and delivering a turnover of £130 million.

The Specialist Transport Division comprises Walking Floor, Chip Liner and Drawbar units. Chip Liners and Walking Floors carry wood co-products and waste paper while the high volume, highly manoeuvrable Drawbars transport packaging and other bulky items.

Chilled Transport Division activities are centred on eight major temperature-controlled 'cross-docking' facilities, strategically located across the UK. This comprehensive network of sites handles a variety of salads, fresh fruit, vegetables and other perishables, serviced by a 270-strong fleet of the latest refrigerated units.

The International Division is responsible for trans-European haulage and storage covering the UK, Republic of Ireland and the Continent. In addition to its fleet of high specification tractors and comprehensive range of specialist trailers, International also operates large scale storage capacity at Lokeren, Belgium.

Finally, the Warehousing Division operates some six million sq ft of storage at key sites throughout the UK. The Group's storage profile includes ambient, chilled, hazardous (ADR approved), conditioned and virtual capacity. Facilities are controlled to the highest GMP standards and are managed by specialist teams using the Group's state-of-the-art in-house warehouse management system.

Inevitably, however, fuel costs and motorway congestion are limiting factors for road haulage and Stobart Group as a whole is developing a wider package of transport solutions with the overall vision of building a fully multimodal transport offering to ensure customers can make the most cost-efficient and environmentally responsible choice for their business.

Stobart Rail, the award-winning and ultra carbon-efficient rail freight service, was joined by Stobart Ports in 2007 following the acquisition of a major port site at Runcorn and a container port at Widnes. Plans are in place to move into all other sectors of freight transport over the next five years.

Recent Developments
While traditionally strong in ambient transport, strategic development and intelligent acquisitions have allowed Eddie Stobart to make a seamless move into the chilled market. The business now has a dominating – and increasing – presence in the crucial FMCG sector and holds distribution contracts with high profile global brands including Tesco, Coca-Cola, Homebase, Nestlé, Sara Lee and Mars.

Promotion
Despite an enviable level of public awareness, the Eddie Stobart branding underwent significant changes in 2004. Heralding a new era for the business, the development saw a complete reworking of corporate colours and the logo itself, while vehicle livery took on a simpler, more cost-effective design. Today, the 'new' look is the driving identity for the parent Group, flexible enough to be applied to the ever-expanding

range of transport options without weakening the brand or reducing recognition.

While the recognisable green and white livery plays a pivotal role in public awareness, the brand's impressive profile can also be attributed to an ongoing marketing and promotional drive that extends throughout the business' culture. The Company operates its own Members' Club with some 20,000 dedicated followers and markets a wide variety of branded merchandise. In sponsorship, Stobart lends its support to Carlisle United FC, Widnes Vikings and Stobart Polo, while also operating a World Rally Team – its consistent success earning valuable TV coverage for Stobart.

Brand Values
Since its inception, the Eddie Stobart brand has built its reputation through a commitment to professional drivers, its high quality fleet and exceptional levels of service. Today, adapting to society's changing needs, the Company has added exemplary employment and environmental practices to its core principles and is working to achieve its vision of building a fully multimodal transport offering to its customers.

stobartgroup.com

MULTI-MODAL
Road Rail Sea Air

2004	2005/06	2007	2008
WA Developments International acquires the company. A major rebrand takes place, from vehicle livery to uniform, heralding a new era for the business.	Eddie Stobart wins its first Tesco Distribution Centre contract. Stobart Rail freight services are launched and a new central control site is built at Warrington.	Eddie Stobart merges with Westbury Property Fund in a £138 million deal that sees the formation of the public limited company Stobart Group.	Through sustained expansion and strategic acquisitions, the business expands to a total workforce in excess of 5,000 and a fleet numbering around 2,000 vehicles.

ExCeL LONDON

An ADNEC Group Company

ExCeL London has staged over 2,500 events since 2000. More than five million people from 200 countries worldwide have visited, experiencing everything from sporting events, gala dinners and religious festivals to award ceremonies, conferences and exhibitions. ExCeL London is home to eight of London's top 10 trade shows; two out of three of the UK's largest consumer shows; and hosts events for blue-chip corporate clients, government organisations and associations.

Market

ExCeL London is one of the UK's premier venues for exhibitions, events and conferences, a market currently worth £20 billion. The venue operates across the sector, marketing itself as able to handle almost any event imaginable and boasting 90,000 sq m of multipurpose space. In May 2008, ExCeL London was bought by the Abu Dhabi National Exhibitions Company as part of its long term vision to create a global network of world-class venues.

ExCeL London works with the biggest names in the exhibition business, including Reed Exhibition Companies, CMPi, Haymarket, Emap, Clarion Events, IMIE and National Boat Shows. The conference and events division, set up in 2004, has built a client list that includes Philips, Tesco, Rolls-Royce, Barclays, Ernst & Young, Symantec, Toyota, the NHS and AstraZeneca. It has also announced some major association

wins including Gastro 2009 UEGW/WCOG London (15,000 delegates), European Academy of Allergology and Clinical Immunology (6,000 delegates), European Hematology Association (7,000 delegates) and the Eighth International Orthodontic Congress 2015 (10,000 delegates).

Achievements

ExCeL London is continually evolving and improving, with its corporate social responsibility programme playing a key role in recent years. This has seen the installation of an on-site Materials Recycling Facility, colour coded recycling bins and the UK's largest and only commercial wormery. In 2007/08 ExCeL London reduced its gas consumption by 56 per cent and electricity by 15 per cent, resulting in a 31 per cent reduction in CO_2 emissions. The venue's wormery and recycling initiatives allowed it to recycle 78 per cent of its waste on and off-site.

Its 'green' credentials were affirmed in 2008 when ExCeL London hosted the first ever event to be awarded the BS 8901 standard for sustainable events management – the MPI European Meetings & Events Conference.

ExCeL London has received many industry accolades over the years and in 2008 was awarded Best Venue Support and the Green Award at the Exhibition News Awards, as well as Best UK Venue Committed to Sustainability in the C&IT Reader Poll. The venue was also awarded Best Venue, Best Event Team and Outstanding Achievement at the 2007 Eventia Awards.

Product

ExCeL London is a £300 million international venue located on a 100-acre, waterside campus in Royal Victoria Dock. It is the largest and most versatile venue in London: its two

1855		1950s	Mid 1960s	1981	1988
The Royal Victoria Dock site, on which ExCeL London now sits, is opened by Prince Albert as a working dock.	It becomes the first dock to take iron steam ships and to use hydraulic cranes, handling shipments of tobacco, South American beef and produce from New Zealand.	Traffic through the Royal Dock reaches its peak.	Containerisation and other technological changes, together with a switch in Britain's trade following EEC membership, lead to the dock's rapid decline.	The dock finally closes.	Architect Ray Moxley is approached by the Association of Exhibition Organisers (aeo) to locate and design a new exhibition and conference centre within the M25.

large halls total 65,000 sq m and can be divided up or used in their entirety. The venue also includes a further 25,000 sq m of meeting space and a host of additional services.

The Platinum Conference Suite can stage conferences and dinners for between 400-1,100 delegates, while an additional 45 meeting rooms can cater for between 20-200 delegates. There are five on-site hotels, providing 1,400 bedrooms that range from budget to four star, more than 30 bars and restaurants, 4,000 car parking spaces and three on-site DLR stations – linking to the Jubilee line.

London City Airport, which is five minutes away from ExCeL London, offers over 350 flights a day from more than 35 European destinations, as well as a business flight to New York starting in 2009.

Recent Developments
In 2008 ExCeL London formally launched its Phase 2 expansion plan. Construction work is underway and when complete will increase

total event space from 65,000 sq m to just under 100,000 sq m. This will include a 5,000-seat semi-permanent auditorium, extra conference and meeting rooms, mezzanine casual dining, permanent production kitchens and additional underground parking. Phase 2 is due for completion in spring 2010, while further plans for a waterside leisure and entertainment district are under consideration.

ExCeL also relaunched its website in 2008, improving functionality for both organisers and visitors. The new website provides interactive maps for travel and visitor services, as well as an online tourism shop through which visitors can book hotels, restaurants, attractions, theatre tickets and order Oyster travel cards in advance.

Promotion
The marketing team targets two distinct audiences – the exhibitions industry and the conference and events market.

UK exhibition organisers are targeted through a variety of communication channels including e-bulletins, sales literature, PR and the ExCeL London website. The venue also undertakes as much face-to-face marketing as possible, through organiser forums, corporate hospitality and strategy days. Its award-winning marketing and PR support package offers benefits such as inclusion in 'what's on' materials, local PR, support with exhibitor days and familiarisation trips. Contra-deals with media partners as well as local and UK-wide organisations are also on offer (including the DLR, Canary Wharf, Archant Media, BBC Club, Borders, Tesco Clubcard and National Rail's 2 for 1 London).

The conference and events marketing campaign targets both UK and international

event planners and is very much focused on promoting the venue in the context of London, a key city in Europe. To this end, much of the international activity is executed in conjunction with Visit London where the destination and the venue are jointly promoted.

In addition, ExCeL London exhibits at international shows and is involved with key industry bodies, hospitality events, speaking at industry seminar programmes and organising UK, European and US road shows, as well as press and client familiarisation trips.

Brand Values
ExCeL London positions itself as more than an events venue, promising its clients and staff 'space to perform'. This promise is underpinned by a commitment among staff to deliver the ultimate environment in which events can flourish; a blank canvas providing creative inspiration and flexibility; a meticulous approach to every aspect of a project; and a caring attitude to the environment and to its neighbourhood.

excel-london.co.uk

Things you didn't know about ExCeL London

ExCeL London is a 2012 Olympic Games venue and will be hosting: boxing, wrestling, judo, Taekwondo, weight lifting, fencing and table tennis, as well as five Paralympic sports.

In 2008, ExCeL London hosted the first ever event to receive the sustainable events certification BS 8901 – the MPI European Meetings & Events Conference.

ExCeL London's economic contribution to London was more than £750 million in 2008 and this is expected to rise to £1.6 billion in 2011 with the completion of Phase 2 (Source: Grant Thornton).

1990	1994	2000	2008
A turning point is reached when the 100-acre Royal Victoria Dock site is found.	The London Docklands Development Corporation launches an international competition to appoint a preferred developer, which is won by the ExCeL London team.	ExCeL London opens in November, as one of Europe's largest regeneration projects.	ExCeL London is bought by Abu Dhabi National Exhibitions Company (ADNEC) and the Phase 2 expansion plan is formally launched.

As the world's largest express transportation company, FedEx Express operates a global air and ground network which aims to provide fast and reliable delivery to more than 220 countries and territories worldwide. All 143,000 employees take on the FedEx Express commitment to 'make every FedEx experience outstanding'.

Market

Despite increasingly challenging global economic conditions, FedEx Express continues to deliver solid financial performance and delivered revenues of US$1,740 million in the 2007/08 financial year. An increase of eight per cent on the previous year, the results show FedEx Express to be reaping the benefits of the continued strong growth of its international express business and from its investments to expand its portfolio of service offerings, drive revenue growth and increase productivity.

Achievements

In 2008 FedEx Express celebrated its 35-year anniversary. FedEx Express, which started life in 1973 as the brainchild of its founder and current chairman, president and CEO Frederick Smith, has amassed an impressive list of 'firsts' over the years. FedEx Express

originated the overnight letter, was the first express transportation company dedicated to overnight package delivery and the first to offer next-day delivery by 10.30am.

FedEx Express was also the first express company to offer a time-definite service for freight and the first in the industry to offer money-back guarantees and free proof of delivery. In 1983 Federal Express made business history as the first US company to reach the US$1 billion revenue landmark inside 10 years of start-up and unaided by mergers or acquisitions.

This illustrious history has resulted in many awards and honours. In 1990, Federal Express became the first company to win the Malcolm Baldrige National Quality Award in the service category. It also received ISO 9001 registration for all of its worldwide operations in 1994,

making it the first global express transportation company to receive simultaneous system-wide certification. In 2008 FedEx Express was ranked sixth in Fortune magazine's World's Most Admired Companies listing and topped the customer service category of the Harris Interactive Reputation Quotient survey.

Product

FedEx Express offers time-definite, door-to-door customs-cleared international delivery services and can deliver a wide range of time-sensitive shipments, from urgent medical supplies, last minute gifts and fragile scientific equipment, to bulky freight and dangerous goods.

Each shipment sent with FedEx Express is scanned 17 times on average, to ensure that customers can track its precise location by email, on the internet or by telephone 24 hours a day. FedEx Express aims to treat

1971	1973	1977	1984	1989	1994
Frederick W Smith buys the controlling interest in Arkansas Aviation Sales and identifies the difficulty in getting packages delivered quickly; the idea for Federal Express is born.	Federal Express officially begins operations with the launch of 14 small aircraft from Memphis International Airport. It delivers 186 packages to 25 US cities on its first day.	Air cargo deregulation allows the use of larger aircraft (such as Boeing 727s and McDonnell-Douglas DC-10s), spurring Federal Express' rapid growth.	Intercontinental operations begin with services to Europe and Asia. The following year, Federal Express marks its first regularly scheduled flight to Europe.	With the acquisition of the Flying Tigers network, Federal Express becomes the world's largest full-service, all-cargo airline.	Federal Express officially adopts 'FedEx' as its primary brand, taking a cue from its customers who frequently refer to Federal Express by the shortened name.

TRUST. To see how FedEx will work behind the scenes to earn your trust and help your business succeed, go to **experience.fedex.com.** FedEx, behind a great experience.

FedEx Express

each package as if it were the only one being shipped that day.

In addition to the international product range offered by FedEx Express, FedEx UK now provides customers with a wide range of options for domestic shipping within the UK including time-definite, next day and Saturday delivery services. All services are supported by free and easy-to-use automation tools, allowing customers to schedule pick-ups and track their packages online.

Recent Developments
In 2006 FedEx acquired the UK domestic express company ANC Holdings Limited. Now rebranded as FedEx UK, the company manages a network of more than 2,000 vehicles and 1.5 million sq ft of operating space across the UK, employing an experienced workforce of over 4,000 employees and contractors. The acquisition of ANC enables FedEx Express to

offer a complete portfolio of both international and domestic express delivery services.

In September 2008, FedEx Express further enhanced its next-business-day delivery service to the US east coast by introducing a new westbound trans-Atlantic flight between Paris and Newark. As a result, many customers across the UK and Europe can now opt for a later pick-up time for their packages, while still having the guarantee of next-day delivery.

Promotion
FedEx Express launched its global 'Behind the Scenes' advertising campaign in November 2007. Aired in nine languages across 13 countries, the multimedia approach included print and digital media. The key objective of the campaign was to help build global leadership in the international express market by reinforcing brand awareness, corporate reputation and FedEx core values consistently across the globe.

The campaign was designed to illustrate how FedEx works behind the scenes to help companies achieve their global objectives. All print and online advertising directed readers to the www.experience.fedex.com website, which provides macroeconomic overviews of international markets and information on how FedEx can help businesses access global opportunities.

Globally, the campaign generated 1.9 billion page impressions and the website won the

Web Marketing Association's 2008 WebAward for Best International Business Website.

Brand Values
The FedEx corporate strategy, known to FedEx Express employees as the 'Purple Promise', is to 'make every FedEx experience outstanding'. The Purple Promise is the long term strategy for FedEx to further develop loyal relationships with its customers. The FedEx corporate values are: to value its people and to promote diversity; to provide service that puts customers at the heart of everything its does; to invent the services and technologies that improve the way people work and live; to manage operations, finances and services with honesty, efficiency and reliability; to champion safe and healthy environments; and to earn the respect and confidence of FedEx people, customers and investors every day.

fedex.com

Things you didn't know about FedEx Express

In May 2008 FedEx Express, in partnership with Heart to Heart International, airlifted 31 tons of relief supplies (valued at more than US$1.5 million) to the devastated Sichuan Province, China, following a magnitude 8.0 earthquake.

In 2006 FedEx Express transported a 3,000 pound piece of the Titanic's hull from Milan, Italy, to Atlanta in the US.

FedEx Express has been known to transport many unusual items, from pandas and penguins to racing cars and even a windmill.

1995	2000	2006	2008
Federal Express obtains authority to serve China, becoming the sole US-based, all-cargo carrier with aviation rights to the country.	The company is renamed FedEx Express to reflect its position within the overall FedEx Corporation portfolio of services.	FedEx Express builds its service capabilities in Europe by acquiring UK domestic express company ANC, rebranded as FedEx UK in 2007.	FedEx Express celebrates its 35th year and is now the world's largest express transportation company, operating 672 aircraft and a ground fleet of over 44,500 vehicles.

First
transforming travel

FirstGroup is a world leader in public transport with revenues of some £6 billion a year. Headquartered in Aberdeen, it employs around 137,000 staff throughout the UK and North America and transports some 2.5 billion passengers a year. First is the leader in safe, innovative, reliable and sustainable transport services – global in scale and local in approach.

Market

First is the UK's largest rail operator, with four passenger franchises – First Capital Connect, First Great Western, First ScotRail and First TransPennine Express – and one open access operator, First Hull Trains. Providing a balance of intercity, commuter and regional services, First operates a quarter of the UK passenger rail network, carrying over 280 million passengers per year. It also operates the Croydon Tramlink network, transporting more than 26 million passengers per year. The Group operates rail freight services through First GBRf.

First is the UK's largest bus operator, with a fleet of nearly 9,000 buses carrying approximately three million passengers every day in 40 major towns and cities. It holds an approximate 23 per cent share of the UK bus service market.

In the North American market, First has four operating divisions: Yellow School Buses (First

Student); Vehicle Fleet Maintenance and Support Services (First Services); Transit Contracting and Management Services (First Transit); and intercity bus services (Greyhound).

Achievements

A FTSE 100 company, First prides itself on innovation and investment and continues to create a new standard of transport services across the UK. It has invested heavily across all of its train companies in order to deliver passenger growth, better performance and increased capacity.

For the third consecutive year, First ScotRail was named Public Transport Operator of the Year at the Scottish Transport Awards 2008, while Transport Scotland also extended the franchise by a further three years to 2014.

Following major investment in new trains and refurbished stations, First TransPennine Express has successfully transformed its business.

Since 2004 passenger numbers have increased from 13.5 million to more than 22 million a year.

In 2008 FirstGroup announced a further £29 million package of investment in its First Great Western franchise, which included recruiting and training additional drivers and onboard staff. This was in addition to a £200 million franchise commitment of investment by First Great Western, much of which has been delivered. For example, the fleet of High Speed Trains has had a complete set of new engines and the West fleet is undergoing a thorough engineering overhaul.

2008 was a milestone year for First Capital Connect with the number of trains arriving on time reaching record levels, while cancellations dropped to a new low. The £5.5 billion Thameslink Programme, funded by the Department for Transport, will transform services further through new and improved stations, track and cross-London routes, as

1995	1996	1997	1999	2003	2004
FirstBus is born from the Grampian Regional Transport and Badgerline Group merger. The two companies merge to form FirstBus plc. The new company is listed on the Stock Exchange.	First acquires a 24.5 per cent holding in Great Western Holdings. The company operates the Great Western Trains franchise.	The name is changed to FirstGroup plc to reflect the growing interests of the business in rail and internationally.	The Group makes a significant entry into the North American transport market, forming FirstGroup America after acquiring Bruce Transportation and Ryder Public Transportation.	Through the acquisition of GB Railways, First acquires GB Railfreight (First GBRf) and Hull Trains.	First is successful in winning the ScotRail bid (the franchise now known as First ScotRail). It also begins operating a new franchise – First TransPennine Express.

well as providing longer and more frequent trains to relieve overcrowding.

Meanwhile, as passenger numbers continue to rise, 2008 saw First UK Bus announce the procurement of more than 700 new buses with an investment of over £100 million – the biggest single order in bus history.

In North America, FirstGroup has grown to become the leading operator of student transportation – with a feet of approximately 60,000 yellow school buses that carry nearly four million students every day – and also operates the iconic Greyhound, the only national provider of scheduled intercity coach services in the US and Canada.

Across the Group, accolades continued throughout 2008 including First ScotRail winning the title of Passenger Operator of the Year at the National Rail Awards and an education, skills and leadership award from the Confederation of British Industry for First UK Bus. First's chief executive, Sir Moir Lockhead, was awarded a knighthood in the Queen's Birthday Honours and was named Director of the Year by IoD Scotland.

Product
First is divided into three principal divisions: UK Bus; UK Rail; and its North American business. UK Bus generates more than £1.1 billion per year in turnover and continues to invest in its fleet to deliver high-quality, low-floor buses that comply with EU IV emission standards. UK Rail, which generated revenues of nearly £2 billion in 2007/08, is the market leader in the UK, running 4,500 train services per day. Furthermore, in the rail freight business, First GBRf is a leading player in the UK, carrying two million letters every day for Royal Mail.

Recent Developments
While addressing environmental matters has been at the heart of First's business for many

years, in 2007 it unveiled its Climate Change Strategy – the first of its kind in the surface public transport sector. First aims to reduce its carbon dioxide emissions by up to 25 per cent by 2020 throughout its UK bus and rail operations, helped by initiatives such as investing in new buses with Euro IV engines. In 2008, First was certified under the Energy Efficiency Accreditation Scheme.

Keeping environmental concerns in mind, First has also established the Yellow School Bus Commission, led by the Rt Hon. David Blunkett MP. It recommends the introduction of dedicated school buses across Britain to all primary and many secondary schools, therefore cutting down on unnecessary car journeys. Indeed, research indicates that 86 per cent of British parents would be willing to send their children to school in a dedicated US-style school bus (Source: raisingkids.co.uk). First Student currently operates over 180 such buses across the UK, carrying more than 8,000 students every day.

Promotion
First has created a strong visual presence across all areas of its business, with its vehicles acting as the strongest representation of its brand.

2008 saw First host its 'First Monster Challenge' for the second successful year; the 120km team relay duathlon attracted almost 1,000 competitors and several celebrities. In 2008 First also rolled out its 'First Mini Monster Challenge' in five cities throughout the UK, aimed at families. All Monster events encourage competitors to raise money for First's charity partner, Save the Children, with some £150,000 raised in 2008.

Brand Values
First has a clear vision: to transform travel by providing public transport services that are safe, innovative, reliable and sustainable – global in scale and local in approach.

It aims to be the 'best in class' in everything that it does, delivering the highest levels of safety and service, constantly building on its reputation for innovation, investment and improvement. Safety is the number one priority for the Group, and it has created a culture of 'Safety First' throughout the business. The message from First is: 'If you cannot do it safely, don't do it.'

firstgroup.com

Things you didn't know about First

By using its buses and trains, First customers help save around one million tonnes of carbon dioxide a year.

First's services help to keep 1.8 million cars off the road each day.

Through its staff training programme, more than 700 First employees have given 7,840 hours of voluntary support to deserving organisations.

2006
First begins operating two new enlarged rail franchises, First Great Western and First Capital Connect.

Also in 2006, First's award-winning articulated tram-like vehicle ftr is rolled out in York. The following year Leeds implements the ftr, with Swansea to follow in 2009.

2007
First completes the acquisition of Laidlaw International Inc. to become the leading transportation provider in North America and the world's leading transport operator.

2008
First now employs 137,000 people globally and transports some 2.5 billion passengers a year.

flybe.

Established in 1979, Flybe is now one of Europe's largest regional airlines; serving five times more domestic routes than any other airline, it also offers more flights from the UK regions to major European cities and regional France. Following Flybe's acquisition of BA Connect in 2007, the airline created a business that, in the 2007/08 financial year, carried seven million passengers on more than 190 routes and generated revenues in excess of £500 million.

Market

The boom in budget airlines over the past decade has led to regional air travel becoming more popular. This has resulted in the market becoming highly competitive, with tight margins. It is also an extremely challenging market, with huge swings in the price of oil, rising taxation on air travel, higher airport charges and growing environmental pressures; all factors that are impacting on the aviation sector.

Achievements

Flybe has chalked up 29 years of continuous operations, evolving from its roots as Jersey European into a successful, innovative market leader within the low cost airline industry. It has continued to differentiate itself in the crowded airline marketplace by flying from the UK regions and focusing on 'low cost travel from your doorstep'.

Following the successful acquisition of BA Connect in 2007, Flybe took another strategic step in 2008 as it extended its brand into new markets through a landmark franchise agreement with Scottish regional airline Loganair. The first of its kind for a low cost carrier, the agreement demonstrates Flybe's commitment to extending its low fare model throughout the UK, increasing accessibility to previously isolated destinations.

The airline has been highly successful in driving ancillary revenue, which is essential for the profitability of any low cost operator. It was the first airline in the world to charge for hold baggage and to reward those passengers travelling only with hand baggage – a pricing structure that has now become an industry standard. In addition, Flybe has become the in-flight sales market leader,

taking a higher spend per passenger than any other regional airline.

Flybe has also spearheaded efforts to reduce the environmental impact of air travel. Investing more than US$2 billion in new aircraft since 2006, Flybe became the first airline to take delivery of the new Embraer 195 jet aircraft. Its performance features include greater fuel efficiency and a reduction in noise levels. This 14-aircraft order – in addition to 60 Bombardier Q400 aircraft – will give Flybe one of the youngest and most environmentally sensitive fleets in the world, part of its drive to reduce fuel consumption by more than 50 per cent per seat by the end of 2009.

In line with this commitment, Flybe was the first airline in the world to introduce an aircraft eco-labelling scheme. Passengers booking via the internet now receive a detailed breakdown of fuel consumption, carbon emissions and noise patterns.

Flybe's achievements have culminated in a number of industry awards, including being ranked first in The Sunday Times Top Track 250 league table in 2008.

Product

Flybe operates services from 34 UK and 29 mainland European airports, with routes to key commercial centres including Paris, Düsseldorf, Frankfurt and Milan. The airline's network is made up of 70 per cent domestic UK routes, 20 per cent business and 10 per cent leisure. Indeed, Flybe is the largest scheduled airline at Birmingham, Exeter, Manchester,

1979	1991	1993	2000	2003	2006
Jersey-based entrepreneur and successful businessman Jack Walker founds Jersey European. The airline is taken over by the Walkersteel Group in 1983.	Jersey European gains its first London route from Guernsey to London Gatwick.	The Business Class service is launched and Jersey European is named Best UK Regional Airline at the Northern Ireland Travel and Tourism Awards, for two consecutive years.	Jersey European changes its name to British European, becoming Flybe two years later.	Flybe is voted Most Recommended UK Low Fares Airline by Holiday Which? It goes on to be named Most Popular UK Domestic and France-bound Airline in 2005.	Flybe becomes the first airline to offer online check-in to passengers carrying hand and hold baggage, along with functionality for online flight changes.

Norwich, Southampton, the Channel Islands, the Isle of Man and Belfast City.

For the business market, a key part of the airline's offering is Flybe Economy Plus. As well as free access to the 13 Executive Lounges across its network, this offers a range of additional features such as a dedicated check-in, shorter minimum check-in times, fully changeable tickets and a generous baggage allowance.

In addition to its passenger service, Flybe is also a major player in Aviation Services. Not only offering aircraft engineering for its own fleet, it provides third-party maintenance for a client list that includes many traditional airlines. The business – which has won several industry accolades – employs more than 500 engineers

at its Exeter site, plus further line engineering teams at an additional 13 bases across the UK.

Recent Developments

In line with Flybe's growth strategy, 2008 brought customers an expanded offering and innovative launches, such as Flybe Connections. A one-stop booking service, it enables customers to book multiple connecting Flybe flights – including those of its franchise partner, Loganair – in a single transaction, effectively creating 117 new route options.

Operating under the 'Spend Once, Fly Free' maxim, the Flybe Spend & Fly MasterCard provides passengers with added value, rewarding cardholders with free return flights. The card is integrated with Flybe's Rewards4all frequent flyer programme – the first loyalty scheme to be introduced by a low fare airline.

Carrying a higher percentage of business passengers than any other UK low cost airline, Flybe has invested £2 million in its business travel product to maintain passenger loyalty and attract new custom: eight of the 13 Executive Lounges are less than two years old and more than 80 self-service check-in kiosks have been introduced across the UK during the past year.

Promotion

With customer relationship marketing a crucial factor in Flybe achieving its goal of increasing customer loyalty, it operates a highly segmented database that allows personalised, relevant communications to be delivered to its key customers.

In addition to its ongoing retail advertising, Flybe's 2008/09 press campaign supports its

product investment, targeting the business traveller. The testimonial-based adverts feature genuine frequent business flyers as advocates for its services. Each represents a key business region and positions Flybe as an 'enabler' for regional businesses. Running across national and regional press, trade press and business magazines, the campaign is also being rolled out online and at airport outdoor sites.

Connecting with the communities it serves is at the heart of Flybe's marketing approach: Local Heroes Awards, Flybe Bursaries, partnering with Cancer Research UK and sponsorship of three football clubs ensure a community-focused mix.

Brand Values

Flybe's brand is built on a vision to be modern, dynamic, passionate and straightforward. Its commitment and contribution to regional economies, investment in local communities, advocacy for regional 'on your doorstep' services, and strong regional heritage all support the Flybe identity. Alongside this, innovation and providing a comprehensive, high quality customer service offering remain key to the ongoing development and success of the brand.

flybe.com

"Our clients expect a presence on-site, with loads of flights from my local airport I can organise my travel to achieve this and be back the same day to spend time with my family."
David McVeigh, Harland and Wolff, Northern Ireland

Visit your customer. If you don't your competitors will. That's the real bottom line.

- High frequency business traveller schedules
- Over 500 flights a day across the network
- Serving 63 destinations from 34 UK airports
- Supporting over 7000 jobs in the UK regions

flybe.com
Powering regional business

2007		2008	
Flybe acquires BA Connect, becoming Europe's largest regional airline. It also launches Rewards4all – its frequent flyer scheme – and pioneers aircraft eco-labelling.	Flybe's acquisition of BA Connect wins it Flight International's Best Management Team award, as well as Achievement of the Year at the Franco-British Business Awards.	Flybe announces a landmark franchise agreement with Loganair, while Flybe Connections creates 117 new route options across an expanded network.	Flybe's CEO Jim French wins the Regional Leadership award at the Airline Strategy Awards and Flybe is ranked first in The Sunday Times Top Track 250 league table.

Things you didn't know about Flybe

If all the tubs of Pringles sold on board in one year were stacked on top of each other, they would be 12 times higher than the world's tallest building, Taipei Tower in Taiwan.

Flybe could fill 15 Olympic-sized swimming pools with all the bottles of mineral water it sells in a year.

Each year the Flybe fleet uses 1,800 aircraft tyres and flies a total of 44.4 million kilometres.

GATWICK EXPRESS

Established in 1984, Gatwick Express is the longest running dedicated airport service in the world and serves the UK's second busiest airport. Offering a non-stop journey time of 30 minutes with trains departing every 15 minutes, it carries more than 14,000 passengers a day between Gatwick Airport and London's Victoria Station.

We're the only non-stop service to central London.

(Which is why we're also the fastest.)

London Victoria in 30 minutes†, every 15 minutes.

GATWICK EXPRESS
Anything else is a risk

Market
Gatwick Airport is one of the top 10 busiest international airports in the world with more than 35 million passengers passing through its North and South Terminals each year. Gatwick Express holds over 70 per cent of the rail market between Gatwick Airport and central London, and it is the fastest way to travel the route; services run every 15 minutes with journey times of 30 minutes.

Achievements
Customer satisfaction has been integral to the success of Gatwick Express and it has scored consistently highly in the independent National Passenger Survey. In the spring 2006 survey, Gatwick Express achieved a 94 per cent satisfaction rating, the highest in the survey's history, followed in 2008 by a rating of 93 per cent, the highest in the country.

Delivering excellent customer service is a constant challenge as customer demands are ever evolving. To meet the needs of an increasingly sophisticated and customer service driven market, Gatwick Express has shifted its focus towards providing flexible, positive and personal customer service. As a result, the innovative and award-winning Leading Lights training programme has been developed. Designed to effectively engage its workforce by using drama and theatrical elements to spark interest and maintain attention in trainees, Leading Lights helps frontline staff identify different types of customers so they can deliver exceptional service that meets the passengers' individual needs. The emphasis is on achieving targeted, long term change in day-to-day behaviour and performance.

Product
Gatwick Express is a dedicated and non-stop, high speed, air-rail link operating between London Victoria Station and Gatwick Airport. It operates purpose built Juniper Class 460 trains that run from Victoria Station between 3.30am and 12.30am and from Gatwick Airport between 4.35am and 1.35am. Gatwick Express trains are air-conditioned and have ergonomically designed seating, generous

1984	1990s	2001	2005	2008	
The first dedicated Gatwick Express service is formed to provide an air-rail link to Gatwick Airport.	Gatwick Airport continues to expand.	All rolling stock is replaced with the modern Juniper Class 460 trains.	Thirty-two million passengers pass through Gatwick Airport throughout the year.	In June, the Gatwick Express franchise is handed over to Southern.	In December 2008, Gatwick Express extends its service to Brighton and introduces Juniper Class 442 trains for the new route.

in 2008 Gatwick Express upgraded its ticket machines to accept euros. Targeting customers travelling to or from Europe, the service aims to save customers valuable time during their journey. Eight ticket machines at Gatwick Airport and two at London Victoria Station now accept euro notes.

Promotion

Gatwick Express uses a range of press, outdoor and online communications in the UK and internationally to reach its customer base and execute its promotional strategy. The current focus for Gatwick Express is on customer relationship marketing, with the objective of ensuring consistent and frequent communication with the customer base, providing news about promotions, new products and service enhancements.

In 2006 it launched its 'Anything else is a risk' advertising campaign, specifically targeted at the time sensitive air traveller. The strapline was underpinned by the essence of 'certainty' associated with the Gatwick Express brand.

International travellers are targeted through airline partners; Gatwick Express has developed solid relationships with growth airlines, such as easyJet, as a mechanism for reaching potential customers during the booking process or during their flight. Jointly branded microsites, reciprocal website links, in-flight announcements and advertising in

in-flight magazines have all been effective methods for generating sales.

Gatwick Express was the first train company to sell visitor Oyster cards in partnership with Transport for London (TfL). This new initiative was launched at a press conference at City Hall with the Mayor of London. Oyster cards for visitors can be bought on board Gatwick Express trains and at the Gatwick Airport ticket office.

Gatwick Express also realises the potential of the ski and snowboard market and is targeting this through sponsorship of the Time Out 'Ski & Snowboard Europe' guide. This sponsorship is supported by concourse promotions at London Victoria Station and online advertising on high profile ski websites. Due to the large number of flights for ski destinations departing from Gatwick Airport, the ample luggage space on board Gatwick Express trains and a 'four for two' promotional offer, this market presents significant growth potential.

Brand Values

Gatwick Express bases its brand promise on the certainty that customers will arrive in a timely fashion; for most air travellers, the consequences of a delay can be significant.

This promise is broken down into rational and emotional benefits of using the service. Rational benefits include the speed and frequency of the service, as well as its punctuality and reliability. Emotional benefits include the dedicated service, trust and reassurance, premium feel and the belief that Gatwick Express is the 'official way' to the airport – anything else is a risk.

The Gatwick Express 'voice' that delivers these brand values in its advertising has been developed to represent that of an airline captain with wit and charm – someone who is confident, comfortable and unflappable.

gatwickexpress.com

luggage areas and onboard catering services. Exclusive platforms at Victoria Station allow customers quick access on and off the trains, while the station at Gatwick Airport is located at the heart of the South Terminal.

In December 2008, Gatwick Express extended its service to run from Gatwick Airport to Brighton as part of the Department for Transport's Brighton Main Line Route Utilisation Strategy.

Gatwick Express is a member of the Airport Express Alliance, a joint alliance between BAA and Southern, which promotes and markets the Gatwick Express, Heathrow Express and Heathrow Connect rail services. The alliance brings together the sales and marketing activities of all three operations to create a single point of contact for airlines, travel trade agents and tour operators.

Recent Developments

In keeping with its commitment to further improve the travel experience for customers,

Things you didn't know about Gatwick Express

Gatwick Express featured in the 2008 edition of National Geographic's travel publication, 'The 10 Best of Everything'.

During the Christmas 2008 period, Gatwick Express offered a free gift wrapping service for customers, using only recycled materials.

Every year 1.6 million miles are travelled by Gatwick Express, the equivalent to more than six times the distance to the moon.

Every day, more than 14,000 customers travel on the Gatwick Express service.

gettyimages®

Getty Images is the world's leading creator and distributor of still imagery, footage and multimedia products as well as a recognised provider of other forms of premium digital content. Bringing ideas to life, Getty Images' photos appear daily all over the world, in newspapers, magazines, websites, books and film – anywhere where there is a story to tell.

Market

Getty Images is the market leader in the provision of creative and editorial still images, footage and music to the world's creative professionals. Serving business customers in more than 100 countries, its core base comprises three key segments: agency, corporate and media.

In recent years the proliferation of affordable digital photographic technology has resulted in user-generated content and 'microstock', impacting significantly on the industry, driving down the cost of traditional commercial stock imagery but without providing the same level of indemnification to the end-user.

In the traditional, premium-priced creative stock imagery arena the brand's nearest competitor is Corbis, but a rapidly changing marketplace poses new industry challenges such as ever more geographically diverse customer groups, the fragmentation of media channels, the growing cult of celebrity and the shift from print to digital advertising.

Getty Images' strategy for success is to diversify into a wide range of digital media products and services, ultimately offering solutions to customers' communications needs at every price point.

Achievements

Today, gettyimages.com serves an average of 3.2 billion thumbnails, 7.3 million visits and four million unique users in addition to an average of 175 million page views each month. Nearly 100 per cent of the company's visual content is delivered digitally.

The company frequently receives industry recognition for both its photography and business accomplishments. In 2005, American Photo Magazine acknowledged its commitment to the industry by naming co-founders Mark Getty and Jonathan Klein

as top of their list of The 100 Most Important People in Photography.

Year after year, Getty Images' photographers and employees have been honoured for their contribution to the industry. In 2008, photojournalist Brent Stirton was named International Photographer of the Year by the Lucie Foundation, joining an elite list of past award-winners including Annie Leibovitz and Cornell Capa. In addition to receiving the prestigious award, Stirton's imagery earned him the title of Editorial Professional Photographer of the Year and topped categories such as Environmental Editorial.

Product

Getty Images provides the most accessible and reliable way to search, download, license and manage the broadest and deepest

1995	1996	1997	2001		2002
Mark Getty and Jonathan Klein establish Getty Communications and the first art-directed 'stock' photo shoot takes place.	Getty Images acquires Hulton Deutsch Collection Limited and lists on NASDAQ as GETY.	Getty Images sells its first image over the internet. Over the next few years, acquisitions see Getty Images grow to encompass editorial imagery and stock film footage.	The launch of gettyimages.com takes place, enabling customers to search, license and download across all of its stills and film collections.	On 11th September, Getty Images' Spencer Platt captures the defining moment when a plane crashes into the South Tower of the World Trade Centre. The image is used by newspapers worldwide.	Getty Images is listed on the New York Stock Exchange as GYI and a partnership with Time & Life Pictures allows it to offer the most extensive collection of archival imagery available online.

selection of relevant still images and film clips. To serve the demands of a fully digital publishing industry it provides instantaneous news feeds, sport and entertainment images as well as painstaking archival research with more than 10 million captioned editorial images and ready-to-use multimedia packages that combine editorial stills and footage with sound.

Working with leading brands such as Canon, HSBC, RBS, Shell, BMW and Vodafone, Getty Images provides bespoke photography to support sponsorship and events programmes, forging similar partnerships across the music and entertainment sector to cover high-profile events such as the Oscars, BAFTAs and Cannes Film Festival.

Getty Images' photographer representation service, Orchard, features a roster of acclaimed international photographers such as Lorenzo Agius, Mitch Jenkins and Tom Stoddart, chosen for their inspiration and creativity. Employing subject-matter specialists with years of experience underlines the brand's integrity.

Getty Images' on-demand digital asset management (DAM) allows business users to access, browse, search and download

the assets they need and distribute digital materials globally.

Recent Developments
In 2008, Getty Images made two significant couplings: it joined forces with Flickr, one of the world's largest photo sharing communities, and it acquired Jupiterimages; a strategic investment in keeping with its commitment to provide long term value to customers by making more digital content easily accessible. Jupiterimages' extensive portfolio enables Getty Images to offer a more versatile and flexible service in the provision of imagery and other content assets to customers, while its partnership with Flickr further extends the choice available by providing more regionally relevant content and a broader range of photography styles.

Promotion
Several recent global campaigns have focused on using imagery to initiate change. 'Change Me' encouraged thousands of people worldwide to select inspirational photographs

from Getty Images and for each submission US$10 was contributed to Friends of the Global Fight Against Aids, Tuberculosis and Malaria – resulting in a total contribution of US$500,000.

The 'Ultimate Pitch' encouraged people to develop a creative idea that they believed could make a difference to the world, using content from Getty Images to communicate the idea online through social networking sites, 24-hour news channels, virals and blogs – creating a digital 'ripple effect'. The people with the top 20 ideas were provided with the high-resolution assets in order to produce their pitch, before an ultimate winner was announced.

Brand Values
Getty Images' success comes from continued innovation in the way it researches, produces and delivers the products and services creative professionals the world over rely on. Central to achieving this is communication excellence, passion and a willingness to embrace change.

gettyimages.com

Things you didn't know about Getty Images

The Getty Images Gallery, opened in 1996, is London's largest independent photographic gallery.

The Getty Images Hulton Archive is home to more than 60 million images dating back to the birth of photography.

Getty Images has offices in 16 key territories including the UK, the US, France, Germany, Australia and Japan, employing 1,800 staff to service the needs of around 250,000 customers.

Getty Images' team of more than 150 staff photographers have won some of the industry's most prestigious awards such as the World Press Photo.

2004
Getty Images launches Grants for Editorial Photography, offering five grants totalling US$100,000 to fund work by established and rising photojournalists.

2005
Getty Images appoints an ombudsman to ensure adherence to photojournalism editorial standards – a first for the imagery industry.

2007
A new music licensing service, Soundtrack, is launched giving customers direct access to more than 20,000 tracks for use in broadcast, film and media projects.

2008
Getty Images enters into a definitive merger agreement to be acquired by Hellman & Friedman LLC in a transaction valued at approximately US$2.4 billion.

Harris®
World Class Decorating Products

Underpinned by a spirit of innovation and high service standards, family-owned Harris has been producing quality decorating products for more than 80 years. Today, Harris is a thriving company that prides itself on its expertise and focuses on originality, ergonomics and aesthetics to produce a broad range of decorating products for the DIY and professional markets.

today it operates a British factory and headquarters in Bromsgrove, Worcestershire alongside a wholly owned foreign enterprise in China. Consisting of a two-site, £5 million factory investment, the Chinese operation provides the company with a competitive proposition and 24-hour global operation; its proactive attitude towards training and development programmes for employees has earned Harris recognition from the Chinese Government.

Harris continually strives to be at the forefront of innovative product design by creating products that outperform market alternatives through ease of use, effectiveness and durability. In 1993, it launched a range of No Loss paint brushes, the first in the world to be guaranteed against bristle loss while painting. This was followed by EasyClean, a range of brushes designed with a unique 'liquiflo' system that reduces drag and enables paint to flow easily out of the brush, which then requires less water to clean.

In 2008, Harris was named Supplier of the Year by both the British Hardware Federation Group and Mica Hardware.

Market

The DIY market continues to be characterised by people wanting to make changes to their home environment, primarily driven by fashion trends and the need to maintain homes. Within the decorating sundries sector of the DIY market, Harris has capitalised on this trend by launching a string of innovative decorating products designed to help consumers bring their inspirations to life.

The economic downturn has seen an increase in the attitude of 'don't move – improve', whereby people are investing in improving the décor of their current property rather than moving home. This has also resulted in a revival of DIY rather than the use of professional tradesmen.

The market value for decorating sundries is estimated at around £58.5 million, of which Harris' share in terms of turnover equates to approximately 56 per cent.

Achievements

LG Harris & Co Ltd was established in 1928, trading from two Victorian houses in Birmingham. Growing from small beginnings,

Product

With a reputation for quality products, the Harris portfolio consists of three main brands that have been strategically developed to cater for a wide range of customer needs.

The Harris range is the core product offering, comprising a comprehensive selection of brushes, rollers, tools and other decorating sundries. The range has been extended to include an international offer with products tailored to suit local environments, paint types

1928	1930	1947	1961	1970	1990s
The Midland Trading Company is founded in Birmingham by LG Harris, buying and reselling paint brushes.	The Midland Trading Company is renamed LG Harris & Co Ltd.	The business develops rapidly with the beginning of the DIY boom and a new 60-acre site is opened.	The company is awarded a Royal Warrant by Her Majesty The Queen, becoming the preferred manufacturer of paint brushes and decorators' tools for Royal Estates.	Household brushes are added with hair brushes, shaving brushes and tooth brushes. Four years later a new warehouse and despatch department is built for the growing product range.	The growth of the large DIY retailers heralds an unprecedented period of growth for Harris, which sees turnover triple in eight years.

and decorating techniques. In supplying customers around the world, Harris aims to achieve 'global brand consistency with local product specificity'.

The T-Class range consists of products designed specifically with the professional decorator in mind and seeks to provide them with the complete solution for any project.

In July 2008 the company strengthened its portfolio with the acquisition of the Victory brand. Under the newly launched Harris Victory name, it now offers a range of brooms and household brushes.

Recent Developments
The Harris ID (Intelligent Decorating) product offering, first launched in 2006, has continued to grow with additions such as the ID Lock 'n' Roll; a unique locking clip holds the roller sleeve securely in place, eliminating slippage while painting. The latest launch for 2009 is the ID Gel range. Spanning brushes, rollers and tools, the unique gel inserts and ergonomic handle shapes have been designed for optimum comfort during prolonged use.

Thanks to the strength of its customer marketing platform, which includes a

bespoke range catalogue as well as a global press and point of sale suite, recent years have seen Harris continue to expand rapidly into export markets. Currently, products are being well received in the Middle East, Scandinavia, South America, Australia and the Caribbean.

Promotion
Harris uses a comprehensive range of marketing communications tools to build awareness and drive demand for its products, both in the UK and in a global market.

Domestically, the Harris website and product-focused marketing campaigns, timed to hit key decorating periods in the UK, have helped to position the brand as a producer of 'World Class Decorating Products'. The 2008 'Feel Inspired' campaign, which ran across press and online, was designed to reignite the 'can-do' attitude towards DIY that was prevalent in the early 1990s.

Internationally, Harris communicates to the retail trade through a select number of industry trade shows, combined with follow-up B2B campaigns and targeted promotions.

Harris has also maintained its partnership with England Squash to continue regional and international

brand building through sponsorship of the Inter County Championships.

Brand Values
Harris is positioned as a producer of 'World Class Decorating Products' and an expert in the field of decorating. The company is proud of its Royal Warrant, which goes hand in hand with the high value placed on the company's heritage, especially as it still remains family owned.

Harris is also committed to upholding the elements of its core brand values of experience, creativity, quality, desirable innovation and leadership, all of which have brought continuing success for the business.

lgharris.co.uk

Things you didn't know about Harris

There are more than 2,000 products in the Harris brand portfolio.

Natural bristle comes from the Chinese hog and comes in both black and white varieties.

At one time in its history, Harris planted and maintained its own forests (covering nearly 5,000 acres) in an effort to create its own raw material supply.

The company's founder LG Harris was awarded an MBE for his work with the Margery Fry Trust, setting up and funding a series of homes for ex-prisoners.

During World War II the company produced brushes for the war effort.

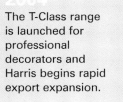

2002
The company's first wholly owned Chinese facility opens, introducing twin manufacturing. The UK facility also grows with the opening of a £1.1 million storage facility.

2004
The T-Class range is launched for professional decorators and Harris begins rapid export expansion.

2006
The ID range is launched as a platform for new and innovative products designed specifically to make decorating easier.

2008
John Palmer Brushes Ltd is acquired and Harris Victory is launched.

Heathrow **express** ⊗

Serving the world's busiest international airport and carrying more than five million passengers per year, Heathrow Express is one of the most successful high-speed air-rail links in the world. The service carries more than 16,000 passengers a day on the 15-minute journey between Heathrow Airport and central London.

15 minutes from Paddington to Heathrow. The airport is closer than you think.
Trains leave every 15 minutes.
Heathrow **express** ⊗

Market

Every year, some 63 million passengers pass through Heathrow Airport. Compared to many other international airports, Heathrow has historically been one of the hardest to get to, with passengers travelling to and from London facing a long journey by tube or risking traffic congestion by car or taxi.

Heathrow Express has tapped into a growing trend among world airports to offer a premium, dedicated and high-speed train service, giving passengers an easy, reliable and fast option for travelling between the city centre and airport. Trains reach the airport in just 15 minutes (services to Terminal 5 take 21 minutes), compared to around 55-60 minutes by London Underground and 30-45 minutes by taxi or car.

Achievements

Since its launch in June 1998, Heathrow Express has established itself as a favoured route for both business and leisure passengers. The service removes approximately 3,000 journeys from the roads every day and when compared to the use of tube, taxi or bus, has made savings to the UK economy (in terms of time) of more than £444 million.

Heathrow Express has eased congestion on London's roads with its Taxi Share scheme, introduced in 1998 and operated in conjunction with the Licensed Taxi Drivers Association. More than 668,000 travellers have shared a taxi so far, saving about 1,608,000 taxi miles and easing the pressure on London's rush hour, while also providing passengers with lower fares and shorter waiting times.

Heathrow Express also extended its global reach by becoming the first ever air-rail link to sign a deal with travel technology provider Amadeus. The deal means travellers in more than 215 geographic markets can book Heathrow Express tickets at the same time as booking their flights and accommodation.

Heathrow Express has won a host of awards and has been recognised internationally as one of the most successful airport rail services. Its corporate identity, developed by Wolff Olins, is among the most comprehensive branding and design projects ever undertaken in transportation. This was recognised when the project became the 2000 Grand Prix Winner of the Design Business Awards.

Heathrow Express has worked hard to translate its customer service ethos into action and in 2006 was judged to have the Customer Service Team of the Year at the National Customer Service Awards. In 2007, Heathrow Express secured a double first by topping the poll in the independent National Passenger Satisfaction Survey and achieving the highest score in the survey's eight-year history. In 2008 Heathrow Express maintained its high position with a 92 per cent satisfaction rating.

1991	1998	2001	2007	2008	
The Heathrow Express Railways Act gives BAA the power to construct the Heathrow Express.	Heathrow Express is officially launched by the Prime Minister, Tony Blair.	Heathrow Express places an order for five new carriages, costing a total of £6.5 million.	In partnership with T-Mobile and Nomad Digital, a WiFi Hotspot service is introduced, providing passengers with 2Mb/s internet access throughout the entire journey, including the 6km tunnel.	Heathrow Express launches services to Terminal 5 and introduces e-ticketing.	Also in 2008, Heathrow Express launches its biggest multimedia campaign to date: 'The Airport is closer than you think.'

Product

Heathrow Express is a dedicated and non-stop, high-speed air-rail link that operates daily between Heathrow Airport and central London, departing every 15 minutes. Services run from London Paddington to Heathrow Central (Terminals 1,2,3) and Terminal 5. Passengers wishing to travel to Terminal 4 can change at Heathrow Central and then board the free inter-terminal rail transfer service.

The Heathrow stations are designed to ensure that customers are provided with swift, convenient access to the train service. Train carriages are air-conditioned and have ergonomically designed seating, generous luggage areas and onboard televisions. There are also Quiet Zones on the trains where the use of mobile phones is prohibited and Express TV is not in use.

Heathrow Express is a member of the Airport Express Alliance, a joint alliance between BAA and Southern, which promotes and markets the Heathrow Express, Gatwick Express and Heathrow Connect rail services. The alliance brings together the sales and marketing activities of all three operations to create a single point of contact for airlines, travel trade agents and tour operators.

Recent Developments

Heathrow Express is an innovative media owner and is constantly looking for ways to give other businesses commercial access to its hard-to-reach business audience.

In January 2007, Heathrow Express launched the first ever 'motion picture videowall' advert in Europe. Four-hundred and fifty 'frames', each holding an individual printed image, were installed in the train tunnel walls, covering a total distance of 1,500ft. Seen from a train travelling at 70mph this created a 15-second moving image advert.

Heathrow Express has also enhanced its groundbreaking onboard television service, Express TV. Created specifically to cater for the Heathrow Express passenger, it delivers a customised bulletin from BBC News 24 covering domestic, international and business news as well as entertainment programmes and travel clips.

The company continues to innovate to meet customer needs and launched an e-ticketing service in 2008. Tickets can be sent to mobile phones in the form of a barcode, allowing passengers to book and board the service without having to queue for paper tickets.

Promotion

Heathrow Express' biggest multimedia campaign, 'The Airport is closer than you think' was launched in 2008 and saw a series of idents run worldwide on Sky News to complement press, outdoor and digital advertising. The campaign set out to reinforce Heathrow Express as the fastest way to the airport. Press advertising featured in key UK business titles while an international campaign ran at JFK Airport in New York and Frankfurt, Schipol and Dublin airports.

The company uses below-the-line media to target its audience, investing in customer relationship marketing to boost frequency of use among its most loyal customers and developing marketing relationships with airlines at Heathrow Airport. For example, Heathrow Express partnered with British

Airways to provide BA Executive Club members with complimentary tickets when booking flights online. Partnerships are communicated via membership packs, media activity and email newsletters.

Brand Values

Heathrow Express' key brand values are speed, frequency and certainty; recent research has shown that these are the service benefits most recalled by customers.

For both business and leisure customers, Heathrow Express aims to provide high levels of comfort and customer service. However, different aspects of the brand's personality are highlighted for each market. For the business traveller, the brand is portrayed as fast, frequent, reliable and convenient. When speaking to the leisure market, the brand is reflected as not being overly formal or austere while being fast, reliable, convenient, approachable and family friendly.

heathrowexpress.com

Things you didn't know about Heathrow Express

Heathrow Express celebrated its 10th anniversary in 2008, carrying over 50 million passengers in the last decade. To mark the event, the BBC Symphony Orchestra played 'Happy Birthday' at Paddington station.

Heathrow Express was the first rail service in the UK to introduce onboard televisions at its launch in 1998.

Heathrow Express trains can travel at speeds of up to 100mph.

THE INSTITUTE
OF CHARTERED
ACCOUNTANTS

IN ENGLAND AND WALES

The Institute of Chartered Accountants in England and Wales (ICAEW) is a leading professional accountancy body, providing premium qualifications, services and support to more than 132,000 members in over 160 countries. It works with governments, regulators and industry to ensure the highest standards in the finance and accountancy profession are maintained. ICAEW members provide technical and ethical financial guidance to individuals and organisations worldwide.

Market

The role of chartered accountants in the world's economies has never been more important. People making financial decisions not only need knowledge and guidance based on the highest technical and ethical standards, but also need to be able to trust in the quality and impartiality of their financial colleagues and advisors.

The ICAEW is the largest professional accountancy body in Europe and its members are therefore well placed to offer clear and thorough guidance and to challenge people and organisations to think and act differently. The Institute provides a supportive environment in which its members' skills can be developed, recognised and valued; after qualification a lifelong relationship is established through the offer of ongoing professional development.

The Institute's thought leadership programme looks ahead at the long term issues for the financial sector and helps to shape government thinking on regulatory business and tax policy. It develops and promotes technical policy in order to enhance the international environment in which its members operate.

Achievements

The ICAEW's members work across the full breadth of the economy, using their expertise in business, practice and the public sector. Among its members are business leaders working in some of the world's most successful organisations; in 2008, 84 per cent of the boards of the FTSE 100 included an ICAEW member. The Institute's membership base also includes more than 700 licensed insolvency

practitioners and over 4,300 audit registered firms; more than any other body in the UK.

The Institute's flagship professional qualification, the ACA, is designed to equip its trainees with the skills needed to become well-regarded professional business advisers. The programme has a reputation for attracting talented people from a variety of backgrounds; in 2008 approximately 89 per cent of the ICAEW's ACA students were graduates, 87 per cent of whom had obtained a 2:1 or first class degree (or international equivalent).

In 2006 the ICAEW was engaged by the European Commission, following a tendering procedure, to undertake a study on the implementation of International Financial Reporting Standards and the modernised accounting directives across the European Union. The study was completed in 2007 and was the most extensive of its kind. In the same year it joined forces with the World Bank and the Bangladesh Government to work towards

raising standards across the country's accountancy profession.

Product

The ACA is regarded globally as one of the leading business and finance qualifications and is recognised and valued in accountancy practice, industry, commerce and the public sector. The ICAEW offers ACA training through more than 2,000 authorised training offices around the world, from the UK to Malaysia, Pakistan, Russia, China, Cyprus and the United Arab Emirates, as well as through partnerships with leading education providers in other countries.

Characterised by its technical rigour, ethical focus, international outlook and multidisciplinary approach, the ACA is designed to reflect modern global accounting practices. Once qualified, members are entitled to call themselves 'chartered accountants' and to use the designatory letters ACA (Associate of the Institute of Chartered Accountants in England

1880	1893	1919	1930	1970
A new professional body, The Institute of Chartered Accountants in England and Wales (ICAEW) is created by Royal Charter.	Chartered Accountants' Hall, in the City of London, is completed and opened by the Institute's president Edwin Waterhouse. It goes on to become a Grade II listed building.	Mary Harris Smith is admitted to the ICAEW, becoming the first female chartered accountant in the world.	Sir William Plender of Sundridge (ICAEW president, 1929-1930) becomes the first chartered accountant to receive a peerage.	The extended and new building at Chartered Accountants' Hall is opened by Her Majesty Queen Elizabeth The Queen Mother.

**THE LABEL.
THE DESIGNER.
THE MODEL.
THE ACCOUNTANT.**

The ACA qualification from the ICAEW gives you access
to amazing career opportunities in any industry.

To find out more:
T +44 (0)1908 248 040
www.icaew.com/careers

THE INSTITUTE
OF CHARTERED
ACCOUNTANTS
IN ENGLAND AND WALES

**THE VOCALIST.
THE GUITARIST.
THE BASSIST.
THE DRUMMER.
THE ACCOUNTANT.**

The ACA qualification from the ICAEW gives you access
to amazing career opportunities in any industry.

To find out more:
T +44 (0)1908 248 040
www.icaew.com/careers

THE INSTITUTE
OF CHARTERED
ACCOUNTANTS
IN ENGLAND AND WALES

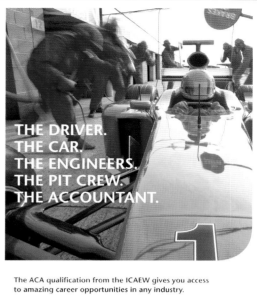

**THE DRIVER.
THE CAR.
THE ENGINEERS.
THE PIT CREW.
THE ACCOUNTANT.**

The ACA qualification from the ICAEW gives you access
to amazing career opportunities in any industry.

To find out more:
T +44 (0)1908 248 040
www.icaew.com/careers

THE INSTITUTE
OF CHARTERED
ACCOUNTANTS
IN ENGLAND AND WALES

and Wales). To retain ACA status, members must participate in continuing professional development every year to ensure their skills and knowledge remain up-to-date and relevant within their industry.

As well as the ACA, the ICAEW provides a range of additional qualifications across various disciplines such as finance, accounting and business (CFAB), corporate finance (CF), charity accounting (DChA), and International Financial Reporting Standards (IFRS certification). Development programmes for professionals are also offered, such as the Financial Talent Executive Network (F-TEN), the Business Sustainability Programme (BSP) and MBA Essentials.

Recent Developments
The ICAEW is constantly developing qualifications, networks, programmes and services for members and the broader business community. In early 2009 it opened a new Business Centre for members and students, providing modern library and business facilities to support its training offering. To widen access to the profession, the CFAB qualification was introduced in 2008 to allow individuals without formal qualifications the opportunity to be certified in the foundations of finance, accounting and business.

The ICAEW also launched the Business Sustainability Programme (BSP), which allows businesses to educate their staff on pressing social and environmental issues, and the first peer to peer leadership network, the Financial Talent Executive Network (F-TEN). Aimed at the

next generation of finance leaders in business and practice, F-TEN is designed to help employers retain their best talent and develop their leadership capabilities.

The Narrowing the Gap programme, introduced in 2008, is designed to help businesses recruit and retain the best female financial talent, as well as helping individuals returning to the workforce after a career break. The programme is supported by the Institute's recruitment portal icaewjobs.com – an all-encompassing career resource for members that showcases the opportunities available to ACAs worldwide.

In addition, the ICAEW is working closely with schools and government on a major national programme to help deliver personal finance education in secondary schools. The Financial Capability programme helps young people develop the basic skills needed to manage their personal finances; skills that are essential in today's economy.

Promotion
A refreshed brand identity was launched in January 2007, supported by a national advertising campaign that also set out to reinforce the premium positioning of the Institute's ACA qualification, as well as the role of the ICAEW in the wider business community. Advertisements featured in national and trade press, online and at cinemas and transport hubs. The response to the campaign revealed a measurable shift in positive perceptions among the Institute's key stakeholders as well as increased recognition of the ACA.

Brand Values
The ICAEW's vision is to promote integrity and professionalism within the finance and accounting profession and to strengthen the Institute's reputation as one of the UK's most influential professional bodies through its dialogue with both government and regulatory bodies.

By setting and maintaining the highest standards and providing access to the latest in-depth expertise available, it aims to ensure that its members are recognised as leaders in their field – acknowledged in the UK and internationally for inspiring business confidence.

icaew.com

Things you didn't know about ICAEW

The Institute is the only international professional body to be invited to join the World Economic Forum in Davos.

The ICAEW is a founding member of the Global Accounting Alliance (GAA), which has more than 750,000 members.

The Institute's Library and Information Service holds the largest collection of UK accountancy, auditing and taxation resources in the world.

The Business Confidence Monitor, a quarterly report from the ICAEW, is drawn upon as an accurate barometer of business thinking by the UK Government and the Bank of England.

Many of the founding fathers of the 'Big Four' accountancy firms were early presidents of the ICAEW – such as Arthur Cooper, William Deloitte, Edwin Waterhouse and William Peat.

1999	2006	2007	2008
Dame Sheila Masters is the first woman to become president of the ICAEW.	The Institute is appointed by the European Commission to study the implementation of International Financial Reporting Standards throughout the European Union.	The ICAEW wins a £1 million tender from the World Bank to raise standards across the accountancy profession in Bangladesh.	ICAEW chief executive Michael Izza chairs the committee recommending to the Chancellor an independent valuer for Northern Rock.

IOD

The Institute of Directors (IoD) has long been recognised as an influential and respected membership organisation in the UK. Its 100-year success is measured by its members who are some of the most skilled and experienced business leaders in the country, representing the full business spectrum – from start-up entrepreneurs to directors in the public sector and CEOs of multinational organisations.

Market

The IoD's most powerful component is the quality of its members; 70 per cent are business leaders from small and medium-sized enterprises and 84 per cent of the FTSE 100 companies are represented. The diversity of professional backgrounds encourages entrepreneurship among the IoD business

community, with members sharing business skills and knowledge with each other while also benefiting from the IoD's support.

Achievements

The IoD's promotion of professional development has opened up many business opportunities for its members throughout 2008. It is recognised for offering creative and flexible training opportunities that can make a significant difference to performance and productivity.

Its exclusive and industry-recognised qualification, Chartered Director, is supported by many major and influential bodies and more than 700 individuals are now qualified. Through IoD International, director training is available in countries as diverse as Japan, India and China, making the IoD a fitting partner for exploring overseas training opportunities.

After celebrating its 60th year as an authoritative and highly regarded business journal in 2007, the IoD's board level publication, Director, was fully redesigned in 2008 to become a contemporary and prestigious business title.

Product

IoD membership aims to offer a real return on investment, improving cost efficiency while increasing long term productivity. The portfolio of benefits includes tangible, measurable business resources that support both individual and operational performance.

The IoD provides its members with many opportunities to meet and connect, with high-profile occasions such as the Annual Convention which hosts more than 2,500 business leaders at the Royal Albert Hall. Smaller, more regular events are held regionally, with local breakfast briefings and seminars.

1903		1921	1950	1976	1987
WA Addinsell, the head of a family-run accountancy firm, becomes the founding pioneer of the IoD.	Also in 1903, the first group of senior directors meet to form the 'Council of the IoD', responding to concerns about the creation of new company legislation in 1900/01.	The forerunner to Director magazine, entitled Advance, is launched.	The IoD holds its first Annual Convention, which moves to the Royal Albert Hall in 1961.	The IoD moves to its current headquarters, 116 Pall Mall, London.	Margaret Thatcher addresses the IoD Annual Convention.

China

"You are a pillock if you don't do business there."

Lord Powell of Bayswater, former President of the China-Britain Business Council

Everyone is shouting about China being the place to do business in the future, but has this boat already sailed? With the speculative global economy, China's economy looks set to remain buoyant, providing a strong consumer base for any company. For those who can navigate the political and cultural maze there are still some golden nuggets for the taking, particularly within the service and retail sectors, but how do you tap into these?

Gain Direction

Breakfast Briefing
Wednesday 11 June 2008
8 – 11am
116 Pall Mall, London, SW1Y 5ED

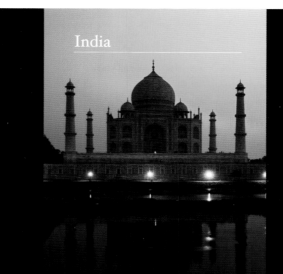

India

"The potential to significantly increase trade, business and investment between Britain and India is remarkable, and the increase is indeed vital to the future strength of our country (Britain)."

Lord Bilimoria CBE DL, Chief Executive of Cobra Beer and UK Chairman of Indo British Partnership

India is inching up the scale in terms of the ease of doing business. The world's largest democracy has an enormous English-speaking population as well as a solid education system, that each year churns out more than a million college graduates. No one is going to argue that India is most definitely making its mark on the world, some even think its economy will outpace fellow Asian giant, China. But with a gloomy outlook for the US economy is the domino effect likely to hit India's booming economy?

Be Inspired

Breakfast Briefing
Friday 20 June 2008
8 – 11am
116 Pall Mall, London, SW1Y 5ED

Members have free access to work space in 10 prestigious city premises across the UK – three of which are in London – and a further two in Paris and Brussels.

The IoD is a reputable source for relevant and accurate information on all aspects of business, and the quality of service is taken very seriously. From confidential, independent business advice to last-minute research on tax issues, its qualified and skilled team is on hand to tackle any business queries that members may have. A popular and practical resource, the legal support line alone received 3,665 calls from members in 2008.

The importance of online resources is also recognised and iod.com is continually developing as a source for business articles, shared ideas, briefing papers and professional forums alongside impartial advice from experienced contributors. It now receives 72,000 visits each month, from both members and non-members.

Recent Developments

2008 was a significant year for the IoD, with many of its members facing a stark company outlook in the wake of the economic downturn. The IoD has placed an increased emphasis on supporting them through the crisis, helping to pre-empt the demands of individual markets and guiding members through unexpected eventualities.

A new online membership benefit was introduced, designed to save members time, money and effort. A private, professional networking forum now allows members to share ideas, opinions, strategies and skills online. Members also have access to a new, private online area that provides a diverse range of material, from articles and fact sheets to information guides.

Promotion

In 2008 a refreshed IoD brand was implemented, following feedback from members that highlighted a need for clearer communications. It was developed through a process of listening to and engaging with key stakeholders, with the resulting strategy utilising imagery to a greater and more creative effect while still preserving the simplicity and heritage of the IoD's well-known mark.

The IoD maintains a strong visual presence across the media as a result of its active promotion of members' interests at government level – from producing in-depth research documents to detailed discussions with civil servants and official responses.

Its own publications further enhance this presence; a new topical publication, Big Picture, provides comment on the full range of policy issues. The introduction of Policy Voice, an IoD policy community, allows members to put their views forward to key policy makers through surveys and forums.

In 2008 the IoD hosted BBC's Masterchef television programme for the first time. The semi-final contestants produced a fine dining meal for a panel of nine business people and renowned food judges, John Torode and Gregg Wallace. The programme aired in early 2009.

Brand Values

The IoD's brand mark represents the essence of the organisation – the 'D' takes precedence over the 'I', illustrating the simple approach that 'Directors come before the Institute'. The elegant, yet commanding design also reflects the IoD's values: professional, inclusive, commercial, enterprising, open and honest.

The IoD attributes its success to the treatment of each member as an individual and to its brand offering of knowledgeable staff, responsive, engaging communication and confident, trustworthy support.

iod.com

It's our business to listen

Our members are our business

You make us the powerful body that we are

1999
The world's first independently accredited qualification for directors, Chartered Director, is launched.

2001
IoD 123 is opened by Tony Blair. In addition, the Business Leaders Summits are introduced and iod.com goes live.

2003
The IoD's commitment to business excellence expands globally with the launch of IoD International.

2008
The IoD Group is launched, a private online networking forum for members.

Already one of the leading forces in the UK design and print market, Kall Kwik continues to add to the range of services offered by its UK-wide network of Centres and is rapidly gaining a reputation for creative design that makes business print even more effective. At the same time, the company has expanded into new markets including email communications and web-to-print.

This growth in design-related business was achieved through support programmes that helped Kall Kwik and kdesign studios to recruit and train skilled design personnel.

Product

For many design and print projects, 85 per cent of the total spend is used on creative design – leaving just 15 per cent for print. Therefore, by placing greater emphasis on selling design services, Kall Kwik is helping Franchisees to increase order values. In addition, as the choice of printer often lies in the hands of a project's designer, Kall Kwik Franchisees that work with customers at the design level have greater ownership of the entire project. This design-led sales strategy is helping to position Franchisees as trusted advisors in design and print; Franchisees are able to engage with customers from the outset of a project, contribute ideas on a consultative basis and oversee every aspect from design through to fulfilment.

This integrated capability, known as Design to Delivery™ (D2D), is of particular benefit to customers with complex campaigns. By covering a wider range of print and design requirements in-house – including specialist print services, such as large-format or outdoor banners – Kall Kwik provides a complete service, from just one supplier. With shorter lines of communication involved, projects are able to run more smoothly and there can be direct economic benefits as a result.

Quick to recognise the potential of new technologies, Kall Kwik continues to adopt the latest in high-definition digital print. Personalised print – whereby printed items include content that is personalised to individual recipients – is just one area where

Market

With virtually every UK business requiring professional design and print services, the total market exceeds £1 billion per annum. Kall Kwik is the UK's largest design and print group – with a seven per cent market share – and the company is proactively helping Franchisees to expand into new market sectors.

Today, as businesses and public sector organisations seek to improve efficiency and focus on their core activities, there's a growing need for suppliers that offer a wider range of services so that administrative burdens are eased and fewer suppliers need to be briefed for each project. While building on its strong position in the traditional print market, Kall Kwik is introducing non-print products that help

Franchisees to respond to customer demand for integrated communications services.

Achievements

Over the years, Kall Kwik has won many awards for its Franchise model. In 2008, Kall Kwik's parent company, On Demand Communications, revealed more than £3.5 million of new investment for its two Franchise businesses: Kall Kwik and Prontaprint. This resulted in the sale of existing Kall Kwik Centres alongside the opening of new Centres.

Kall Kwik has also accelerated the development of its design services offering. During 2008, Franchisees undertook record levels of design and consultancy work and the number of Kall Kwik's kdesign studios grew by 20 per cent.

1978	1979	1999	2005	2007	2008
The company is founded by Moshe Gerstenhaber, who purchased the master franchise from the US Kwik Kopy organisation.	The first Kall Kwik opens in Pall Mall, London.	Kall Kwik UK is acquired by Adare Group, the leading provider of print, mailing and data management solutions throughout the UK and Ireland.	Kall Kwik UK is named Franchisor of the Year by the British Franchise Association. Kall Kwik also launches D2D and the first kdesign studio is opened in Winchester.	The 33rd kdesign studio is launched and the 154th Kall Kwik Centre is opened in Stockport.	Kall Kwik celebrates its 30th year trading and the number of kdesign studios grows by 20 per cent.

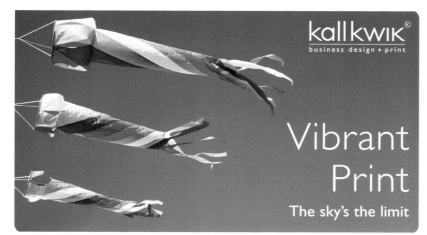

kall kwik ®
business design + print

Vibrant Print

The sky's the limit

kall kwik ®
business design + print

Large Format

Big, bright ideas

kall kwik ®
business design + print

Dynamic Design

Ideas with impact

kall kwik ®
business design + print

Direct Mail

To suit you

Kall Kwik helps customers to ensure that items, such as direct mail, stand out from the crowd.

Recent Developments

Long established in printed direct mail services, Kall Kwik is now helping clients to execute email-based communications. The emphasis is on offering an integrated service with help at every stage – from sourcing targeted email address lists to design, copywriting, email distribution and monitoring click-through rates.

Web-to-print is an innovative service whereby Kall Kwik offers clients an online ordering facility and works with them to create a portfolio of standard templates for a range of printed items. The online templates enable clients to offer their employees a self-service facility for the generation of new brochures, business cards or promotional materials; logos and key design elements are fixed within the template in order to ensure consistent layout and branding. The customised items can then be checked online before the final order is placed. The web-to-print service helps to streamline the entire design, proofing and

ordering process, which helps customers to reduce administration overheads, cut costs and eliminate errors.

Promotion

Kall Kwik continues to focus on generating sales leads for its Franchisees. While many new campaigns promote specific products and services, Kall Kwik's marketing team has used a range of techniques to help Franchisees publicise their consultative approach to solving business communications issues.

Kall Kwik's Franchise Sales Team works closely with potential Franchisees, selecting only those candidates that have the necessary qualities to build a successful business and support Kall Kwik's reputation for consistently high customer service. The Franchise Sales Team oversees Kall Kwik's Marketing Launch Programme (MLP), which provides business and marketing support. Following the 12-month MLP, Kall Kwik Centres continue to receive direct access to specialist marketing and business expertise in order to help generate demand and manage growth.

Brand Values

Brand image is vitally important – both in attracting new Franchisees and promoting services to each Centre's customers. To Franchisees, Kall Kwik represents an established, respected brand with a proven business model. For customers, Kall Kwik offers a convenient range of local, trusted, on-demand services combined with the support of the Kall Kwik nationwide network.

The company strives to ensure consistency across the Franchise network. Each Kall Kwik Centre provides customers with access to an approachable team of design, print and communications experts, capable of contributing ideas to transform a concept into a finished product that achieves better results.

kallkwik.co.uk

Things you didn't know about Kall Kwik

Kall Kwik arranged for its Putney Centre in south west London to print the 'Feed Me Better' petition that was presented to the then Prime Minister, Tony Blair, by TV chef Jamie Oliver.

Across the group, Kall Kwik employs more graphic designers than any other UK private sector company.

2009 sees the 30th anniversary of the opening of Kall Kwik UK's first franchised Centre, located in London.

kall kwik ®
business design + print

LandSecurities

As the leading commercial real estate brand for more than 60 years, Land Securities has focused on delivering a customer offering which provides its occupiers with quality accommodation and high levels of customer service. Three signature qualities exemplify the Land Securities brand: expert – recognisably an expert in commercial real estate; progressive – genuinely changing in a changing world; and accessible – easy to talk to and do business with.

Market

Land Securities is the UK's leading Real Estate Investment Trust (REIT). Its national portfolio of commercial property, worth many billions of pounds, includes some of Britain's best-known retail outlets, including Leeds' White Rose Centre and Gunwharf Quays in Portsmouth, as well as London landmarks such as the Piccadilly Lights and Westminster City Hall. Land Securities has a multibillion pound development programme with projects in Cardiff, Leeds and Glasgow city centres as well as key sites in central London. It is also one of the leading names in property partnerships and through urban community development is involved in long term, large scale regeneration projects in the South East.

Leading competitors in the market are institutional investors such as Prudential Property Investments Management, Legal and General, Standard Life and Morley Fund Management, quoted competitors such as British Land and Hammerson, together with private commercial companies such as The Crown Estate and Grosvenor.

Achievements

The Group's investment portfolio was valued at £12 billion at its half financial year on 30th September 2008, maintaining its position as one of the world's largest REITs. Land Securities is also a member of the FTSE4Good and Dow Jones Indices, which acknowledge its commitment to corporate responsibility.

The Group is a regular recipient of industry awards and in 2008 the highly acclaimed Cabot Circus development in Bristol, developed in partnership with Hammerson, won the Supreme Gold at the British Council of Shopping Centres' awards – the BCSC Golds. A Land Securities development has now received the accolade for five consecutive years.

Product

Land Securities operates mainly in the £500 billion UK commercial property market and, measured by market capitalisation, represents 20 per cent of the UK quoted property sector. Its business model is diversified, focused on retail property, London offices and property outsourcing. In the core markets of retail property and London offices, the Group provides about 5.8 per cent and four per cent respectively of the market floorspace and it is recognisably the market leader in property outsourcing by number of contracts. Within its core market segments, Land Securities' activities include property

1944	1950	1968	1982	1987	1994
Harold Samuel buys Land Securities Investment Trust Limited, which at this point owns three houses in Kensington together with some Government stock.	Shares purchased for 44p in 1945 are now worth £6.15. The following year, Associated London Properties is purchased for £2 million. This marks the first big take-over by the company.	In Britain's biggest property deal of its time, Land Securities takes over City Centre Properties, which has assets of £155 million.	The name of the company is changed from Land Securities Investment Trust Limited to Land Securities plc.	The total income of the Group exceeds £200 million and the portfolio valuation tops £3 billion.	Following the recession, the portfolio increases in value to more than £5 billion.

management, investment, development and the provision of property related services.

Recent Developments
In 2008, the Retail team completed a major regeneration project in the heart of Bristol in conjunction with Hammerson. Designed to seamlessly integrate with the city through a series of open streets and squares, the scheme has been a notable success since opening in September. Featuring 140 new shops, with some 75 retailers making their city centre trading debut, the project has been credited with playing a key role in the city's transformation into a top shopping destination.

The development at One New Change, in the heart of London's financial district, will open for business in 2010. The mixed use scheme will bring a long awaited retail focus to the area to the east of St Paul's Cathedral, accommodating 70 retailers on the lower three levels and a roof terrace on the sixth floor which will open up new views of the Cathedral and its surroundings.

Following a review of the structure of the business, in November 2007 the Land Securities Board announced the conclusion that, over the long term, the Group's component businesses and shareholders would benefit from separation and therefore proposed to demerge the Group into three specialist, separately quoted entities. In November 2008, however, the Company announced that despite the Board's continued belief in the benefits of specialisation, given the current financial environment it would not be in shareholders' interests to proceed.

Promotion
During 2008, Land Securities continued to build its brand at corporate, business unit and individual scheme levels using all aspects of the marketing mix.

At Group level, print advertising was aimed at key target audiences and illustrated the breadth of impact that the Company has on the UK's infrastructure. Using the tagline, 'Evolving Britain', the campaign showed examples from each of the main business units across the Group and highlighted the innovation and thought behind Land Securities' developments – from the positioning of a library in a new school to make it more accessible to the pupils, to ensuring that independent retailers feature alongside high street brand names in shopping centres.

Sponsorship continued to be a key tool with the retail business emphasising its market leadership and expertise by sponsoring Retail Week's 'Stores' book, celebrating the best of retail interior design.

Proactive PR campaigns also kept the brand prominent, as demonstrated by the extensive coverage achieved for the Ebbsfleet Landmark Project and the competition to find Kent's equivalent to Gateshead's Angel of the North.

Land Securities used its own media property for further promotion, displaying brand messages on the newly reformatted Piccadilly Lights – and even added a giant Land Securities light switch to the hoarding while the lights were undergoing redevelopment.

Brand Values
Land Securities' values are: excellence – striving to achieve the very best; customer service – never forgetting that its customers are the source of its strength; innovation – new ideas inspiring the Group to new heights; integrity – people trust Land Securities; and respect for the individual – everyone has the power to help, to grow, to influence and to contribute.

These values are reinforced by the Group's Values into Action initiative which recognises and rewards employees and key stakeholders whose behaviour reflects the core values. They are also reflected in all marketing and communication materials to ensure that the brand the Company presents and the brand that people experience are aligned.

landsecurities.com

2000	2005	2006	2008
With the purchase of Trillium, Land Securities enters the new property outsourcing market. Pre-tax profits rise by 11.7 per cent to £327.7 million and the portfolio is valued at £7.5 billion.	Land Securities acquires Tops Estates – a quoted shopping centre company – and LxB, an out of town retail specialist. Its portfolio is valued at £14.5 billion.	Land Securities enters into a joint venture with the Mill Group. It also acquires Secondary Market Infrastructure Fund, marking an entry into the primary and secondary PPP markets.	Jointly developed with Hammerson, Bristol's Cabot Circus opens. It is one of the UK's largest retail-led city centre urban regeneration projects.

Founded in 1922, Leyland Trade has grown from humble beginnings to become the UK's second largest trade paint brand by volume. Known as 'The Professional's Paint', Leyland has a long and distinguished history as a trusted and reliable brand for the trade. Its 2008 acquisition by PPG Industries created one of the biggest coatings manufacturers in the world.

Market

According to the British Coating Federation (BCF), in 2007 the UK trade paint market was worth £325 million and 150 million litres. In comparison to its retail equivalent (the DIY market), the trade paint market is mature and relatively stable, tending to remain unaffected by changing trends in colour and fashion.

Merger and acquisition activity over recent years now leaves the UK decorative paint market dominated by three manufacturers – PPG Industries, AkzoNobel and Crown Paints. Products are predominantly stocked and sold though manufacturer-owned Decorating Centres as well as decorators' and builders' merchants.

There are three main market sectors in which trade paint is used: industrial (such as factories), commercial (such as offices and retail premises) and domestic (households). End-users range from one-man decorating firms to large decorating contractors; with time such a precious commodity for any decorator, product performance is paramount.

Achievements

Leyland was one of the first manufacturers to pioneer the development of emulsion paints for the homeowner with the introduction of its Leytex product in 1922 – still recognised as a market leader today. For many years, products were entitled to display the Royal Warrant accreditation, 'By Appointment to Her Majesty The Queen'.

The brand's early success paved the way for a period of growth. By the mid 1960s the business had grown from a modest 24 employees at the original site in Leyland, Lancashire, to a workforce of over 1,000 and a network of more than 80 retail outlets across the UK and Ireland. Factories across South Africa supported the exporting arm of the company.

A testament to the strength and heritage of the Leyland brand is its survival through four separate company buyouts, remaining an attractive acquisition at each stage and continuing to deliver both to the business and customers. Over the last 40 years, Leyland has evolved from a UK-based listed company to become part of the portfolio of PPG Industries,

1922	1956	1984	1985	1990	1995
FW Jones founds The Leyland Paint and Varnish Company in Leyland, Lancashire and its flagship product, Leytex, launches.	Leyland floats as a public company. By the mid 1960s it has over 80 branches, more than 90 salesmen on the road and also produces varnishes, wallpaper and sundry products.	The Leyland Painter of the Year competition is launched.	Kalon takes over Leyland and becomes Kalon Group plc. It closes the Leyland factory in 1987.	The first Leyland Complements tinting system is launched in the UK.	Kalon merges with Euridep (part of Total SA), incorporating Johnstone's Paints, Manders and Windeck Paints into the newly enlarged Group.

a global leader in coatings with a presence in more than 60 countries.

Leyland products are now manufactured to strict BSI standards in Birstall, West Yorkshire. The factory site – one of the largest paint manufacturing sites in Europe, covering 63 acres with warehouse space at 350,000 sq ft – is ISO 9001 and ISO 14001 certified.

Product

During its lifetime, the Leyland portfolio has reflected numerous trends and developments within the industry, with many of its original product names – such as Super Leytex and Truguard – becoming industry bywords.

Today the comprehensive Leyland range offers a wide selection of trade-quality paints including emulsions, glosses and undercoats, floor paint, the Contract range – specifically designed for new work – and the BBA (British Board of Agrément) accredited Truguard exterior range. In total, Leyland produces more than 600 individual product lines, while in-store tinting machines offer customers a choice of over 16,000 colours, wholly integrated with its ColorXpress colour matching service.

Behind the scenes, the Leyland brand is fully supported by a team of experienced advisors, on hand to provide colour schemes, specifications and technical assistance where required.

Recent Developments

January 2007 saw a modernised Leyland Trade identity rolled out into the market. The packaging design, website, literature and point

LET'S GET ON WITH IT!

of sale materials were brought up-to-date with a fresh new look. With customers at the heart of the design brief, focus groups of trade users and stockists took place across the UK to ensure that the new packaging aided ease of use through colour representation, both in stores and on site.

Changes in volatile organic compounds (VOC) legislation are also having a substantial impact on the coatings industry. The first steps came into force in 2007, with major changes due in 2010 when the use of current solvent-based products will be prohibited. Leyland is carrying out extensive research and customer trials to develop solvent-based technologies that meet the new targets, while ensuring that customer expectation and product performance are not compromised.

In January 2008, Pittsburgh-based PPG Industries acquired the Leyland brand as part of the SigmaKalon Group. A global supplier of paints, coatings, chemicals, optical products, speciality materials, glass and fibreglass, PPG Industries operates in over 60 countries and has more than 150 manufacturing facilities and equity affiliates.

Promotion

Leyland applies a split channel strategy to its promotional activity; as its range is supplied direct to trade users as well as via third party stockists, two individual approaches are essential. For the direct Leyland user, trade press is the preferred and most successful advertising channel. Recent campaigns featured the 'Get On With It' slogan, which was also used across Rugby Super League advertising, in-store point of sale materials and promotional giveaways.

The complementary campaign, targeting stockists, employed the 'Bank On It' message to promote the margin benefits of stocking the brand. Leyland is predominantly sold through its national chain of more than 170 Johnstone's Leyland Decorating Centres and a mix of independent and national merchants

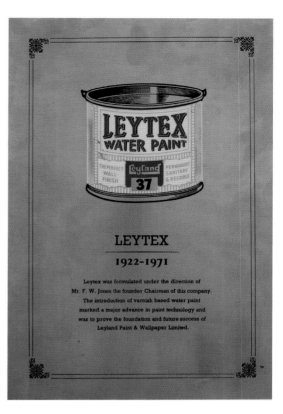

LEYTEX
1922–1971

Leytex was formulated under the direction of Mr. F. W. Jones the founder Chairman of this company. The introduction of varnish based water paint marked a major advance in paint technology and was to prove the foundation and future success of Leyland Paint & Wallpaper Limited.

– all supported by in-store point of sale materials, bimonthly and bulk promotions, product literature and colour cards.

The latest product news and brand developments are further communicated through two quarterly customer magazines, Brushstrokes for trade users and Independent News for stockists.

In keeping with its mantra, 'The Professional's Paint', Leyland ran the 'We Want You' competition in order to find the 'real' face of Leyland for its 2009 advertising campaign.

Brand Values

Leyland's values are based on the brand's foundation as 'The Professional's Paint': it is committed to delivering honest, trusted and reliable products to the trade.

leylandtrade.com

Things you didn't know about Leyland Trade

In the UK there are more litres of Leyland paint sold each year than there are males over the age of 16.

In a year, enough Leyland paint is sold to cover more than 300 million sq m of surface.

During World War II, Leyland's manufacturing capacity was largely taken up with paint production for HM Forces and government departments.

Leo Baxendale, the artist behind The Beano's 'The Bash Street Kids' cartoon strip, started his career designing paint labels for Leyland.

1999	2003	2007	2008
Total's Kalon Group merges with PetroFina's Sigma Coatings. Leyland Floor Paint is launched and the Leyland Contract range launches the following year.	ISO 14001 environmental management systems standard is attained and Kalon is named Top Newcomer at BITC's Environmental Awards for Excellence. Bain Capital buys SigmaKalon Group.	A new Leyland Trade identity is unveiled. Parent company SigmaKalon wins the BCF Coatings Care award for commitment to the environment, health and safety.	PPG Industries buys SigmaKalon, creating one of the biggest coatings manufacturers in the world.

MINTEL

Mintel International is an industry-leading supplier of market research. Its wide-ranging products and exclusive expert insights have proved invaluable for clients looking to grow their business. Through Mintel, clients also have access to world-renowned analysts who evaluate global trends in areas as diverse as consumer goods, retail, financial services, leisure and lifestyle.

Market

As much in prosperous times as in more challenging ones, market research forms the crucial foundations of sustainable growth and profitability, making it an extremely rewarding area in which to operate.

Today more than ever, clients are looking to research companies for direction. They need reliable data and inspiring opinions that can easily be integrated into their business strategy. Mintel is committed to providing services and solutions to meet these needs.

Achievements

Mintel has been a Business Superbrand for more than eight years and aims to remain at the forefront of innovation and development in the research industry. It has continuously adapted and improved its offering to ensure clients get exactly what they need, when they need it.

The company has successfully retained the entrepreneurial family culture of its early days, despite growing its workforce to more than 500 full-time and 17,500 associated employees globally. At every stage of the employee lifecycle Mintel aims to bring out the best in its staff, making it a fast-paced and highly productive working environment.

Product

Mintel's product portfolio is the result of years of client feedback and the innate ability to sense exactly what the market needs.

From marmalades in Guatemala to Vietnamese milk chocolate, the Mintel Global New Products Database (GNPD) monitors product innovation in the consumer packaged goods market. Covering 48 of the world's major economies, this online platform is updated with more than 20,000 new launches every month. Clients can also access analysis of the latest trends, product innovations and much more.

Mintel Oxygen is the online delivery platform for Mintel's consumer and market reports. It focuses on enhanced content, insight and exclusive opinions from Mintel analysts across 13 sectors, ranging from food and finance to beauty and travel.

Mintel Comperemedia monitors print advertising as well as all communications sent to consumers' mailboxes and email inboxes. Mintel uses a panel of US and Canadian households and covers financial services, insurance, telecommunications, automotive and travel.

Mintel Menu Insights tracks more than one million food and drink items on 2,400 menus in the US, monitoring the most popular flavours, ingredients and dishes.

Mintel Inspire is a global resource for trends influenced by consumer behaviour, culture and society, offering inspiration for new concepts and product development.

Mintel Global Market Navigator underpins the entire Mintel portfolio. It allows clients to identify, compare and export critical market size and market share data for thousands of categories worldwide.

1972	1997	1998	2000	2001	2004
Mintel is established in London, providing food and drink research in the UK.	Mintel Reports go online as Mintel becomes the first research supplier to provide instant internet access.	The US office opens in Chicago and Mintel GNPD goes online. The following year, Mintel Comperemedia is launched in the US.	The Australian office opens in Sydney.	Mintel publishes the first European and US reports.	Mintel Menu Insights is launched.

Mintel Research Consultancy offers bespoke services including mystery shopping and product pick up, sales promotion tracking and price audits. The experienced team also carries out extensive consumer research and analysis on markets around the world.

Recent Developments

Constant innovation and improvement is the key to Mintel's offering, as it recognises its clients' need to stay ahead in an increasingly competitive global market.

Mintel GNPD now features further improved navigation and search functions, making competitor monitoring, idea generation and new product development even simpler and faster. Clients can now customise the Mintel GNPD website and gain a greater understanding of key trends, thanks to category, company and claim analysis pages.

In 2008 Mintel also launched Mintel Beauty Innovation, which focuses on enhanced analysis of new launches in the beauty industry, covering niche, prestige, 'masstige' and mass-market products.

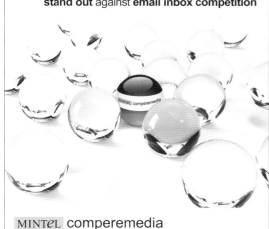

stand out against email inbox competition

MINTEL comperemedia

New for Mintel Oxygen is the Multicultural America series, which helps marketers understand how Hispanic, Black and Asian Americans spend their money. Meanwhile, Mintel Inspire now has a greater number of trends and connections and Mintel's experts have also added insightful blogs to the site.

Mintel Comperemedia has been updated to monitor landing pages so companies can more closely track their competitors' offers, while recent developments for Mintel Menu Insights include an interactive interface, instant analysis and innovative trends.

As the result of the recent acquisition of Snapshots, in early 2009 Mintel launched the Mintel Global Market Navigator. A one-stop-shop for preliminary research into categories, countries or regions, it enables clients to quickly understand global market conditions before investing in further detailed research.

Mintel's new all-encompassing website, www.mintel.com, has been designed to showcase all that Mintel has to offer the business world and is the central hub for Mintel clients and prospects alike.

Promotion

Media coverage is an integral part of Mintel's brand communication and the company's research boasts daily coverage across all media, including Bloomberg News, The Wall Street Journal, the FT and BBC News. Activity focuses on providing commentary to the media, highlighting Mintel's in-depth understanding of up-to-the-minute trends in consumer markets worldwide.

Mintel regularly organises exclusive events for its clients and attends the major industry trade shows around the world, allowing businesses to experience the products, meet key analysts

and see them present on the latest Mintel findings. The company has also formed successful affiliations with trade associations and industry bodies across the globe.

Brand Values

Mintel believes that every member of its team is a brand ambassador. Every contact Mintel makes with a client should leave them with a consistent message of how Mintel can help them make informed business decisions. However, it is the continuing support and loyalty of its clients, many of whom had their first Mintel experience while studying at university, that lies at the heart of the company's branding success.

mintel.com

Things you didn't know about Mintel

Results from Mintel GNPD show that at least one new consumer packaged goods product is launched somewhere in the world every two minutes.

Mintel once shipped 200 kilos of ice cream from the UK to Australia for a focus group session – ensuring it was still edible on arrival.

Mintel's latest chocolate report shows that the British spend almost £6,700 a minute on chocolate while the US, with a population almost five times the size, spends more than US$32,000 every minute.

Mintel Comperemedia has collected more than five million pieces of direct mail in the US, in just over 10 years.

In the last year alone, Mintel has been mentioned more than 11,000 times in the global print media.

Since its launch in 2000, npower has become a household name and leading UK energy supplier with more than 6.6 million residential customer accounts and a prime position in the sector. Despite the energy industry as a whole facing a period of unprecedented change, npower has risen to the challenge and remains committed to its positioning as 'Britain's Brightest Energy Company'.

Market

2008 has been a challenging year for the energy industry with the credit crunch and turbulent economic climate increasing pressure on consumer household spending.

Over the last few years the UK has become a net importer of energy, changing the face of the domestic market. The UK now imports 40 per cent of its gas and is part of a global market; instead of getting gas from just the North Sea or Europe it has to compete for fuel with emerging economies such as China and India. This increased global demand has resulted in energy price rises.

The UK is also experiencing an energy gap that has opened up as older power stations have been forced to close. By 2020, up to 20 new power stations will be needed to meet existing levels of consumption. To help tackle these challenges, npower's spending on energy efficiency measures increased dramatically in 2008 with npower contractors installing cavity wall and loft installation in more than 270,000 homes to reduce their CO_2 emissions. npower is working to reduce its generation CO_2 emissions intensity by a third by 2015, requiring a total investment of around £1.7 billion.

Achievements

Over and above maintaining its strong positioning as a major residential and business supplier, with key business accounts that include Wembley Stadium, Sainsbury's and TSB, npower has had other notable successes in 2008.

The company was awarded the CommunityMark standard by Business in the Community (BITC) in recognition of its long term commitment to, and investment in, community schemes and partnerships including Urban Cricket, Climate Cops, Health Through Warmth (HTW), Skills for Life, Warm Wales, The National Trust and Macmillan Cancer Support.

Skills for Life, HTW and Warm Wales have also received BITC Big Tick awards in their own right while Climate Cops – a programme for 4-14 year-olds that encourages more sustainable living – won the IVCA Clarion Climate Change Communication award. npower's graduate scheme was listed in The Times Top 100 Graduate Employers and the company made The Times Top 50 Where Women Want to Work list.

Product

With energy being a necessary commodity, industry offerings have at times been criticised

2000	2001	2003	2004	2005	2006
npower is launched – subsequently combining the former electricity and gas supply businesses of eight companies.	In partnership with Greenpeace, npower launches npower Juice – a pioneering clean electricity product using identified renewable sources at no extra cost.	The creation of the npower Juice Fund is announced, designed to assist the development of projects in other renewable energy fields such as wave and tidal energy.	npower signs the world's biggest green energy deal with BT – equivalent to supplying more than 100,000 homes with electricity each year.	npower wins two Hollis Awards – Best Sports Sponsorship and, in partnership with the Federation of Disability Sports, Best Grassroots Sponsorship.	npower launches Urban Cricket in conjunction with the England and Wales Cricket Board (ECB) and extends its sponsorship of Test match cricket to 2009.

for their complexity. In 2008, npower unveiled a raft of products aimed at addressing these concerns, such as npower ONE which offers a fixed dual fuel energy price combined with the security of gas boiler breakdown cover.

As a way of helping its consumers take control of rising energy costs, npower launched Price Protector, a capped product that prevents price hikes and could benefit consumers through lower bills if wholesale energy prices fall. It's not only domestic consumers that are reaping the benefits, however, with the newly launched m3 – measure, monitor, minimise – portfolio of energy management products providing npower's medium to large business customers with a comprehensive toolkit to better understand and manage their energy use.

As a company, npower remains committed to combating rising fuel poverty amongst the most vulnerable energy customers. The Spreading Warmth social tariff is targeted at this group, in some cases providing an annual discount of up to £250 for people in need.

Recent Developments
After a successful start in 2007 the brand's own central heating division, npower hometeam, has gone from strength to strength, with new offices opening in Burton,

and a sponsorship deal with Burton Albion Football Club extending the brand's already extensive sponsorship activities.

A further area of brand expansion is npower's Solar programme, which saw the addition of Solar Thermal Solutions and marked the launch of Solar PV (photovoltaic) panels through a one-stop-shop installation service for residential customers.

Throughout 2008 npower continued its programme of investment in energy generation: the £100 million plus investment in sulphur cleanup equipment at Aberthaw coal-fired power station was completed; a £60 million replacement programme of old turbines at Didcot B gas-fired power station commenced; and construction started on the 1650MW, £600 million Staythorpe gas-fired power station in Nottinghamshire.

Promotion
When it comes to brand promotion, npower responds to the ever-changing and increasingly competitive marketplace. Its advertising strategy took on a new and distinctive style for 2008, delivering consumer-centric product benefits in a different, more engaging style by combining real life and 2D imagery. The resulting commercials addressed modern consumer concerns by showing elements of daily life to be out of sync with reality, to which npower was able to offer solutions.

Cricket sponsorship has for some time helped drive npower's brand awareness and with a new England captain and the introduction of the IPL and the Stanford series, the sport is currently creating plenty of buzz, making

npower uniquely positioned to capitalise on its growing popularity; expected to escalate further when the Ashes returns to the UK in 2009.

Joining forces with household names such as Piers Morgan and Fearne Cotton through the launch of its Green SOS competition (an extension of npower's Climate Cops activity which set out to find the UK's top 100 'greenagers') raises the brand profile further, especially with younger demographic groups – the future energy consumers.

Brand Values
In everything it does, npower strives to bring its 'personal, rewarding and forward-thinking' brand values to life and live up to its claim of being 'Britain's Brightest Energy Company'.

npower.com

Things you didn't know about npower

npower's one-stop-shop installation service now includes the original Solar PV (photovoltaic) panels and Solar Thermal Solutions.

npower was the first energy company to produce a domestic green energy tariff at no extra cost.

Macmillan Cancer Support has been npower's corporate charity since 2004 and the partnership is now valued at around £1.9 million to Macmillan.

npower was the first company in the world to 'star-vertise' – by buying stars to form a constellation of its logo.

2007
The summer solstice on 21st June sees npower launch a one-stop-shop installation service for Solar PV (photovoltaic) panels in residential homes.

In September, a groundbreaking partnership with The National Trust is announced; npower will supply all Trust sites and help to neutralise its carbon footprint.

2008
e-force, npower's team of energy advisors, launches its mission to save money and energy for small businesses in the UK.

The team carries out free energy makeovers for four businesses, installing low-cost energy efficiency measures that could save them more than £250 on annual energy bills.

With almost 100 branches, Office Angels is the UK's leading recruitment consultancy specialising in secretarial and office support staff. Each week 8,000 people find short-term assignments, while more than 9,000 people are placed in permanent jobs every year – all guided through the recruitment process by experienced and qualified consultants.

Market

The UK recruitment market is dominated by temporary and contract business, with industry turnover valued at a record US$27 billion between April 2007 and March 2008 (Source: Recruitment Employment Confederation (REC) Annual Industry Turnover & Key Volumes Survey).

The most significant growth in the UK market was the increase in permanent placements, growing from a value of £3.514 billion to £4.276 billion, a rise of 21.7 per cent. The REC survey also showed the number of temporary and contract workers to have fallen from 1,377,310 placements to 1,220,310 – a drop of 1.8 per cent.

The international recruitment industry is closely linked to the strength of the economy and changes in labour supply and demand, such as the rise in home and freelance working and people working for longer. Other trends, such as the influx of well-qualified workers from new EU Member States and the current world economic climate, also have an impact.

Achievements

Office Angels is consistently regarded as one of the UK's best employers, as recognised in 2008 when, for the third time in four years, it was voted eighth in The Sunday Times 100 Best Companies to Work For survey. Based on employees' views, the company's success in the survey reflects its efforts to listen to its

people and to create a strong and supportive organisational culture.

Office Angels also upholds the principles of equality and fair treatment for workers in and out of the workplace environment, operating a diversity monitoring and reporting system that complies with industry best practice.

Furthermore, Office Angels has made a conscious effort to minimise its environmental impact. In order to monitor its carbon footprint in the UK and Ireland, green policies are being implemented that encompass travel, recycling, energy use, waste, stationery and carbon offsetting.

Product

Office Angels provides clients with both assignment and permanent staff across a wide range of secretarial, administrative, financial, call centre and customer service positions. Candidates, meanwhile, are provided with a wide range of services free of charge, with each jobseeker following a thorough and formal procedure from registration through to assignment, including an in-depth interview, skills evaluation and online training courses.

Consultants undergo training and development to ensure they are equipped with the latest and necessary skills, resulting in a highly motivated workforce. To assess candidates' abilities, Office Angels uses a skills evaluation system that allows consultants to assess the fundamentals, such as PC skills, but can also create tailored tests to reflect a client's exact requirements. Through working closely with candidates and providing them with continued support, Office Angels lives by its belief that

1986	2003	2005	2006	2007	2008
Office Angels is founded and the first office opens in London.	Office Angels joins Race for Opportunity (RfO), a government-backed initiative for UK organisations committed to race and diversity issues.	Office Angels is voted as one of The Sunday Times 100 Best Companies to Work For, sitting in eighth position.	Office Angels celebrates its 20th anniversary.	Office Angels opens its 100th branch in the UK and Ireland.	Office Angels is once again voted eighth in The Sunday Times 100 Best Companies to Work For survey.

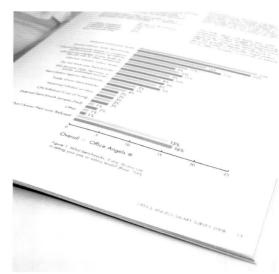

it is in the business of finding 'jobs for people' rather than 'people for jobs'.

Integral to Office Angels' commitment to its assignment staff is its ongoing candidate care programme. Initiatives such as regular social and networking events, Angel of the Month and Year awards, pension schemes, competitions and training ensure that candidates are rewarded for their dedication and professionalism.

At office-angels.com candidates are able to view all current vacancies and obtain further information on the services offered. This is not, however, a substitute for the personal, one-to-one service that remains the cornerstone of the Office Angels philosophy.

Recent Developments

In response to increasing demand from clients for other specialist services, Office Angels established two divisions: executive and call centre.

The Office Angels executive division has established itself as a strong presence in the London marketplace, as well as in Scotland and the Midlands, specialising in permanent and interim senior support and middle management recruitment. Placing candidates with a variety of clients, from small boutique businesses to global corporations, a unique consultative approach has helped form longstanding relationships with clients and candidates alike.

The Office Angels call centre business grew from a demand for quality call centre support and is devoted to temporary and permanent staffing solutions for contact centres, tackling the most complex or basic call centre needs. Doors first opened in late 2007, growing to six offices in the UK and Ireland today.

Office Angels has created a suite of training opportunities to help its staff learn new skills and achieve their work ambitions. This includes Office Angels Training Solutions (OATS), which consists of more than 60 online courses including MS Office software, accountancy packages, languages, customer service, IT and psychometric testing. Ascent, a year-long programme, exposes potential management trainees to every aspect of the company to equip them with the necessary experience to become branch managers. Finally, the Aspire senior management development programme builds the skills required to manage an Office Angels region.

Promotion

The Office Angels marketing strategy aims to capitalise on the brand's position as an industry leader. Activity encompasses press, outdoor and radio advertising, direct mail, event marketing, public relations, sponsorship, corporate social responsibility, internal communications, research, the internet and an extensive programme of client and candidate care.

Further brand exposure is gained by conducting regular research studies and publishing reports on a range of employment-related issues, including flexible working, employee benefits and managing communications in the modern office. An example of this is the Office Angels 2008 Annual Salary Review which regularly attracts wide media coverage in the consumer and trade press.

Brand Values

The professional and contemporary style of Office Angels attracts clients and candidates alike. It has a passion for recruitment and is dynamic and forward thinking. At the core of Office Angels' service proposition is the brand tenet, 'Be More', which reflects its desire to provide clients and candidates with the opportunities and advice that will help them to achieve their best.

office-angels.com

Things you didn't know about Office Angels

In a poll conducted by Office Angels, 93 per cent of managers nominated trust as the single most important trait in their assistants. The second sign of secretarial excellence is the ability to organise, according to 88 per cent of managers.

Working closely with the Royal National Institute for the Blind (RNIB), Office Angels has introduced technical testing equipment for use by its blind and visually impaired candidates.

Office Angels has a broad spectrum of candidates, of whom one in four are male and one in five are over 45 years-old.

In 2008, Office Angels initiated 'Facemail Day' which saw employees turn off their email and only use traditional methods of contact instead: the telephone and face-to-face meetings.

Black n' Red

Black n' Red was first produced in 1964 as a quarter-bound book with a black cover and a red cloth spine. In 1984 the brand was relaunched in its current casebound format and a wide range of sizes and formats followed to meet the broader needs of the business professional. Oxford Black n' Red is now the UK's leading business notebook.

Market

The target market for Oxford Black n' Red is business people between 25-60 who pride themselves on their professionalism. The brand is a staple of the office stationery cupboard for companies, offering a range of value for money, high quality notebooks. The brand prides itself on being suitable for use by a wide range of companies and individuals – from taxi offices and on-site surveyors to chief executives. This universal appeal is attributed to the robust nature and high quality of the product.

Oxford Black n' Red notebooks are available through retail outlets (high street and grocery) and the office products channel including wholesale and contract stationers. More recently, there has been huge growth in the ecommerce channel, triggered by both current distributors and new suppliers entering this arena.

Oxford Black n' Red is the brand leader in its sector with an 80 per cent share of the branded manuscript book market, which has an estimated total (brand and own label) market value of £19 million at manufacturer selling price (Source: MPA 2005).

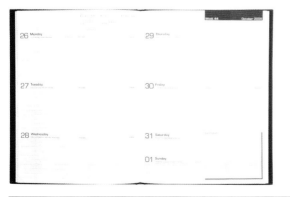

Achievements

In 2005 Black n' Red won the Brand Awareness Award at the industry Oscars, the BOSS Awards. This was followed in 2006 by a commendation for Oxford Black n' Red at the Campaign Media Awards for its integrated advertising campaign. The high level of competition in the category reinforced the brand's achievement in terms of its effective and creative use of a relatively small media budget to drive sales through the office products channel and major retail customers.

Product

Attention to detail is a key attribute of Oxford Black n' Red products. All books (including recycled) are made with smooth, premium quality 90gsm paper, reducing show-through and allowing the user to write on both sides of the page – even with a fountain pen. The paper also resists yellowing which helps maintain the quality of archived notes.

All books include metric conversion tables as standard, while the classic A4 and A5 hardback casebound books also feature a range of maps and travel information.

In addition, the range includes a hardback wirebound calculator book – which has a full function, solar powered calculator built into the inside cover – as well as books with polypropylene covers, 'smart ruling' for the 'organised note-taker' and the recently added recycled variant.

1964	1984	1989	1991	1996	2002
Spicers launches a quarter-bound book with a black cover and red cloth spine.	Black n' Red is relaunched in its current casebound format.	A hardback wirebound variant is introduced.	A soft cover range is launched, taking Black n' Red into the notepad market.	DS Smith, owner of Spicers, purchases John Dickinson Stationery and Black n' Red becomes a John Dickinson brand as Spicers refocuses on wholesaling.	Paper in Black n' Red products is upgraded to premium 90gsm and a wirebound polypropylene variant with an elastic closure strap is launched.

Recent Developments

Due to a dramatic increase in the demand for eco-friendly office products, in 2006 the first Oxford Black n' Red Recycled book was launched – an environmentally friendly version of the iconic notebook that remains faithful to the original. Following the success of this single product, an additional five Oxford Black n' Red Recycled lines have been added: A4 hardback and polypropylene wirebound books and A5 hardback wirebound, polypropylene wirebound and casebound books.

The brand is innovating further in order to ensure that the covers of its polypropylene notebooks are as environmentally friendly as possible. The paper stock has also been improved to achieve a better whiteness without the need for chlorine-based bleaches.

In 2007 the brand introduced a range of diaries designed with the professional's organisational needs in mind – easy to use with a unique page layout which has been specially developed to help manage and plan time more effectively. Oxford Black n' Red diaries also feature Quicknotes™, a planning tool which is useful for prioritising tasks or setting personal reminders. The diaries feature a full-colour map section, reference information and address book as well as perforated page corners and ribbon markers to ensure that the current week can be accessed quickly and easily.

Promotion

In May 2007 Oxford Black n' Red launched a major media campaign in The Times and City A.M. The campaign also ran in the trade and PA press, such as Executive PA and OS Magazine and on websites including Times Online, Telegraph.co.uk and Guardian Unlimited. Oxford Black n' Red also became the sole sponsor of the Alex cartoon strip in the business section of The Daily Telegraph and even went mobile, with fans downloading their daily dose of Alex's wry wit direct to their mobile phones for free.

The campaign aimed to inspire and attract the attention of PAs, office workers and city professionals who might be looking to buy a notebook, whether for themselves or for the office.

Online consumer attitude magazine surveys and exhibition questionnaires are used for new product development and promotional strategy.

Recent press advertisements continued to reflect the style and professionalism of the brand, featuring striking, hand-written quotations such as 'Excellence is not an act but a habit' and 'Success is preparation meeting opportunity'. These were designed to provoke thought and express humour with Oxford Black n' Red's target audience.

Brand Values

Fundamentally, loyalty to the product is built on its functionality and heritage. It is a high quality product but offers value for money, durability, reliability and dependability. Oxford Black n' Red is 'the classic notebook for serious professionals'.

blacknred.com

There are dreams and there is reality, and there are those who turn one into the other.

www.BlacknRed.com

Black n' Red
...means business

Oxford

2004
The Black n' Red digital writing solution is created (now part of an exclusive range under the Oxford Easybook brand) in partnership with Anoto and Nokia.

2006
Black n' Red becomes a range in the Oxford portfolio following Groupe Hamelin's purchase of John Dickinson in 2005. Recycled variants are launched under Oxford Black n' Red.

2007
Oxford Black n' Red returns to consumer media with a high profile press campaign. Oxford Black n' Red Diaries are launched for the 2008 calendar year.

2008
A4 Project books are added to the Oxford Black n' Red Portfolio.

Portakabin®

Quality - this time - next time - every time

As the UK market leader in high-quality accommodation solutions, Portakabin aims to provide peace of mind for its customers. Portakabin provides added value services such as data communications and security systems, to ensure that the working environment is of the highest standard. Its Customer Charter, pioneering warranty package and broad product range ensure that Portakabin is able to provide value-added, flexible solutions.

Market

A member of the Shepherd Group, Portakabin is part of one of the leading private and family-owned businesses in the UK. With turnover in excess of £700 million, the Group's operations cover national and international markets, encompassing construction and engineering, manufacturing, and property development.

The Portakabin Group is split into a number of divisions that allow customers from a variety of market sectors to choose to hire or buy a specific working environment. Portakabin employs more than 1,300 people throughout the UK and continental Europe. This well-established infrastructure allows it to fulfil its commitment to providing a rapid response and a comprehensive support service.

Already market leader in the UK, Portakabin is a multinational organisation and is actively pursuing a European development programme through the expansion of its network of hire centres. Portakabin offers one of the widest and most comprehensive ranges of modular building solutions from its businesses across the UK, Ireland, France, Belgium and the Netherlands.

Achievements

Portakabin is proud of its track record in delivering buildings on time and on budget, particularly when its statistics are compared to the construction industry average of only 63 per cent of projects being delivered on time and just 49 per cent on budget (Source: Research carried out by BCIS on behalf of the Royal Institution of Chartered Surveyors Construction Faculty, September 2004).

Portakabin, however, has delivered 99.6 per cent of its buildings on time and on budget, based on orders from January 2004 to June 2008.

Introduced in 2004, the Portakabin 'On time, on budget' promise was the first (and remains the only) in the industry. It means that if the company fails to meet a client's contracted start date, it will provide a week's free hire for every day that it is late on a hire contract or an additional twelve months' warranty on the building on a sales contract.

Portakabin has earned the ISO 9001:2000 quality management systems standard – awarded for everything from office procedures right through to its zero tolerance manufacturing process – and ISO 14001:2004 environmental management systems accreditation for its continued commitment to the improvement of its environmental performance.

1961	1965	1980	1991	1998	2000
Portakabin launches its original site accommodation building, the PK16. Success leads to the formation of Portakabin Ltd and registration of the trademark in 1963.	Portaloo is launched, providing mobile toilet and shower facilities.	After receiving the Queen's Award for Export Achievement in 1978, Portakabin is awarded a British Board of Agrément (BBA) certificate – the first for a building module system.	Portakabin earns the BS 5750 quality systems certification; this is the forerunner to ISO 9001:2000, the quality management systems standard.	Lilliput Nursery from Portakabin becomes the first and only modular building to be awarded Millennium Product status by the Design Council.	Portakabin expands its service with building access, air conditioning and furniture hire businesses. Titan – the largest single modular building in Europe – is also launched.

You can hire it....

But you'll want to keep it

When a building makes you feel this good, you won't want to leave it. Here's why...

The Ultima Vision is an outstanding, head-turning building that adds prestige as well as functionality to any organisation's work environment.

Unbelievably, quality styling and design like this, can be yours to hire!

When you hire the Ultima Vision, you get more than just a prestigious development, even your bottom line will benefit with 90% of employees saying that office design has a direct effect on their productivity. So when you need additional workspace, you'll want the design features and quality of a permanent building, with the flexibility of hire terms.

The Ultima Vision model was created to motivate and inspire - the result is the ability to increase an occupant's productivity by up to 26%.**

Floor to ceiling, double-glazed wall panelling floods the interior with natural light, a crucial factor which influences performance in the workplace. Space is just as important, so the Ultima Vision building boasts a two-storey capacity to accommodate up to 1000 people in total comfort.

Portakabin will always give you one point of contact who will work with you to create your complete environment - from climate control and groundworks, to furniture hire and more. So you can be sure of a complete solution.

For your complete peace of mind, you can be certain that we'll be there when we say we will. In fact, we'll deliver your Ultima Vision building on time and on budget or we'll give you a week's free hire for every day we're late.*

To ensure you have a workspace environment that motivates and has the ability to increase productivity, find out more about the Ultima Vision building. Call your local Hire Centre now on 0845 401 2020 and receive your free DVD. Alternatively, visit www.2020ultimavision.co.uk for a virtual tour.

Portakabin
Quality · this time · every time

* Terms and conditions apply. A copy is available on request. Prime Thresholds Ultima and Ultima Ultra are registered trade marks.
**Research conducted by Microsoft Study conducted by the Heshong Mahone Group 1999. Gut Orku, California.

Product

Having originally conceived his idea of a relocatable building in the 1940s, Portakabin founder Donald Shepherd developed the concept, beginning production of the first Portakabin building in 1961. Today, as market leader and pioneer in the development of relocatable and modular accommodation, Portakabin manufactures some of the most sophisticated building solutions available.

Designed and produced at the 250,000 sq m Portakabin site in York, solutions are offered for a wide range of uses, from office space, marketing suites and classrooms to surgeries and clinics, toilets and showers as well as storage facilities.

The broad Portakabin product range includes modular buildings such as: Ultima and Ultima Vision, which can accommodate between one and 1,000 people within individual offices or large open-plan spaces; Portakabin Solus,

which offers up to 30 sq m of office space with improved aesthetics, including larger windows and doors; and Titan, the largest single modular building in Europe that can be sited with minimal groundwork required. Portakabin also provides a range of classroom and nursery products, such as the Lilliput Children's Centres, which are delivered complete with nappy-changing rooms, junior toilet facilities, vibrant colours and wipe-clean surfaces.

Recent Developments

In keeping with its reputation for pioneering innovation, recent years have seen Portakabin launch two industry-leading products. The highest performing floor option for a modular building, its new factory-installed concrete floor has a point loading of 7kN and a uniformly distributed load (UDL) of 9kN/m^2 – beneficial for areas of high footfall or heavy point loading.

Its Ultima Vision modules, meanwhile, are designed with increased productivity in mind. Incorporating floor-to-ceiling, double-glazed wall panelling to maximise natural light inside the building, they are the first of their kind available for hire. Studies have shown that natural light can increase the productivity of occupants by up to 26 per cent (Source: Research carried out by Microsoft and the Heshong Mahone Group, 1999).

Portakabin is also making strides in sustainability, with product development that includes the introduction of the new Titan Solar building. Taking its responsibility to the environment seriously, Portakabin has achieved a 17 per cent year-on-year reduction in carbon emissions, a 50 per cent reduction in the cost of waste

sent to landfill over the past three years, and now recycles 78 per cent of its waste.

Promotion

To launch its innovative Ultima Vision product, Portakabin developed a dedicated advertising campaign to raise awareness of its availability to hire. Under the 'You can hire it… But you'll want to keep it' strapline, creative executions highlighted the product's unique pairing of high quality design features – more typically associated with permanent buildings – with the flexibility provided by hire options.

Brand Values

The essence of the Portakabin brand is to provide peace of mind for its customers across Europe, through quality buildings and services.

portakabin.co.uk

Things you didn't know about Portakabin

Portakabin uses 5,000 tonnes of steel every month to produce its buildings.

Since 1998 Portakabin has built more than 120 Lilliput Nurseries and Children's Centres.

Yorkon, a subsidiary of Portakabin, manufactures Tesco Express stores. Yorkon has also manufactured restaurants for Pizza Hut and 200 restaurants for McDonald's.

Since the launch of its warranty package in January 2004, Portakabin has sold more than 2,000 buildings and only 0.17 per cent of customers have made a claim.

Portakabin was first to market with a high performance concrete floor with a point loading of 7kN and UDL of 9kN/m^2.

2004	2005	2007	2008
Portakabin becomes the first and only modular manufacturer to launch a Customer Charter and to offer five-year product and 20-year structural warranties.	Titan Building System is launched, allowing more flexibility. Ultima Vision follows in 2006 – a contemporary building for hire, designed for greater productivity.	Portakabin launches glazed Titan (featuring a fully glazed wall), Titan Solar – with solar powered capability – and a suite of biometric site access management solutions.	Portakabin launches the highest performing floor option for a modular building and earns environmental management systems ISO 14001:2004 accreditation.

prontaprint
trusted to deliver, every time.

Prontaprint has maintained its position at the forefront of the corporate print-on-demand market by delivering distinctive design and print solutions, underpinned by a commitment to first class customer service. Through its ability to evolve and adapt to changing customer needs, Prontaprint has grown to become the largest and best-known brand in the business.

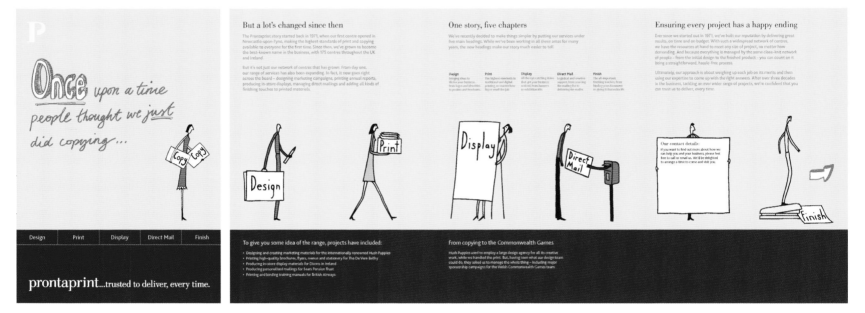

Market

In an age where design and print technology is rapidly developing, the business print world demands the very latest digital know-how the minute it hits the market.

Prontaprint is exploiting its commercial design and print expertise, concentrating on tailored communications for business clients – and the number of centres with turnover in excess of £1 million is growing rapidly.

Prontaprint is committed to adopting a completely client-focused role to ensure that its network is in a strong position to capitalise on major changes within the B2B market. Understanding clients' businesses is crucial to satisfying a greater proportion of their needs. Delivering exceptional standards of client care and relationship management are key to the total service offering.

In recent years, clients have increased in-house capabilities, becoming digitally enabled and web-smart. In response, Prontaprint has repositioned itself to provide an enhanced business offering comprising design, print, display, direct mail and finishing services.

Achievements

Established over 35 years ago, Prontaprint has a fully integrated European network of more than 150 digitally linked centres across the UK and Ireland and employs over 1,100 people with an annual turnover nearing £50 million.

The company is a founder member of the British Franchise Association (BFA) and played a crucial role in establishing a regulatory body for the franchise industry. A former winner of the BFA Franchisor of the Year award, Prontaprint remains a strong supporter of the BFA and was appointed to the board in 2005.

It is also affiliated to the British Print Industry Federation, the British Association of Printers and Copy Centres, the Institute of Printers and XPLOR International (the Electronic Document Systems Association).

Furthermore, it was the first national print-on-demand network to sign a formalised licensing agreement with the Copyright Licensing Agency. This allows licensed copying of specified material within agreed limits. Prontaprint is therefore able to offer advice on copyright issues and help protect businesses from potential copyright infringements.

Prontaprint won prestigious Franchise Marketing Awards in 2007 and 2008 for the work it had done repositioning the brand to appeal to higher value business clients: the awards for Best Overall Marketing Campaign and Best Brand Management were judged by

1971	**1973**	**1980s**	**1990s**	**2000s**	**2009**
The first Prontaprint centre is opened in Newcastle-upon-Tyne, aiming to overcome the high prices, large minimum orders and long lead times associated with traditional commercial printers.	Following the signing of the first Franchise Agreement, the Prontaprint business model goes from strength to strength.	The company continues to expand widely across the UK, as well as into international markets.	Prontaprint focuses heavily on the B2B print-on-demand sector.	Prontaprint is now the largest design and print network in the UK and Ireland and repositions to consolidate its place at the forefront of the corporate print-on-demand market.	Prontaprint completes the roll out of a new brand positioning, following an investment of more than £3 million and almost two years of research into the market.

a panel of experts from the franchising industry and the Chartered Institute of Marketing.

Product

Prontaprint offers a comprehensive portfolio of business communication solutions to businesses of all sizes including design, print, display, direct mail and finishing services. An ongoing programme of investment in the latest digital technology ensures its centres feature the latest design tools as well as black & white and colour high-volume digital print equipment alongside traditional print capabilities.

With most documents now produced digitally, clients' original designs can be enhanced, updated and amended. Work can also be securely stored electronically at Prontaprint centres, where it can be easily accessed. The versatile nature of the Prontaprint digital network means that material can be supplied to one centre and sent out digitally across the network to be produced at different centres simultaneously, simplifying distribution and increasing capacity and efficiency. This not only saves the client time and money with reduced wastage and storage costs but also improves competitive advantage by enabling clients to respond to market opportunities quickly.

Prontaprint's direct mail service focuses heavily on the use of variable data printing, enabling images and text to be customised to the recipient. This service, offering one-to-one marketing solutions, underpins Prontaprint's consultancy approach to servicing clients.

Recent Developments

Proud of its heritage, Prontaprint consistently evolves the brand to meet changing client needs in the commercial design and print market. With a corporate client base including British Airways, NEXT, Hush Puppies and Dixons, Prontaprint has rolled out a new brand positioning to develop this market further, following an investment of more than £3 million and almost two years of research, brand development and training.

The new brand positioning was initially piloted at seven Prontaprint centres across the country, chosen to represent a cross-section of the print market in terms of size, offering and service. The six-month trial delivered a sales growth seven times higher than the rest of the network.

The roll out includes a new corporate identity, training for Franchisees and their staff and enhanced business services. A powerful new positioning statement – 'trusted to deliver, every time.' – has been introduced alongside the strong use of illustration and a warm aubergine corporate colour, reinforcing the human face of the brand.

Promotion

Prontaprint has been transformed from a high street print and copy shop into a key player in the B2B print-on-demand sector through continual investment in the development and promotion of its brand on a local, national and international level. It has maintained its market-leading position through a sustained and structured approach to business planning, sales and marketing strategy at both macro and micro levels.

Marketing activity is based on extensive client feedback and market research. Independent in-depth surveys of existing, lapsed and potential customers help to identify changing factors of importance among small, medium and large businesses when buying print and related products and services. Results provide Franchisees with a greater understanding of buyer behaviour as well as identifying new market opportunities.

Prontaprint believes that consistent and regular external sales and marketing activity is central to the ongoing profitable growth of each centre. This activity is focused on the acquisition, retention and development of business clients. It also provides Franchisees with a wide range of central sales and marketing tools and resources to enable them to grow their businesses locally, as well as providing external sales support.

Brand Values

Prontaprint has four key brand values – Close, Connected, Can-do and Collaborative.

'Close' focuses on building long term relationships with clients on a one-to-one level. This is achieved through close contact with clients and close understanding of their needs.

'Connected' refers to Prontaprint's network of talented and experienced people as well as the use of technology. Prontaprint harnesses these connections, aiming to ensure clients get the best results with their business communications on time, every time.

'Can-do' reflects the business culture of getting things done. Whatever the job, large or small, Prontaprint aims to go the 'extra mile' to ensure it is 'trusted to deliver, every time.'

Finally, 'Collaborative' reflects that talking to clients is the start of a two-way conversation, rather than a one-way sales pitch. By working in partnership with clients and each other, Prontaprint consistently offers distinctive design and print solutions.

prontaprint.com

Things you didn't know about Prontaprint

Prontaprint was the first print brand to be named a Business Superbrand.

Prontaprint is a former winner of the British Franchise Association's Franchisor of the Year award.

In 2007, Prontaprint's central marketing was accredited with a prestigious Franchise Marketing Award. This was followed in 2008 by the award for Best Brand Management, judged by experts from the franchising industry and the Chartered Institute of Marketing.

RIBA

As the voice of architecture in the UK since its foundation 175 years ago, the Royal Institute of British Architects (RIBA) champions good design to Government, the public and the construction industry. It believes that everyday life can and must be improved through better designed buildings and communities, and that the architect's role is crucial. RIBA Enterprises, the RIBA's principal commercial arm, is the leading information provider to the UK construction industry.

Market

The RIBA's founding mission, 'to advance architecture by demonstrating public benefit and promoting excellence in the profession', holds true to this day, but has evolved to meet the needs of its members and the society they serve. The growing demand for sustainable buildings, new-built and 'retrofitted' is currently transforming the marketplace for architects, while in today's uncertain economic times, the RIBA's role as a source of information and business guidance for its members remains key.

The Institute validates architecture courses around the world, with one third of the world's architects qualifying through a RIBA validation system.

Achievements

The RIBA has had considerable success in highlighting the importance of design to the Government, its lobbying instigating significant change in legislation. In 2008 the Government agreed to amend legislation to ensure that the new Homes and Communities Agency, which is responsible for building and providing social housing, must actively promote good design. It also agreed to amend the Planning Bill so that all major infrastructure projects, such as an airport or new rail project, must outline design criteria from the outset. Most importantly, further changes to legislation mean that all local authorities must actively promote good design. As a result of the RIBA's consistent campaigning, communities will benefit from better designed houses, schools, shops and other public buildings.

Product

Although many architectural icons such as 30 St Mary Axe (the Gherkin), London Eye and Gateshead Millennium Bridge were created by RIBA members, most of the RIBA's work does not centre on big design statements, setting out instead to raise the standards of buildings and spaces everywhere by supporting the designers of everyday architectural necessities. RIBA Client Services helps clients commission the right architect for their project, while the

1834	1837	1863	1931	1934	1996
The Institute of British Architects is founded.	The Royal Charter is bestowed upon the Institute.	The first formal (but voluntary) exams in architecture by appointment of a board of examiners are introduced by the RIBA.	The RIBA is instrumental in establishing the Architects' Registration Act – the first UK register of practicing architects.	The RIBA moves to its Art Deco headquarters at Portland Place, London.	The RIBA Stirling Prize is inaugurated.

RIBA Competitions Office is dedicated to helping clients run competitions to select architects for their project. Clients are also benefiting from the RIBA Client Design Advisor scheme, which provides independent, expert advisors to guide clients through the, often complex, public sector procurement process. RIBA Awards, given to buildings that have high architectural standards and make a substantial contribution to the local environment, are the industry's benchmark and culminate in the televised RIBA Stirling Prize.

Within the RIBA Enterprises portfolio is a thriving publishing and bookselling business. Through its National Building Specification (NBS) sub-brand, RIBA Enterprises supports the technical side of architecture. As well as being the de facto specification system for buildings in the UK, NBS provides access to technical and regulatory information and publishes the UK Building Regulations on behalf of the Government. Its RIBA Product Selector offers a range of advertising options that provide the interface between product manufacturers, the architectural community and construction professionals. RIBA Bookshops provide one of the largest selections of both UK and international titles covering architecture, the built environment and design.

Recent Developments

Not all architects are members of the Institute. RIBA chartered membership is widely considered to be the gold standard, recognising architects practicing at the top of their profession. The RIBA and RIBA Enterprises help them to excel by providing leading-edge information; the recent acquisition of four online video-based 'learning channels' is the latest investment in 'life long learning' not only for architects but surveyors, engineers and planners. The RIBA has also led the way with services to help its members design 'greener' buildings and following the 2008 roll-out of the RIBA Climate Change Toolkit, the series has now been enhanced with a further three titles.

The RIBA continues to grow in other areas. The sharing of expertise among architects and the construction industry has a new online home in RIBA Knowledge Communities, with sustainability the first topic to be covered. Through the online Carbon Buzz initiative, the RIBA has partnered with leading architects and engineers to create a sector-by-sector monitor of UK buildings' energy use – essential information for the carbon-conscious practice.

Promotion

The RIBA brand is driven through its press and marketing activity and public relations as well as its lobbying of Government. In addition, its members play a vital role in developing the brand as they trade using the 'RIBA' name. The RIBA works collaboratively with bodies such as the Construction Industry Council, Institution of Civil Engineers, Royal Town Planning Institute and on the consumer front, with the housing and homelessness charity, Shelter, through the annual RIBA Architect in the House scheme.

The RIBA Trust, the Institute's cultural arm, partners with other organisations to help promote interest in architecture, as well as devising its own programme of exhibitions and a talks programme which attracts world-renowned speakers. The RIBA Library, housed at the RIBA headquarters and now with free admission, holds a collection of some four million items devoted to the study of architecture. Its virtual gallery RIBApix.com has a growing collection of more than 30,000 viewable images.

The RIBA president, who stands for two years, acts as the spokesperson for the Institute to the media, representing the RIBA when talking to Government and at industry and public events.

Brand Values

The brand is crystallised in the letters 'RIBA', which represent architecture's gold standard and which are valued by RIBA members and the public alike. The RIBA aims to be responsive to its stakeholders and audiences; to be influential through its advocacy and campaigning; to be bold as it addresses 21st century challenges of design and construction; and to be authoritative at all times. In all that it does, it aims to inspire trust, demonstrate competence and show leadership.

architecture.com

Things you didn't know about RIBA

Every year some 20,000 students emerge from schools of architecture, both in the UK and worldwide, whose courses have been validated by the RIBA.

In 1983 the RIBA presented its first Design for Energy Efficiency award, to a gas service depot in Manchester.

Throughout the 1990s the RIBA lobbied Government to recognise the importance of listing post-war buildings, resulting in a change in legislation.

The RIBA Library holds 350 original drawings by renowned Italian Renaissance architect Andrea Palladio – more than 80 per cent of his total portfolio in existence today.

1997	2004	2007	2009
The US chapter of RIBA is launched in recognition of the 700 plus RIBA members who are at work across the US.	The V&A+RIBA Architecture Partnership is launched at the Victoria and Albert Museum.	Sunand Prasad is elected RIBA president.	The RIBA celebrates its 175th birthday.

Every person in the UK, at home and at work, is a Royal Mail customer. Its vast network also extends overseas, transporting 900 million items annually to 240 countries. Despite increased competition Royal Mail continues to deliver a comprehensive service and remains committed to providing top class support to its social and business customers.

Market

Royal Mail's unique 'one price anywhere' service means that everywhere in the UK is accessible at a price and time that suits individual customer needs. Each working day, mail is collected directly from 113,000 post boxes, 11,500 Post Office® branches and some 87,000 businesses. These items pass through a network of 69 mail centres, eight regional distribution centres and 1,400 delivery offices; transported via a fleet of more than 30,000 vehicles, before being delivered by some of the 156,000 dedicated postmen and women.

The liberalisation of the postal market in 2006 brought new challenges for Royal Mail, demanding a proactive response to identify new markets and channels in which to operate. Online trading, bulk-mailing and mail media consultancy are all areas where Royal Mail is taking a lead in order to exploit growing trends.

Achievements

Royal Mail Group picked up several prestigious awards in 2008 for its corporate social responsibility (CSR) policies. Its Carbon Neutral Payroll Giving Scheme, which offsets personal carbon emissions through a tax-efficient plan, won the Institute of Fundraising's award for the Best Use of Payroll Giving while its Carbon Management Programme took the Group to the top of the CSR category at the World Mail Awards. Royal Mail's commitment to reducing the environmental impact of its operations has seen its normalised emissions (based on the distribution of a single item) reduced by 31 per cent since 2003.

Awards were also won at the 'Oscars' of the global direct marketing industry, the 2008 ECHO Awards. Two campaigns, 'Chocolate Letter' and 'Mr Complete' both achieved Gold, and a USPS Gold Mailbox Award was also given to Chocolate Letter for the most innovative use of mail, highlighting how engaging and effective direct mail can be.

Furthermore, Contact – Royal Mail's quarterly magazine for senior marketers – won Best Designed Magazine at the Association of Publishing Agencies' (APA) Creative Awards 2008 and was also named the Most Effective B2B Title at the APA Effectiveness Awards. At the same awards ceremony, monthly title Courier was voted Most Effective Internal Communication.

Product

Royal Mail's offering is diverse, aimed at delivering services that meet its customers' needs. Its product range is not limited to conventional mail, however, with end-to-end logistics, data and media services available to help large and small businesses find, grow and retain customers. Areas such as direct mail and data services already generate large revenues, but Royal Mail continues to introduce initiatives that allow businesses to target their audience.

Mailshots Online, for example, has been specifically developed for small business customers, allowing them to produce mailshots of any quantity; from initial design needs through to final delivery, via a single tool.

1635	1840	1883	1919	1924	1968
Charles I makes his Royal Mail available to the general public, with postage costs covered by the recipient.	The Penny Black is introduced. Any item can be sent anywhere for a penny, paid in advance by the sender.	Postmen walk Britain's streets for the first time.	The first publicly available overseas airmail service begins operation on 11th November between London and Paris.	The first commemorative Special Stamp is issued.	Two-tier postage is introduced, giving customers the choice between sending mail First Class or opting for cheaper, but slower, Second Class delivery.

The introduction of 'Matter®', meanwhile, takes direct mail to a new level. A box containing a range of physical brand representations, Matter® enables advertisers to get products into the homes of their target customers – all of whom have opted in. A test mailing to 1,000 men led to more than 30,000 people registering to receive the follow up, rising to 65,000 for the third box.

Royal Mail also introduced one of the world's first digital stamps, SmartStamp®, enabling customers to buy personalised postage online for printing directly onto envelopes.

The more traditional Special Stamp programme celebrates British heritage through an eclectic range of subjects. 2008 highlights included designs celebrating Ian Fleming's James Bond, the 50th birthday of the Carry On films and the historic handover of the Olympic flag from Beijing to London.

Recent Developments
Customer needs are paramount for Royal Mail and this has led to many new developments. One example is 'Ask Sarah', an enhanced online customer assistance tool, which provides instant answers to queries from customers, making their interaction with Royal Mail easier and more effective.

In October 2007, Royal Mail initiated a commercial strategic partnership with eBay, focusing on their shared customer base. The result is a range of mutually beneficial initiatives, such as 'eBay Day' events in Post

Office® branches (providing expert advice on effective trading) and a joint marketing strategy for the time-saving Online Postage system that has seen increased monthly volumes of items sent by eBay sellers throughout 2008.

In response to increased public concerns, Royal Mail is a key stakeholder in the development of a new environmental standard (PAS 2020) for direct marketing. The standard sets out objectives to improve environmental efficiency in direct marketing materials, promoting better targeting through suppression, as well as the inclusion of an opt-out facility. Royal Mail's commitment to this is demonstrated through its Responsible Mail programme which rewards mailers who use recyclable and sustainable materials.

Promotion
In 2008 Royal Mail launched a substantial multimedia advertising campaign that focused specifically on business customers. Building on the promise to help British businesses prosper and grow, the 'Partners for Growth' campaign features real-life customer stories and invites companies to go online to royalmail.com/growth to create a free, individually tailored growth pack. The positive response to the campaign led to more than 200,000 unique website visitors and 12,000 tailored customer growth packs.

A precursor to the 'growth' theme was the 'DM Seedbox' campaign, launched to heighten awareness of Royal Mail's portfolio of direct marketing solutions and sent to an

audience of 14,000 media agency staff. Over the past year alone, Royal Mail has introduced innovative new services within the direct mail medium including Sensory Mail, developed in conjunction with BRANDSense.

Brand Values
Royal Mail's key brand values are defined as expert, proud, together, trustworthy and hungry. It aims to help the nation thrive and grow by connecting businesses with their customers and people with people.

royalmail.com

Things you didn't know about Royal Mail

As postage stamps were invented in the UK, Royal Mail's stamps are the only ones in the world that do not have to include a country name on them – just the monarch's head.

The first British pillar boxes were introduced as an experiment in Jersey in 1852 following a suggestion made by Post Office surveyor's clerk (and latterly popular Victorian novelist), Anthony Trollope.

The words 'Royal Mail' first appeared on a British pillar box in 1991.

In 2008 Royal Mail was inducted into the Design Week Hall of Fame for its creative work on stamps.

1974
A postcode is designated for every UK address.

2008
Royal Mail introduces its new 'pricing in proportion' system; mail is priced according to the weight and size of each item.

Also in 2006, a revolutionary new service is introduced that uses GPS technology to track deliveries online. The UK postal market is fully liberalised.

Since Ryman was established in 1893 it has become a household name, recognised for its quality products, value, reliability and service. With a multi-channel and nationwide chain of 240 stores, Ryman is the high street's market-leading specialist commercial stationery retailer. Turnover for the group is estimated at £140 million, with substantial growth in online and business account sales.

Market

Building on its longstanding history of innovation and customer service, Ryman combines high street accessibility with a mail order service and website, offering a complete multi-channel solution. Targeting the small office, home office and consumer stationery markets, Ryman's range comprises more than 4,000 items which extends to over 20,000 available to buy online or through special order. In addition, it offers a dedicated business account service with credit facilities and bulk discounting.

Despite difficult trading conditions, the UK market for personal and office stationery remains relatively constant. According to Key Note research, it is valued at just over £3 billion, made up primarily of core products such as paper and board, writing instruments, filing and storage solutions. However, digital storage, home printing and social categories including journals, notebooks and note cards are experiencing significant growth, as are security products such as shredders, tamper-

proof ink and forged note identification equipment, fuelled by rising instances of identity theft. More recently, the credit crunch has generated marked growth in home safes and cashboxes.

Due to the wide appeal of stationery, Ryman has a broad spectrum of competitors ranging from electrical retailers to supermarkets as well as more traditional stationery retailers such as WHSmith, Viking and Staples.

Achievements

Ryman continues to show strong performance in the stationery sector; since 1995 the business has increased fourfold and today Ryman has a turnover in excess of £140 million.

Not only diversifying into new product areas as the market changes, Ryman's success can also be attributed to consistent investment in its people, its store estate, information technology, warehousing and distribution.

In the last year, Ryman has opened 12 new stores in key areas around the UK and refurbished the majority of its existing estate. Furthermore, Ryman has successfully completed the integration of three separate stationery businesses – Partners the Stationers, Stationery Box and Ryman – into one national chain, remodelled its merchandise profile to suit regional customer needs and has implemented a modern operating platform from which to trade.

1893	1970s	1995	1996	2001	2007
Henry J Ryman opens his first store on Great Portland Street, London.	The family business is sold. Over the next 20 years its owners include Burton Group, Terence Conran, Jennifer d'Abo and Pentos.	Ryman is acquired by Chancerealm Ltd (later known as Ryman Group Ltd), in which Theo Paphitis is the controlling shareholder.	A direct mail order catalogue is launched. Two years later Ryman enters the ecommerce market with the launch of www.ryman.co.uk.	Ryman acquires Partners the Stationers, comprising 86 stores.	Ryman acquires 61 Stationery Box stores, which are rebranded to Ryman by October 2008.

Product

Ryman sells a wide range of office supplies, from writing equipment, paper and filing solutions to office furniture and high-tech items such as flash drives, multi-function printers and a wide range of own-brand remanufactured, compatible and high capacity ink cartridges.

As a specialist stationer, Ryman is able to offer products not normally found in generalist stationery stockists, such as grades, colours and sizes of products to suit many specific needs. Ryman continually strives to introduce new lines and to be first to market with innovative products.

A full business service is provided in a number of stores including photocopying, binding, laminating, bulk printing and business and personalised stationery. Self-service photocopying is also available in most outlets. In addition, business account holders are offered a credit facility which combines the convenience of delivery for large orders with the flexibility of visiting one of 240 local high street stores for smaller top-up purchases.

Recent Developments

It's not only Ryman's product offering that is driven by innovation and improvement; the business itself is in the midst of a major initiative to lessen its impact on the environment, with the ultimate aim to become carbon neutral by March 2010. In order to achieve its goal, Ryman is reducing its carbon emissions across all areas of the business.

In product development, Ryman is committed to growing its range of environmentally friendly products using new technology, recycled paper

and materials from sustainable forests. On the shop floor, meanwhile, degradable carrier bags have been introduced which due to their light weight, have a smaller carbon footprint than an equivalent sized paper bag. A reusable carrier bag made from non-woven polypropylene is also available.

At the company's warehouse and packaging and logistics operations, cardboard and plastic waste is compressed and recycled, while the Ryman delivery fleet uses Euro 4 vehicles to reduce carbon emissions and developments in eco-friendly fuels are monitored. In addition, all Ryman suppliers must comply with guidelines from the Ethical Trading Initiative Base Code and standards are regularly reassessed.

Promotion

Ryman's promotional strategy rests on its consistent 'value for money' offering across its ranges. Multi-purchase discounts are made

available on key lines and special items, while price-led promotional activity features heavily during seasonal consumer peaks such as 'back to school' and Christmas.

Charity work – such as Ryman's support of Comic Relief in 2009 – and continued sponsorship of the Ryman Football League maintain visibility for the brand.

Brand Values

Acknowledged as a specialist in its field, Ryman has developed and nurtured its standards of quality, value, reliability and service over 115 years, building and retaining a loyal customer base. Ryman is proud of its record of investing in its people, training them to be able to deliver a high standard of service, backed by expert knowledge of Ryman's range of products and their applications.

ryman.co.uk

Things you didn't know about Ryman

Ryman recycles more than 150,000 cartridges every year on behalf of its customers. Many of its own-brand cartridges also use remanufactured materials.

Ryman sells two million pens every year; enough ink to draw along the length of the Great Wall of China almost 300 times.

At present there are 13 members of staff who have been with Ryman for more than 25 years, 25 members of staff who have celebrated at least 20 years' service and 76 members of staff who have been with the company for over 15 years. One member of staff has been with the business for 52 years.

Ryman opened its first stationery shop in 1893; sales were £50 in the first week.

SKANSKA

As part of one of the world's largest construction groups, Skanska UK is a construction service business operating under two clear business streams – Construction and Infrastructure. Its business model is to integrate its core disciplines to deliver project solutions in its chosen market areas. By integrating all disciplines and working together with its clients, partners and supply chain, the company's aim is to make a difference to the way construction is normally delivered.

Market

Skanska is a multinational construction and development company headquartered in Sweden. Founded in 1887 as Aktiebolaget Skånska Cementgjuteriet manufacturing concrete products, Skanska quickly diversified into a construction company and within 10 years received its first international order – which happened to be in Leeds.

The company played an important role in building up Sweden's infrastructure including roads, power plants, offices and housing. Growth in Sweden was followed by international expansion. In the mid 1950s Skånska Cementgjuteriet made a major move into international markets, entering South America, Africa, Asia and in 1971, the US market. In 1965 the company was listed on the Stockholm Stock Exchange and in 1984 'Skanska', already in general use internationally, became the Group's official name.

During the latter part of the 1990s and early 2000s, Skanska embarked on its most expansive phase ever and sales doubled in just a few years. While the major portion of this growth was organic, a string of successful acquisitions also paved the way for Skanska's development into a global company. One of these acquisitions, in November 2000, was the Construction arm of Kvaerner – a Norwegian conglomerate – which has become today's Skanska UK.

Skanska is a local player in many countries. Primary markets are the Nordic region, the UK, the US, Central Europe and Latin America. The Group's operations are based on local business

units which have good knowledge of their respective markets, customers and suppliers. These local units are backed by Skanska's common values, procedures, financial strength and Group-wide experience. Skanska is thereby both a local construction company with global strength and an international builder with strong local roots.

Skanska's mission is to develop, build and maintain the physical environment for living, working and travelling. The company's aim is to be a leader in the markets in which it operates.

Achievements

Skanska UK undertakes more than £1.3 billion of work each year and prides itself on being able to draw on a combination of the best in British engineering with the best in Swedish innovation and design. All operating units

have certification to the management systems ISO 14001, ISO 9001 and OHSAS 18001 and work strictly in accordance with the Skanska Code of Conduct.

Skanska has worked on a wide range of notable contracts. In London, recent examples include 30 St Mary Axe (the Gherkin), Moorhouse, the Southbank's Palestra and Heron Tower.

1887	1897	1927	1965	2000	2009
Aktiebolaget Skånska Cementgjuteriet, later renamed Skanska, is founded by Rudolf Fredrik Berg.	Great Britain's National Telephone Company places Skanska's first international order; more than 100km of hollow concrete blocks are supplied to hold telephone cables.	Sweden's first asphalt-paved road is constructed in Borlänge in central Sweden – a milestone in Skanska's role in building Sweden's infrastructure.	Skanska is listed on the Stockholm Stock Exchange.	Skanska enters the UK construction market by acquiring Kvaerner's Construction business, which had previously been part of the Trafalgar House Group.	Current projects include Heron Tower, Barts and The London new hospitals redevelopment and National Grid's North London gas mains replacement programme.

Skanska has undertaken more infrastructure projects for the Channel Tunnel Rail Link than any other contractor and is currently carrying out major civil engineering works for the new Docklands Light Railway (DLR) extension to Stratford, which is expected to play a key role in transport plans for the London 2012 Olympic and Paralympic Games.

Skanska is a UK leader in the development and operation of Privately Financed Initiatives (PFI) and is currently undertaking the UK's largest hospital development – Barts and The London. The company is also one of the largest providers of utilities and infrastructure services in the UK.

During 2008, Skanska received numerous accolades for its progress in sustainable development, including being ranked fifth overall in The Sunday Times Best Green Companies awards.

Product
Skanska UK is a leading PFI provider. From the successful completion of the country's first PFI scheme in the late 1980s – when it built the Queen Elizabeth II Bridge on the M25, crossing the Thames – Skanska's portfolio is now in excess of £3 billion, covering healthcare, custodial, education, transportation and defence.

Complex civil engineering projects are often involved in developing and improving Britain's physical environment for living, working and travelling. The need to improve the infrastructure of roads, railways and utilities has led to upgrades that draw upon a wide range of expertise and experience. Skanska combines civil engineering and utilities expertise with its specialist businesses to provide total solutions to its clients.

In the market of commercial construction, Skanska UK's capability and experience, encompassing the entire scope of construction, is unique. Skanska offers its clients more than just a traditional construction service.

Recent Developments
Skanska UK employs more than 5,500 people and operates across design, construction, civil

engineering, PFI/PPP, piling, steel decking, mechanical and electrical, facilities services, utilities, infrastructure services and ceilings as well as decorative plasterwork units. The company works throughout the UK, integrating the skills of its operating units in a collaborative style in order to provide a construction service to its clients that delivers real benefits.

Promotion
Skanska's approach to brand promotion in the UK could be described as a 'little bit different'. While the company does occasionally promote its services and skills in the traditional way with advertising and exhibitions, this is secondary to the way in which the company prefers to be seen and recognised.

At Skanska, it's much more about being truly recognised for the way it lives up to its brand values. This is by the performance and behaviour of its people – Skanska people are 'team players who care and want to make a difference to the way construction is delivered' – creating projects that its staff, clients, partners and the communities in which it works are proud of.

Every office and major Skanska construction site in the UK is planned using a bespoke approach to meet the needs of its teams, partners and clients – creating a 'shop window' for the company's visual brand identity.

Skanska is proud of its third party recognition which it considers a true measure of the value and performance of the company and the brand. In the last few years, Skanska has received more than 100 external awards not only for the projects it has constructed, but also for key areas of its performance including health and safety, the environment and sustainability. Skanska has received a string of awards from the Considerate Contractors Scheme and has achieved Business Superbrands status for the second year running.

Brand Values
Skanska's key responsibility is to develop and maintain an economically sound and prosperous business. It is committed to the countries, communities and environments in which it operates, as well as its employees and business partners.

Skanska stands for technical know-how and competence combined with an understanding of its customers' needs. The ability to apply these skills to new areas enables it to produce the innovation that its customers demand. Skanska aims to develop, build and maintain the physical environment for living, working and travelling and to be the client's first choice in construction related services and project development.

skanska.co.uk

Things you didn't know about Skanska

LEGOLAND Windsor's Miniland London was built with Skanska's help.

Skanska is the only Swedish contractor in the UK.

More than 56,000 people work for Skanska worldwide.

In 2008 Skanska completed the UK's first Building Schools for the Future (BSF) project, in Bristol.

Founded in 1920, Snap-on is a leading global innovator, manufacturer and distributor of tools, vehicle diagnostics and equipment solutions for professional users. Product lines include hand and power tools, tool storage, diagnostics software, information and management systems and workshop equipment.

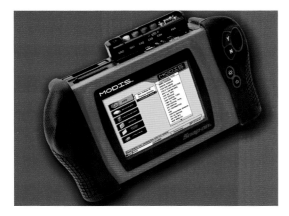

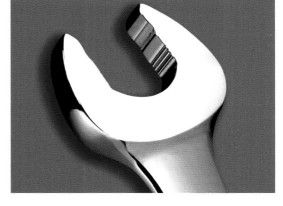

Market

Snap-on has a history of more than 85 years of one-to-one relationships with professional tool users. The company sells its products and services in more than 130 countries worldwide. Consistently delivering high value-added products and services, its customers include automotive workshops and their technicians, manufacturers, users in aerospace, commercial aviation, the marine industry, construction, agriculture, mining, the oil and gas industries, and military forces around the world.

Achievements

In 2007 Snap-on received the coveted Frost & Sullivan Technicians' Choice Award for Overall Best Brand of Automotive Tools, emerging as the leader in all service and product categories tested. Its top performance in services encompassed the Best Quality, Innovation and Retailer Customer Experience categories, while US technicians voted Snap-on the best in all four major product groups – hand tools, power tools, diagnostics and tool storage. The company was also recognised by the diagnostics survey as the clear market leader

for automotive hand-held scan tools. The award was presented to Snap-on for its tradition of excellence, as well as the company's ability to distinguish itself through proactive strategies that have helped it to become known as an industry leader.

Snap-on is one of the longest serving members of the British Franchise Association (BFA), the self-regulating governing body for the UK's £12 billion franchising industry. In 2007 the company was celebrated as the top UK franchise, winning the BFA's Franchisor of the Year gold award.

Product

Snap-on's products command enduring allegiance, often becoming treasured objects for virtually every type of professional tool user. With a focus on innovation and quality, Snap-on's designers and engineers, whether working on the latest screwdriver design or vehicle software development, are continuously looking for ways to improve the company's products and customer efficiency. The company currently holds 2,000 active and pending patents.

One of Snap-on's most recent innovations has been a revolutionary new ratchet with Dual80™ technology. A ratchet is not only one of the most constant components of the technician's toolkit but also one that takes the most stress. Building on its successful sealed head design, Snap-on has now developed a twin pawl technology, which makes this ratchet one of the smoothest and strongest in the world today.

In 2008 the company celebrated its 2,000th UK MODIS™ sale. MODIS™ is a complete premium-price hand-held diagnostic solution which aids the technician to pinpoint and diagnose problems on today's complex vehicles. In 1985, cars with engine management systems made one calculation per second. Today, however, even the most basic car calculates at a rate of one million times a second. Snap-on is at the forefront of this technology with products such as MODIS™ maintaining this technology-led ascendancy.

Recent Developments

Snap-on is driving for even faster customer responsiveness and is strengthening internal processes to advance its competitive position

1918	1920	1945	1959	1965	1978
Snap-on co-founder Joe Johnson develops the interchangeable socket set.	The Snap-on Wrench Company is formed.	Salesmen for the company start carrying inventory.	Joe Johnson retires.	Snap-on forms its UK subsidiary, Snap-on Tools Ltd.	Snap-on Tools Corporation lists on the New York Stock Exchange.

and increase sales and earnings. Its Rapid Continuous Improvement (RCI) process has been adopted throughout the organisation. The process focuses on four principles – safety, quality, delivery and cost – which aim to help drive profitable growth and financial performance.

Snap-on's enhanced long range planning process facilitates growth through internal development, growth of its customer base – particularly in the emerging markets – and a continuous stream of innovative new products.

The company recently acquired ProQuest Business Solutions, a world leader in electronic parts catalogues. Rebranded as Snap-on Business Solutions (SBS), its products transform complex technical data for parts catalogues into easily accessed electronic information for the world's automotive, power equipment and power sports manufacturers and their dealer networks. SBS also provides warranty management systems and analytics to help vehicle dealerships manage and track performance.

Promotion
The one-to-one relationship that Snap-on franchisees have with customers is the primary way that the quality of Snap-on is sold, the

values of the brand having been handed down from generation to generation. Snap-on franchisees pay weekly visits to customers to keep them up-to-date on new products and services. They also handle warranty repair and replacement when necessary and provide affordable programmes for technicians to build their tool kits and their capabilities.

Snap-on's brand is also visibly associated with motor sports, most notably Formula One, MotoGP, World and British Superbikes and the World Rally Championship. In addition to its existing sponsorship portfolio, in 2008 Snap-on announced a three-year deal with Aston Martin Racing – the 2007 and 2008 title holders of the GT1 class Le Mans 24 Hours endurance race.

The company's staff spend time with some of the best racing teams in the world to understand exactly what they need from tools and equipment under extreme race conditions.

Snap-on monitors how products perform at the track to consistently enhance the quality, durability and performance of the tools for the professional tool user. The company is continually developing new motor racing-themed products in tool storage, hand tools and power tools, inherently linking the modern vehicle technician with the pinnacle of his profession.

Brand Values
The word 'Snap-on' aims to project an image of quality, service and innovation, as well as conveying superior workmanship. There is a distinct pride of ownership among customers who use Snap-on products. The essence of the Snap-on brand can be distilled into seven key attributes: high-quality products, exceptional service, innovation, expertise, premium price, productivity and leadership.

snapon.com

1992	2005	2007	2008
Snap-on acquires the Sun Electric Corporation.	Snap-on customers donate more than £35,000 to its UK 'Gissa Quid' campaign for The Prostate Cancer Charity.	The 'Gissa Quid' campaign raises more than £53,000 for The Prostate Cancer Charity. Snap-on wins the BFA's UK Franchisor of the Year gold award.	Snap-on UK achieves record sales and profits, and also announces a three-year sponsorship deal with Aston Martin Racing.

Things you didn't know about Snap-on

Snap-on co-founder Joe Johnson pioneered the interchangeable socket set for professional mechanics, using the 'Five do the Work of Fifty' slogan.

As part of the 1941 Lend-Lease deal, Snap-on products were sent by the US to the UK in support of the World War II war effort. One of these tools was a tappet adjuster for use on the Supermarine Spitfire's Merlin engine.

The longest tool Snap-on ever made was a square drive extension wrench, which was used in a nuclear reactor. The wrench was 25 feet long and always had to float upright in water.

Snap-on tools accompany the majority of US voyages into space and were most conspicuously used as part of the Apollo space programme.

Making every day a better day

In the UK and Ireland, Sodexo is a leading food and facilities management provider with clients in the corporate, education, healthcare, leisure and defence sectors. Its 43,000 employees provide a diverse range of quality of life services from catering and hospitality to grounds maintenance, laboratory services and reception at more than 2,300 locations.

Market

A global specialist in quality of life services, the Sodexo Group is a leader of food and facilities management services in all of its markets and number two worldwide in service vouchers and cards, with an issue volume of 7.5 billion euros. With relatively low outsourcing rates in many of its markets, Sodexo's activities offer considerable growth potential, with estimated markets of more than 650 billion euros in food and facilities management services and over 70 billion euros in service vouchers and cards. The Group is listed on Euronext Paris.

With an annual UK turnover in the region of £1 billion, Sodexo leads the way in creating added value by integrating the management and delivery of services that aim to improve the quality of daily life for customers.

More and more organisations are recognising the benefits of outsourcing all of their non-core activities to one supplier. Sodexo is an organisation with a heritage built on catering expertise, but now more than 40 per cent of its turnover in the UK comes from other services; a strong indication of the confidence clients have in its ability to effectively co-ordinate a multitude of services.

Achievements

Sodexo is proud of its many achievements and for being recognised as a responsible global business.

In the UK, Sodexo received three awards at the prestigious BIFM International Investors in FM Excellence Awards 2008: Innovation in Systems and Services, Facilities Manager of the Year and the Special Recognition Award. 2008 also saw it win Cost Sector Catering's Event Catering Award, the British Hospitality Association's Environment Award and the title of Workplace Sandwich Supplier of the Year from the British Sandwich Industry.

Furthermore, and for the third year running, Sodexo was named as one of Business in the Community's (BITC) Top 100 Companies that Count (published in The Sunday Times), following its inclusion in BITC's Corporate Responsibility Index.

1966	1971-78	1983	1985-93	1995	1997
Pierre Bellon launches Sodexho; the Bellon family has more than 60 years' maritime catering experience. Operations initially serve staff restaurants, schools and hospitals.	International expansion begins with a contract in Belgium. The Remote Site Management business develops and Sodexho's Service Vouchers business starts up.	The initial public offering of Sodexho shares on the Paris Bourse takes place.	Sodexho establishes activities in the Americas, Japan, South Africa and Russia and reinforces its presence in the rest of Central Europe.	Sodexho becomes the world market leader in food service thanks to alliances with Gardner Merchant in the UK and Partena in Sweden.	The Group's holding company changes its name to Sodexho Alliance.

The Sodexo Group has been a member of the FTSE4Good Index since its creation in 2001 and is listed in the Dow Jones Sustainability World Index and the Dow Jones STOXX Sustainability Index (Europe) as Industry Leader and Worldwide Super Sector Leader.

Product
Sodexo's quality of life services centre on two core activities: food and facilities management; and service vouchers and cards.

Its food services are specifically tailored to its customers, whether they are schools, hospitals, military bases, offices, factories or even special events like Royal Ascot. For facilities management services, Sodexo works in partnership with its clients to help them reduce costs, improve service delivery and give them the assurance to focus on their business.

Sodexo service vouchers and cards offer corporations and public authorities a range of innovative and secure solutions that help make life easier for 20 million beneficiaries throughout the world.

Recent Developments
In 2006, the Sodexo Group launched a major project to support its strategic ambition: to become the benchmark for services that improve the quality of daily life. A first step was to develop a common visual identity to be shared

across 80 countries and by employees representing 130 nationalities. This new identity was rolled out globally in late 2006, underlined with a new brand signature: 'Making every day a better day.'

In 2008, the word 'Alliance' and the letter 'h' were removed from the company name to help accelerate the development of a single global brand across all activities, sectors and countries where Sodexo operates.

Promotion
Through its 'Ambition 2015' strategy the Sodexo Group seeks to become the leading global expert for quality of life services, doubling its revenue and evolving its business portfolio to confirm its expertise in facilities management services. The plan sets out a clear three pronged strategy.

Firstly, to reinforce Sodexo's leadership in food services: its 40 years of experience give the company a clear advantage in a market in which the outsourcing rate averages at just 45 per cent.

Secondly, to accelerate development in facilities management services: Sodexo already offers a wide range of services, from landscaping and the maintenance of green spaces to CAT or MRI scanner maintenance, from building climate control to energy management.

Thirdly, to become the world leader in service vouchers and cards: the ability to innovate and optimise synergies with its other activities provides Sodexo with a distinct competitive advantage in this changing

market. Sodexo is the number two worldwide in service vouchers and cards.

In 2008, Sodexo launched Abetterday.tv – a web TV channel that uses more than one hundred video clips to illustrate the brand's activities throughout the world.

Brand Values
Three enduring values guide Sodexo's business and its 355,000 employees: service spirit; team spirit; and the spirit of progress. These values reflect the brand's aim to grow organically and contribute to the development of countries in which it operates.

sodexo.com

Things you didn't know about Sodexo

Sodexo provides more than 45 different integrated facilities management services from patient feeding to hospitality at Royal Ascot; from repairing electron microscopes to reprographics; from tree maintenance to building and asset management.

At the 2008 Chelsea Flower Show, Sodexo served 93,000 drinks and 95,000 food items.

Sodexo was selected as an official nutrition partner for the Year of Food and Farming 2008 campaign.

Through consolidation of its supply chain Sodexo estimates around 280,000 fewer deliveries, meaning a reduction in its delivery miles of 1.5 million a year. This is estimated to save 9.68 tonnes of CO_2 per week, which is 465 tonnes over a year.

1998	2000	2005	2008
Sodexho Marriott Services is founded, with Sodexho holding 48.4 per cent of the outstanding shares.	In the UK, Gardner Merchant changes its name to Sodexho.	On 1st September, Michel Landel becomes chief executive officer and Pierre Bellon continues as chairman of the Board.	Sodexho Alliance becomes Sodexo and a new dynamic, modern logo is adopted globally.

The **co-operative** bank
good with money

As a pioneer of ethical finance, The Co-operative Bank is the only UK high street bank with an Ethical Policy that is voted on by customers and which seeks to ensure their money is invested in line with their ethical values. It is a stance reinforced by the bank's longstanding principles of value, fairness and commitment to social responsibility that lie at the heart of its business.

Market

The Co-operative Bank forms part of The Co-operative Financial Services (CFS). Under the brands of The Co-operative Bank, The Co-operative Investments, The Co-operative Insurance and smile, the internet bank, CFS offers a complete range of financial products and has more than 5.5 million customers. Within the UK's highly concentrated banking marketplace (comprising approximately 60 million current accounts) The Co-operative Bank holds a 1.6 per cent share; the 'big five' – HSBC, Lloyds TSB, Barclays, Halifax and NatWest – claim more than 66 per cent of the remaining market share.

The banking sector has had a turbulent year with unrest likely to continue for some time.

Against this difficult financial climate, however, The Co-operative Bank has seen a 40 per cent increase in both its personal savings and corporate deposits over a 12-month period. The Co-operative Bank, which screens potential corporate and business banking customers for practices that may conflict with its Ethical Policy, stands out as an innovator within the market.

Achievements

The Co-operative Bank has a proud history of corporate responsibility – as recognised by CFS winning Business in the Community's (BITC) Company of the Year award in 2008 – central to which, is managing and developing the business in a sustainable manner. While other companies are beginning to tackle their contribution to

climate change, CFS' operations have already gone 'beyond carbon neutral', offsetting 110 per cent of the business' remaining carbon dioxide emissions (after already significantly reducing emissions through the procurement of green electricity and investment in high-quality renewable energy and energy efficiency projects). It is a pioneering approach that has seen it reach Platinum status in three separate BITC indices: Corporate Responsibility, Environment and Community.

In 2007 The Co-operative Bank celebrated 15 years of its Ethical Policy and remains market leader among socially responsible organisations. As one of the seven co-operative principles, 'concern for the community' is at the core of the bank's approach, with its work in this field covering five key areas: climate change, social inclusion, tackling crime, food ethics and modern co-operation. As part of this, in 2007 The Co-operative Bank raised more than £1.5 million through its 'affinity' credit card in support of a range of national charities and non-governmental organisations. Affinity partners receive a donation from the bank for each new card that is issued and a donation each time the card is used.

Product

The Co-operative Bank's product range – from current and savings accounts to credit cards, loans and mortgages – reinforces its commitment to ethical investment. The 'think' credit card, for instance, launched in 2007, was the first aimed at ethical shoppers; the first time the card is used, The Co-operative Bank makes a donation to protect an area of rainforest in the customer's name, after which 25p is donated to rainforest protection for every £100 spent on the card. Similarly,

1844		1867	1872	1992	1997
A group of 28 weavers – the 'Rochdale Pioneers' – create a local store to avoid exploitation by unscrupulous shopkeepers.	Other groups follow suit and co-operative businesses begin springing up, first in the north of England, then throughout the country.	The Co-operative Insurance Society is formed. It goes on to build a broad customer base with a wide portfolio of insurance services and a reputation for social responsibility.	The Co-operative Wholesale Society's Loan and Deposit Department is founded – the origins of The Co-operative Bank.	The Co-operative Bank becomes the world's first bank to introduce a customer-led Ethical Policy.	In partnership with Greenpeace, The Co-operative Bank launches the world's first biodegradable credit card.

The **co-operative** bank
insurance
investments

Good with money

Join us make a difference
goodwithmoney.co.uk

through its mortgages The Co-operative Bank funds several 'climate care' projects around the world; for every year a customer holds a Co-operative Bank mortgage, the bank pays to offset a fifth of a typical UK home's CO_2 emissions – in 2007, mortgage customers contributed more than £280,000 to combat climate change in this way.

The Co-operative Bank also has a corporate arm that, in addition to offering the full range of financial services expected from any corporate bank, provides tailored solutions to meet the most complex funding requirements.

The **co-operative** bank
good with money

the cat's whiskers

**Voted No.1 on the high street
for customer satisfaction**

See why – open a new **Current Account Plus** with linked savings

Current Account Plus

Call in today
co-operativebank.co.uk

Recent Developments

Through a significant rebranding programme, the different sectors of The Co-operative Group – from bank, insurance and investments to pharmacy, funeral services, food, travel and legal services – have recently been united under one master brand, 'The Co-operative'. The rebrand clarifies the range of financial services on offer and enables The Co-operative Bank to promote its 'good with money' ethos to a wider audience. The intention of the unified approach is to highlight to consumers the benefits of being part of a group of businesses with shared values and principles.

An unprecedented investment has been made to promote the scale and importance of the changes ushered in by the rebranding programme, including CFS' first national television advertisement for nearly 13 years and direct mail to customers that personally informs them of the changes and what to expect in the future.

Promotion

Over the course of its history The Co-operative Bank has used a wide range of communication channels to promote products and services, such as TV, press, outdoor, direct mail, online and in-branch. A diverse community engagement programme supports these communications and ranges from its Trees for Schools initiative to the arts and charitable causes, partnering with the likes of the Henley Literary Festival and Oxfam.

In 2008 CFS launched a new campaign that repositioned its three main financial services brands – The Co-operative Bank, The

Co-operative Insurance and The Co-operative Investments – with a consistent look and tone clearly espousing its ethical stance. The campaign focused on the relationship between banking and money and featured a powerful icon, the globe of televisions, positioned in an unbroken background of blue – the CFS brand colour. The strategy was to convey the purity of the ethical positioning at the businesses' core. The accompanying scripts, voiced by the actor John Simm, underlined The Co-operative Bank's operational differences compared to those of other institutions and invited viewers to compare the ethics of their own financial services providers.

Brand Values

The Co-operative Bank's customer experience statement – 'We will always offer value, fairness and social responsibility' – supports its key principles which are to be trustworthy, open and honest; customer focused; community focused and socially responsible; and willing to champion causes.

co-operativebank.co.uk

Things you didn't know about The Co-operative Bank

The Co-operative Bank has turned away more than £900 million of loans to businesses in conflict with its Ethical Policy.

The Co-operative Insurance's solar tower in Manchester is the UK's biggest solar project and generates enough electricity every year to make nine million cups of tea.

The Co-operative Financial Advisers offer the opportunity to discuss CFS products face-to-face anywhere in the UK – even as far afield as the Outer Hebrides.

2002		2007	
The Co-operative Financial Services is launched, encouraging a stronger working relationship between The Co-operative Bank and The Co-operative Insurance.	The Co-operative Insurance becomes the first insurance company in the world to launch a customer-led Ethical Engagement Policy.	The Co-operative Group and United Co-operatives become one organisation, The Co-operative. It is the world's largest consumer co-operative.	The Co-operative Bank and CIS rebrand under The Co-operative Bank, Insurance and Investments brands.

The Daily Telegraph

Launched in 1855, The Daily Telegraph has grown from Britain's best-selling quality daily newspaper into an award-winning, integrated, multiplatform brand that reaches one in three of the UK population every year and 10 million adults worldwide every week. The Daily Telegraph's popularity stems from its reputation to break news stories with honesty, accuracy, depth and intelligence, and from the quality of its writers, commentators and contributors.

860,298 and an average daily readership of 2.06 million adults (Source: NRS July 2007 to June 2008, Mon-Sat).

Market

The combined circulation of UK national daily newspapers in August 2008 was 10.4 million, of which the four qualities accounted for 2.036 million per day on average. The Daily Telegraph takes 42.2 per cent circulation share of the quality market, 248,000 copies ahead of The Times. According to ABC figures for August 2008, The Daily Telegraph achieved an audited average daily circulation figure of

Achievements

Telegraph Media Group (TMG) was awarded the title of Best Online Consumer Publisher in the Association of Online Publishers' (AOP) 2007 awards, for leading the field in applying the strengths of traditional publishing to digital platforms. TMG was nominated for a total of 11 awards, more than any other publisher.

Furthermore, The Daily Telegraph was voted the Personal Finance Newspaper of the Year at the 2007 Bradford & Bingley Personal

Finance Media Awards. Your Money, the Telegraph's Personal Finance section, was praised for its combination of excellent news delivery, presentation and objectivity. Faith Archer, deputy Personal Finance editor, was also named the Personal Finance Consumer Mortgage Writer of the Year.

Product

The Telegraph is committed to providing the latest business news and expert analysis from the City and around the world in print, online, via video or direct to mobile devices in an ever-evolving and engaging way. As such, in September 2008 the Telegraph relaunched its online and print Business products at a time when business and finance news was more in demand than ever before.

The Daily Telegraph's separate, dedicated Business section is now printed in full colour and along with its online counterpart, continues to be recognised for its accurate, bold and insightful coverage. Its team of award-winning journalists includes Jeff Randall, Ambrose Evans-Pritchard, Ian Cowie, Tracy Corrigan, Edmund Conway and Roger Bootle, with Damian Reece as group head of Business across all three Telegraph titles (The Daily Telegraph, The Sunday Telegraph and Telegraph.co.uk).

One of the most popular features of The Daily Telegraph's Business coverage has long been its Alex cartoon. A stalwart of the Business section since his creators joined the Telegraph in 1992, Alex is held in great affection amongst the business community. In 2007 Alex was brought to life on stage in London, with Robert

1855	1862	1897	1947	1987	1994
The first Daily Telegraph & Courier is published, having been founded as a vehicle for its proprietor, Colonel Sleigh, to wage a vendetta against the Duke of Cambridge and his conduct in the Crimea War.	The Daily Telegraph's championing of charitable causes sees the newspaper raising £6,000 for starving cotton workers in Lancashire.	A young Winston Churchill reports from the North West Frontier for the Telegraph.	In April, Telegraph sales exceed one million.	The Telegraph moves from Fleet Street to the Isle of Dogs, leaving in 1992 for Canary Wharf.	The Telegraph becomes the first British newspaper to launch an internet presence – the Electronic Telegraph.

Bathurst in the title role. Since then, the play has toured Australia, Hong Kong, Singapore and the Middle East.

Also in 2007, Telegraph TV was launched. Today, the schedule includes: News Now; The Business Bullet – a must-watch in the City every weekday; and Your Money, Their Hands, which offers expert investment advice without the fee.

Recent Developments

Exceptional events demand exceptional coverage and in response to changing times The Daily Telegraph has introduced more financial news, both in its Business section and online. New content includes BreakingViews.com – previously only available to those in investment banks, where it was widely regarded as a must-read to give City insiders the low-down on every deal – and an integrated Questor column, which places expert share-buying tips alongside relevant business news. Online, Telegraph.co.uk/finance now features useful tools including best-buy tables and a portfolio tracker to help everyone from private investors to small businesses make the most of their money.

For those on the move, The Daily Telegraph's finance content is optimised for viewing on mobiles and handheld devices via Telegraph.co.uk/mobile. Furthermore, the Telegraph's extensive portfolio of widgets, including specialised Finance widgets, means that anyone in the world can receive the latest business headlines from Telegraph.co.uk, updated by the minute and delivered directly to their desktop, social network profile or blog.

Promotion

In September and October 2008, the Telegraph ran a campaign promoting its Business portfolio. Fronted by Sir Philip Green, Martin Sorrell and Paul Walsh, it asked, "Where do the stars of business get their business news?" and gave the answer, "The Telegraph of course." The campaign was executed outdoor, online, in trade and consumer press and via email. Following the campaign, the Telegraph celebrated its new-look, new content and relaunched Finance channel at an event attended by more than 300 global business heavyweights – including Gordon Brown, Sir Philip Green (pictured above right) and Royal Bank of Scotland CEO, Stephen Hester.

The Telegraph's coverage of Alistair Darling's first Budget speech as Chancellor of the Exchequer in 2008 demonstrated the versatility of the Telegraph's integrated multimedia newsroom. Coverage included exclusive interviews on Telegraph TV with industry experts and the most recent Conservative Chancellor, Kenneth Clarke. Telegraph.co.uk ran up-to-the-minute news and instant reaction, helping readers to understand what the Budget really meant for them, with expert analysis and Budget calculators to bring it all to life.

Budget Day was followed up with an eight-page broadsheet Budget special featuring in-depth commentary and insight from Jeff Randall, Roger Bootle, Edmund Conway and Ian Cowie. To support the Telegraph's Budget coverage, thousands of 'Budget Box' flyers were distributed at mainline and underground stations in London's business districts during that morning, followed by a four-page Budget special featuring news and analysis for commuters travelling home in the evening. An extensive online advertising campaign, targeting business and political websites, helped raise awareness of the Telegraph's online coverage throughout the day.

Brand Values

The Daily Telegraph brand values are accuracy, honesty, integrity, quality and heritage. Its brand personality is intelligent, British, trusted, good-humoured, authoritative and engaging.

telegraph.co.uk

Things you didn't know about The Daily Telegraph

In 1925, The Daily Telegraph became the first British newspaper to publish a daily crossword.

The Telegraph launched a fund in 1937 to buy Christmas presents for children whose parents were unemployed.

In 1988, Matt Pritchett's cartoon – Matt – appeared in The Daily Telegraph for the first time.

In 2006, the annual Telegraph Christmas Charity appeal raised more than £1 million – this sum, donated by Telegraph readers, was divided between the three charities selected for support that year.

2004
The Barclay Brothers buy the Telegraph Group.

2005
The Daily Telegraph relaunches with a standalone broadsheet Business section and a separate compact Sport section. It also becomes the first British newspaper to have a daily podcast.

2006
The Group rebrands to Telegraph Media Group and moves into state-of-the-art offices on Buckingham Palace Road, London. Telegraph TV launches the following year.

2008
The Telegraph relaunches its Business offering with a full-colour Business section and mobile and online Finance channel.

WARWICK
BUSINESS SCHOOL

Warwick Business School (WBS) is a leading 'thought-developer' and innovator, in the top one per cent of global business schools. Its students come from more than 140 countries to learn at undergraduate, masters, MBA and PhD level. WBS educates and develops global citizens, and promotes new knowledge to benefit business and society, through its executive education and applied research. WBS is consistently top-rated for teaching quality and research.

Changing lives, challenging minds

Achievements

WBS has achieved a global reputation for excellence in just 40 years. It has one of the broadest subject bases and most highly regarded faculties of any business school in the world. The December 2008 Research Assessment Exercise rated 75 per cent of WBS research at three stars and above, placing it third in the UK. WBS submitted 130 academics for assessment, nearly 90 per cent of its total, making this statistic an accurate reflection of the quality of the breadth and depth of research at WBS. These research credentials are fundamental to its culture and differentiate it from teaching colleges or commercial training companies.

The performance of its degree programmes continues to excel. The Guardian University Guide 2008 ranked its undergraduate programme in the top two business and management degrees in the UK and has given it 10 out of 10 for job prospects. In addition, its portfolio of 11 masters courses provides highly specialised learning in areas of business that are increasingly important in the search for sustainable competitive advantage.

More than 20 years of combined learning experience enable WBS to deliver the Warwick MBA to over 2,400 experienced managers each year, wherever they are in the world. Furthermore, its long-standing commitment to work across the private, public and voluntary sectors created the Warwick MPA – the UK's first MBA for the public sector. In 2009, WBS will launch the Warwick Global Energy MBA, a groundbreaking programme bringing together energy industry professionals.

Market

There are more than 3,900 business schools across the world, aiming to develop the next generation of business leaders. Warwick Business School is one of the largest in Europe and ranks in the top one per cent worldwide. As the largest department of the University of Warwick, WBS aims to offer its students both excellent facilities and a prestigious reputation.

A high quality business education is valued by employers and employees alike; employers can gain competitive advantage by recruiting and developing talent with knowledge and critical thinking skills, while individuals can gain new options for career progression, both sideways and upwards. With thousands of schools offering MBAs worldwide, the business school market is incredibly competitive. To be a success and to attract successful people, a respected brand is essential. WBS was the first among fewer than 35 schools to be endorsed by all three international business school accreditation bodies: AMBA, EQUIS and AACSB.

WBS academics work to produce world-leading research in all fields of management. With recognised research leaders across disciplines as diverse as pensions, industrial dispute resolution, business strategy, customer service, enterprise, corporate social responsibility, sports management, public sector governance, sales marketing and energy policy, people go to WBS to explore grounded, well researched ideas that work in the real world. WBS research and expert opinion is valuable, sometimes crucial, to the success of corporations, not-for-profit organisations, Government and society.

1965	1981	1989	1997	1999	2000
The University of Warwick is founded by Royal Charter. Two years later, WBS is created as the School of Industrial and Business Studies, with five staff, 24 students and three courses.	The Warwick MBA brand is launched. In 1986 the distance learning option launches.	WBS achieves five star rating for research excellence.	On its 30th anniversary, WBS has 3,160 students, 263 staff and a turnover of £12.4 million.	WBS becomes the first business school in the world to hold accreditation from all three international management education bodies: AMBA, EQUIS and AACSB.	The Warwick MBA by distance learning celebrates its 2,000th graduate.

Warwick Business School's reputation means WBS graduates are highly sought after by business leaders and can be found in senior positions around the world. Its expertise is clear from its diverse list of clients and sponsors, including Accenture, AT Kearney, The Bank of England, BP, The Cabinet Office, Capgemini, Deloitte, Deutsche Post, WorldNet, GKN, GlaxoSmithKline, Grant Thornton, HSBC, IBM, Islamic Bank of Britain, Johnson & Johnson, J.P.Morgan, Nestlé, PepsiCo, Procter & Gamble, SABMiller, Santander, Siemens, UBS Investment Bank, Unilever and Vodafone.

Product

Warwick Business School has something to offer individuals at every stage of their career. It offers a range of business and management undergraduate degrees; 10 specialist masters courses; a generalist MSc in Management; the new Warwick Global Energy MBA as well as the popular and flexible Warwick MBA; its public sector equivalent, the Warwick MPA; and one of the world's most respected PhD programmes. For corporate clients and individuals, it also offers a range of diplomas, short courses and customised programmes.

WBS consults with industry to keep its programmes fresh, relevant and accessible. The fact that many graduates return for further study at WBS later in their career demonstrates its effective blend of academic research with the practicalities of the workplace. Learning by sharing experience and insight is key to the student experience at WBS. Alumni members, who number 23,500 in total, have cited the combination of a highly intelligent and internationally diverse cohort as being a major benefit of their learning experience as well as their future careers.

Recent Developments

Warwick Business School celebrated its 40th anniversary in 2007. It has grown from offering three courses to 27 and now has more than 8,000 students enrolled, with a turnover of £40 million. The course portfolio continues to refresh, expand and diversify, with an ongoing contract to customise delivery of the Warwick MBA for multinational solutions provider IBM, as well as brand new courses in global energy, business analytics, and international management.

WBS has established a Fund for Academic Excellence to invest in future leaders, faculty and its learning environment. Since August 2003, the fund has helped to support many students, recruit 16 new professors and expand facilities, with a £9 million building recently completed and £20 million earmarked for further development. WBS recognises that in order to retain competitive advantage, it is essential to continue to gain funding for growth.

Promotion

WBS maintains a solid global presence with a range of below- and above-the-line segmented international marketing. Its 'extremely usable' website (according to the independent WebWorks 2007 study by CarringtonCrisp) attracts in the region of 2,500 visitors a day and is an essential platform for communicating. However, for many people its brochures are still an important channel, providing tangible evidence in a knowledge-based sector.

WBS is no stranger to using creative channels, having used airport advertising, taxis and sports events sponsorship to attract attention. Currently it is exploring 3D TV advertising. But, ultimately, its graduates are its best adverts and its best advocates.

Brand Values

Warwick Business School has simple core values: excellence in all it does, nurturing fresh-thinking in staff and students, ensuring a positive impact from the ideas it creates, and continuing to be international in outlook and approach. From these foundations WBS aims to continue to challenge minds, change lives, and create tomorrow's leaders.

wbs.ac.uk

Things you didn't know about Warwick Business School

Every FTSE 100 company has employed a WBS graduate.

In the last seven years, WBS academics have written, edited and contributed chapters to nearly 800 books and published almost 3,500 articles and papers.

WBS has 180 academic and teaching staff, supported by a team of management and administrative staff.

2003
The Guardian survey of top employers rates WBS graduates as the most employable in the UK.

2006
The Times Good University Guide rates WBS as the best overall undergraduate business education provider in the UK.

2008
The WBS masters portfolio reaches 11 courses.

2009
WBS launches the Warwick Global Energy MBA.

WEBER SHANDWICK

Advocacy starts here.

Weber Shandwick is a full service public relations agency, helping clients to manage their reputation and achieve their business goals. Part of The Interpublic Group of marketing companies, Weber Shandwick puts its creative talent, communications expertise and specialist teams to work for some of the biggest companies and most innovative brands in the UK and around the world, across the private, public and not-for-profit sectors.

Best PR Campaign at the inaugural MediaGuardian Innovation Awards for KFC's 'Face from Space' campaign, where the London team created the world's first logo visible from space as part of a global brand relaunch.

Market

The UK public relations market is growing in size and diversity, with an estimated 50,000 people now working in the industry. It is also growing in terms of spend, with many companies and organisations switching marketing resources from traditional advertising to PR, digital and other marketing disciplines.

The key growth areas for public relations are digital, corporate responsibility, healthcare, multicultural communications, technology and corporate reputation.

The consultancy sector varies from one-man bands to UK-only agencies and international players. Weber Shandwick is the UK's largest consultancy, employing around 350 people in the UK and Ireland and some 2,000 internationally in a network of offices and specialist consulting groups. Internationally, Weber Shandwick has 83 owned offices in 39 countries and affiliates that expand the network to more than 127 offices in 77 countries.

Achievements

In 2008, Weber Shandwick won praise from peers across the world when it was recognised as Best Communications Department/Organisation at the International Business Awards. Weber Shandwick also won the prestigious United Nations Grand Award for Outstanding Achievement in Public Relations for the three consecutive years from 2005 to 2007.

In the UK alone, the agency has won more than 20 industry accolades for client work during 2008, including five European SABRE Awards, two IPRA Golden World Awards, two European Excellence Awards, two PRWeek Awards and

High-profile assignments have included: creating Lewis Hamilton's ultimate F1 circuit to generate unprecedented online engagement for Mobil 1; launching an integrated campaign aimed at saving the British pig farming industry by raising awareness and increasing the price of pork; devising a European public advocacy campaign for the US-based Save Darfur Coalition, to raise awareness about the humanitarian crisis; helping Oxford University with a communications strategy to attract and retain Britain's brightest and best ethnic minority students; turning motorcycle journalists across EMEA into enthusiastic advocates for Harley-Davidson; organising the first conference on HIV testing in Europe on behalf of Gilead Sciences for more than 300 advocates, physicians and policymakers; and devising a lobbying programme to help IKEA turn fellow retailers, the media and MPs

1974
Shandwick International is founded in London with a single client and a global vision.

1987
The Weber Group is founded in Cambridge, Massachusetts as a communications agency for emerging technology companies. In less than a decade it goes on to become a top 10 PR firm.

1998
Shandwick International is acquired by The Interpublic Group.

2000
Shandwick International merges with The Weber Group and becomes Weber Shandwick.

2001
BSMG Worldwide merges with Weber Shandwick.

2008
Weber Shandwick continues to win awards and is recognised for its work internationally.

**An audience of millions.
Thousands of languages.
Hundreds of channels.**

**One good reason
to speak to us?**

Weber Shandwick is a leading global public relations agency with offices in over 79 markets around the world. With a deep commitment to client service, creativity and collaboration, we harness the power of Advocates – engaging stakeholders in new and creative ways to build brands and reputation.

www.webershandwick.com
www.webershandwick.co.uk

WEBER SHANDWICK
Advocacy starts here.

into firm supporters, enabling the Swedish company to gain planning permission for its first store in Ireland.

Product

Weber Shandwick is a full service public relations agency. Its policy of recruiting the best media and PR professionals means it now possesses some of the strongest teams of experienced senior ex-journalists and industry-specific communications specialists in the business.

In the UK, Weber Shandwick has six specialist practice teams in technology PR, healthcare PR, financial communications, corporate communications, consumer marketing and public affairs and also offers cross-practice consultancy in digital, multicultural and internal communications, lifestyle marketing, over 50s marketing, broadcast PR, sports PR and corporate social responsibility.

The UK and Ireland business employs around 350 people across nine regional offices in London, Manchester, Leeds, Glasgow, Edinburgh, Aberdeen, Inverness, Belfast and Dublin. Globally, the company is part of the extensive global IPG network with a strong PR presence across the US, Europe, Asia Pacific and in the emerging economic giants of China, India, Russia and Brazil.

Recent Developments

During 2008, Weber Shandwick built on its reputation for excellence in traditional PR to set a new agenda for the future of the public relations industry. The agency's focus shifted to advocacy and Weber Shandwick invested in new ways to create, identify and harness the power of advocates for clients' brands, causes, products and services.

Harnessing the power of the digital revolution, Weber Shandwick invested heavily in its pan-European digital practice, Screengrab, to ensure digital communications and relations are seamlessly integrated into all client campaigns.

Weber Shandwick's corporate responsibility and sustainability practice, Planet 2050, launched globally, to help international clients to prepare for the challenges of a planet under social and environmental stress. DNA Medical Communications, a new medical education practice, was also established to add scientific communications expertise and help build advocacy for healthcare clients globally.

In November 2008, Weber Shandwick strengthened its sports PR offering with the launch of Weber Shandwick Sport, a dedicated UK sports practice with experience of winning Olympic bids, maximising sports sponsorships, driving successful sports public affairs campaigns and leading the debate for sports organisations and bodies.

The agency's London and US offices achieved the environmental standard ISO 14001 as part of a move towards becoming a more sustainable business, and the UK operation has been awarded the prestigious Investors in People accreditation.

Promotion

Following the launch of its 'Advocacy starts here' positioning in 2007, which illustrated the agency's shift in focus to communications programmes that forge emotional bonds and higher levels of involvement with stakeholders, Weber Shandwick has embedded advocacy

into all of its agency work with the aim of creating an army of believers and fans for every client.

Weber Shandwick's investment in its specialist offering has also led to a number of high-profile new appointments and internal promotions including: a new worldwide chief digital creative officer; a strategic insight and planning specialist; a head of practice integration; and a head of crisis and issues management.

Brand Values

Weber Shandwick's values are creativity, passion and commitment. It has a pool of specialist talent and strong European and international networks. Its clients are among the top brands, companies and organisations in the UK and around the world.

Weber Shandwick makes a significant investment in staff development every year to ensure the consultancy continues to develop added value services and to deliver real business results for its clients. In the past year alone, the agency has delivered more than 500 individual learning opportunities and introduced a 'digital university' training initiative to drive digital PR skills across the agency.

webershandwick.co.uk

Things you didn't know about Weber Shandwick

Weber Shandwick partnered with Henley Business School, one of the largest business schools in Europe, to create a Senior Executive Development Programme.

Weber Shandwick has created an employee volunteering scheme in partnership with The Media Trust to help small charities with pro bono work worth thousands of pounds.

Weber Shandwick is one of the few leading UK PR agencies with a dedicated strategic planning team.

Weber Shandwick is one of the biggest graduate recruiters in the UK public relations industry.

Business Superbrands Brands to Watch

On the pages that follow you will find brands that have been identified as Brands to Watch, i.e. brands that are enjoying significant momentum and positive progression. These brands are making considerable headway and their drive is likely to lead to them attaining Business Superbrand status in the near future.

Full details of the Brands to Watch selection process can be found on page 136.

Cass Business School
CITY UNIVERSITY LONDON

Cass Business School is one of the leading business institutions in London, delivering innovative, relevant and forward-looking education, training, consultancy and research. Located on the doorstep of one of the world's leading financial centres, Cass is ideally positioned to be the City's intellectual hub; its dialogue with business shaping the structure and content of programmes and research that has gained a reputation for excellence in professional education.

Market

The business school market is highly competitive and attracting and fostering success requires vision. Cass Business School combines international academic talent with years of experience in industry. Its strategic move in 2003, to a new state-of-the-art building in the heart of London's financial district, further cemented its mutually beneficial partnership with the City – one which attracts industry experts, thereby offering a highly sought after practical dimension to programmes.

Cass Business School's main competitors in the UK include London Business School, London School of Economics and Political Science, Warwick Business School, Cranfield School of Management, Said Business School and Judge Business School. Its key international competitors are world renowned establishments such as Wharton, Columbia, Stanford, Harvard, INSEAD and HEC. The Cass global reach extends to more than 140 countries and its faculty speaks 22 different languages.

Achievements

Cass Business School is built around innovation, an ethos that has moved it up the business school ranks year-on-year, both in the UK and

abroad. In 2008 the Financial Times ranked its Executive MBA (EMBA) second in the UK, third in Europe and 13th in the world, while its PhD programme has been ranked as one of the world's top 30 for the past three years.

A flexible approach also sets Cass apart from many other business schools; flexible MBA options, for instance, enable students to study full-time or part-time at the School in London, or remotely from Europe or Dubai. Both its full-time MBA and EMBA programmes are ranked among the best in the world by the Financial Times.

The School has one of the largest finance faculties in Europe, led by Professor Alec Chrystal, former adviser to the Monetary Policy

Committee of the Bank of England, and its finance research has been rated second best within Europe and fourth in the world (outside of the US) by Financial Management Magazine. In 2003, the Worshipful Company of Actuaries awarded its Gold Medal to the Cass Faculty of Actuarial Science and Insurance for outstanding contributions to teaching and research over a 30-year period – it currently has the largest actuarial science and insurance faculty in Europe, led by Dr Ben Rickayzen.

Product

Cass Business School has 3,000 students studying a range of specialist programmes that balance theory and thinking with practice and understanding – skills and capabilities highly valued by employers. An emphasis on

The London Olympics: Who Wins?

Can the business benefits of the London Olympics
really justify the cost?

constant dialogue with business feeds into the structure and content of all study programmes, be it BSc, MBA, MSc or PhD.

Cass offers seven undergraduate degree options (either general or specialised) with the opportunity to spend a year studying abroad or working in industry. It also has the widest portfolio of specialist masters programmes in Europe, offering a diverse spectrum of subjects. The MBA programme offers a range of degrees: a full-time MBA, Executive MBA, Modular MBA and an EMBA in Dubai. In addition, the Cass Exec programme has been delivering executive education to the business world for more than 15 years, working in partnership with clients to construct bespoke programmes to meet their business needs.

Recent Developments
In February 2007, Cass launched its Dubai-based Executive MBA in collaboration with the Dubai International Financial Centre (DIFC), offering a general EMBA and two specialist streams in Islamic Finance and Energy. The Islamic Finance stream is the first of its kind in the world.

In 2008 three new research centres were created. In April, the Cass Private Equity Centre (CPEC) was set up to promote understanding and provide evidence of the key issues and challenges facing participants in the private equity industry. In October, Cass went on to

establish its Centre for Professional Service Firms (PSFs) – bringing together academics and professionals to collaborate on innovative research – and an M&A Research Centre (MARC), the only active one at a major global business school.

The ESRC Research Centre for Charitable Giving and Philanthropy was also launched. Based at Cass Business School, the facility's aim is to provide crucial evidence that can be used by UK charities and Government to inform policy making and strategies concerning donation giving and effective distribution.

Future Plans
Cass is driven by an aim to become one of the top five business schools in Europe and one of the top two in the UK; an ambition that seems achievable in the not too distant future given its current ascent through the business school ranks. Cass Business School is also striving to become the leading intellectual resource for the City of London, with the ultimate goal of being the best educator of young business graduates in the European market.

Promotion
In keeping with the establishment's emphasis on innovation, Cass uses a range of creative promotional strategies, including a large emphasis on online marketing. In a nine-month City-based campaign (pictured right) promoting MBA and MSc programmes, the School

combined traditional marketing channels with more visible experiential artwork, displayed in key business locations such as Canary Wharf and the Docklands Light Railway. To raise brand awareness further, the School organises around 120 events each year, with high profile speakers such as Chancellor of the Exchequer, Alistair Darling and Conservative Party Leader, David Cameron.

Other promotional strategies include the use of advertising at trade events and fairs – to boost international recruitment – and producing an in-house bi-yearly business magazine focusing on the School's academic research (InBusiness, pictured left). In addition, Cass spokespeople regularly provide expert commentary across the international media – print and broadcast – speaking on issues relating to global finance and international business strategy.

Brand Values
A forward-thinking approach defines Cass Business School. Its location allows the School to draw inspiration not only from the world of academia but from the everyday realities of global business. Companies cannot thrive on knowledge alone, they need people with experience, ideas and vision – qualities that Cass always strives to deliver.

cass.city.ac.uk

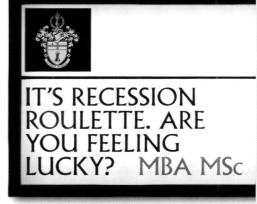

IT'S RECESSION ROULETTE. ARE YOU FEELING LUCKY? MBA MSc

In these risky times, make yourself a
better bet with a world-class Executive
MBA or MSc from Cass Business School.
www.cass.city.ac.uk/skillup
0207 040 8744

chartered
management
institute

inspiring leaders

As the only chartered professional body dedicated to management and leadership, the Chartered Management Institute (CMI) is committed to raising the performance of business by providing the necessary skills to address new practices and challenges. Through engaging with the wider management community, the CMI provides training and development, disseminates knowledge and promotes best practice.

Market

The essential skills required to survive and prosper in the modern business environment are constantly changing, impacting significantly on the way in which organisations structure and develop themselves and their managers.

The Chartered Management Institute helps to set and raise standards in management by encouraging development in order to improve performance. The breadth and depth of the Institute's offering is unrivalled in the marketplace and caters for individuals and employers in a variety of sectors across a number of distinct markets: training and development, qualifications and management consultancy.

Achievements

For more than 60 years, the Chartered Management Institute has been supporting individual managers and developing organisations. It is the only institution dedicated to management and leadership to acquire 'Chartered' status, granted in 2002,

and is home to the Management Standards Centre, the government-recognised standards-setting body for management and leadership.

The Institute is seen as the leading body for developing and promoting best practice in management and leadership. Its research agenda continues to produce data that identifies the management skills needed now and in the future and demonstrates the impact of management and leadership on individual and organisational performance. The research benefits those within the workplace, those delivering development needs, the media and key policy makers.

As the 'champion' of management, the CMI is regularly consulted on a range of management and legislative issues and frequently engages in discussion with government and senior business leaders.

Awarded by the CMI, Chartered Manager status offers independent recognition and endorsement of an individual's management

and leadership credentials. It has been cited, by independent analysis of Labour Force Survey data, as a route towards higher earnings potential and greater employability.

Product

The Institute is committed to supporting managers across the globe throughout their careers and learning, from individuals seeking to enhance their career to employers looking to develop staff and training bodies seeking accreditation.

CMI members have access to a comprehensive online information resource as well as books, articles, journals and trade publications via the Management Information Centre.

Regional and branch events offer opportunities to develop new skills and network with like-minded professionals, while the online Continuing Professional Development service allows members to assess their needs, plan their development and record their progress.

ManagementDirect is an online support facility which uses videos and podcasts, featuring business leaders' real-life experiences, to bring subject matter to life. Members can search by topic or content – or even by the amount of time they are able to devote to finding the required information.

The online media centre presents the latest news on management and leadership as well as providing access to research, reports, policy, management facts and figures and information on current topics.

The CMI's network of Approved Centres in the UK and overseas enables organisations to deliver and access their choice of qualifications from a comprehensive range of full certificates, diplomas and S/NVQs.

Recent Developments

The Institute's recent focus has centred around the launch of independent research based on Labour Force Survey (LFS) data. The LFS demonstrates how professionalism pays – namely, how membership of professional bodies and undertaking professional qualifications has a direct impact on earning power and employability. CMI believes that driving up the demand for professionalism in the UK has immense potential; not only can individuals benefit at a personal level but the spill-over effect as they influence colleagues can have a significant impact on UK productivity.

Future Plans

Aware that the skills required for an organisation to succeed and prosper are constantly changing, the Institute has begun to implement a number of strategic initiatives to address evolving workplace conditions; a supporting role aimed at equipping managers and organisations with the necessary tools to tackle new challenges as they arise.

Continued investment in new and media-rich resources feature heavily in the brand's future plans as does the rolling out of a new group membership package, aimed at making it easier for employers to engage their managers

with the range of products and services available within the Institute. A particular emphasis is also placed on extending collaborative working and partnership relations that will see relationships with higher education establishments forged in order to engage potential career managers earlier.

There is a growing recognition of the need to raise awareness and understanding of the Chartered Management Institute through continued investment in integrated marketing activities, not only to help promote its future pivotal role in establishing and reviewing management and leadership standards but also to ensure a world-class benchmark of best practice.

Promotion

Promotion of the Institute to raise the brand profile remains vital and takes place through a full range of marketing and promotional activities, from branch events and regional conventions to more targeted PR activities. Brand marketing activities focus around three key areas: opinion forming, influencing and brand building.

A recent campaign – 'However do you manage?' – focused on individuals and employers within the management community and highlighted the totality of the Institute's offering by directing respondents to a purpose-built micro site from where resources aimed at improving management skills could be downloaded. The campaign theme was used across the Institute's PR activities and was also rolled out across various advertising media, from national press to adverts on the London Underground and online advertising.

During 2008, media coverage (both traditional and more innovative) has promoted the Institute's work to more than 197.5 million people. National coverage, specifically, increased by 53 per cent with mentions in over 40 items of broadcast news.

Brand Values

The Chartered Management Institute is built around key brand values that look to develop, support and recognise the skills and achievements of managers. It works with employers to identify and promote the necessary management and leadership skills to drive performance – through a combination of innovation and authority. The Institute looks to influence stakeholders to address the challenges faced by today's managers and leaders and in doing so, aims to provide guidance to help managers choose the most appropriate strategy for their business.

managers.org.uk

C CLEARCHANNEL
OUTDOOR

Clear Channel Outdoor is the UK's leading outdoor advertising company, providing more than 70,000 advertising opportunities across its four premier sub brands: Clear Channel Pinnacle, Clear Channel Billboards, Clear Channel Adshel and Taxi Media. Over the last two years Clear Channel Outdoor has emerged as a power brand in the UK media through quality of product, innovation, accountability and strong brand positioning.

Market

The UK outdoor advertising market was worth £975.8 million in 2007, representing nearly 10 per cent of display advertising spend (Source: Outdoor Advertising Association). The digital outdoor sector, meanwhile, is growing rapidly and has seen a 60 per cent increase in revenue from 2007 to 2008.

Clear Channel Adshel is the UK's leading supplier of 6-sheet advertising with 65 per cent of the UK roadside market while Clear Channel Billboards is the market leader in 96-sheet billboards and provides a national offering of 48-sheet billboards across the UK and Ireland.

In terms of the global market, Clear Channel Outdoor is the world's largest outdoor advertising company with close to one million displays in 49 countries across five continents. In the US, the company operates just under 200,000 advertising displays and has a presence in 49 of the top 50 designated market areas.

Clear Channel Outdoor is part of CC Media Holdings, Inc., formed in May 2007 by private equity funds sponsored by Thomas H. Lee

Partners LP and Bain Capital Partners LLC. CC Media Holdings is a global media and entertainment company specialising in mobile and on-demand entertainment and information services for local communities as well as premier opportunities for advertisers. The company's businesses include radio and outdoor displays.

Achievements

Clear Channel Outdoor made its way to the top of the premium end of the market through its acquisition of Van Wagner in 2006 and a commitment to developing quality sites in prime locations. It now has the UK's largest quality portfolio, including two iconic digital sites at Piccadilly Circus in London – one sold long term to LG and one sold to short term advertisers in 30-second slots.

Simultaneously, Clear Channel Outdoor has developed its Adshel 6-sheet portfolio, winning such contracts as Glasgow city centre, South Yorkshire, Portsmouth and Oxford to add to its existing client list of more than 350 local authorities and Transport for London's street furniture contract.

For the past 10 years, Clear Channel Outdoor has worked hard to ensure high standards of environmental management and in The Sunday Times 2008 Best Green Companies listing, was ranked 22nd overall and fifth in category. The company was highly commended at the Green Business Awards 2008 and was a finalist at the 2008 National Energy Efficiency Awards. It was also a finalist for Campaign magazine's Outdoor Sales Team of the Year award for three consecutive years in 2006, 2007 and 2008.

Product

Clear Channel Adshel is the UK's leading supplier of 6-sheet advertising, encompassing a roadside network, point of sale panels at Sainsbury's supermarkets and panels in more than 80 UK shopping malls.

Clear Channel Pinnacle offers premium advertising at more than 200 high-profile sites, such as London's Cromwell Road and the M4 Towers and introduced large format digital roadside LED screens in London in 2008.

Clear Channel Outdoor pioneered the move to audience planning and offers customers highly flexible targeting and planning options. Its Audience Solutions system, for instance, provides an accessible planning guide for all campaigns, from outdoor broadcast to niche lifestyle and destination targeting. It was also the first media owner to offer a full and transparent proof of posting system, WAVe.

The company continues to provide research and insight to demonstrate the effectiveness of outdoor advertising, is a strong supporter of Poster Audience Research (Postar) and aims to provide high quality products and services that benefit its clients, serve a need and help ensure that outdoor is an effective and innovative broadcast medium.

Recent Developments

Recent successful company launches include premium roadside panels, digital screens and interactive mobile services. The launch of the large format digital LED roadside network in London in June 2008 was a notable success for the brand, as was the Piccadilly Lite digital LED screen at Piccadilly Circus; both have brought new flexibility, quality displays and instant copy changes to advertisers.

In terms of mobile services, Clear Channel Outdoor launched a full service mobile marketing brand, Interact, in 2008 with a dedicated SMS short code number and a range of unique services for advertisers.

Its most recent development is a pioneering dry-posting technique that is not only environmentally friendly but also weather resistant; it was tested for six months in severe weather conditions including a force 10 gale.

Future Plans

During 2009, Clear Channel Outdoor will unveil the next generation of landmark outdoor advertising sites in Glasgow: 10 gateway locations with substantial, bespoke architectural structures housing large format backlit displays. The sites will complement Clear Channel Outdoor's existing portfolio of bespoke structures such as Wandsworth Bridge Roundabout, Chester Road Roundabout in Manchester and the Millennium Arches in Birmingham. The project, developed in partnership with Glasgow's Mackintosh School of Architecture, reflects Clear Channel Outdoor's commitment to creating the highest quality structures.

Clear Channel Outdoor recently launched digital panels in shopping malls in a joint venture with Vision Media Group (VMG). Expansion into the world of digital media

will continue in 2009 with the launch of Clear Channel Socialite – the first premium in-bar advertising screen network of high quality, portrait digital poster sites with the capability of streaming static, animated, full motion video and real-time content into pubs and bars.

Promotion

Clear Channel Outdoor not only communicates with its key audiences of clients, agencies and specialist outdoor agencies through events, email, newsletters, its website, presentations and printed marketing material but also seeks to promote the outdoor advertising industry as a whole. In partnership with Media Week, it launched the Outdoor Planning Awards in 2006, now in their third year. It has also championed creativity in outdoor advertising through the Clear Channel Student Design Awards, which it has run for 21 years.

Brand Values

The company strategy has been to consolidate the brands under the Clear Channel Outdoor umbrella, with a coherent message and consistent strong brand values of leadership, innovation, quality, flexibility and accountability guiding everything the company does and says. The company mantra is to put the customer at the heart of all communication.

The Clear Channel products, services and people are the embodiment of its brand values and are trusted not only by a large and rapidly-growing client base but also by more local authorities and city councils for the provision of street furniture than any other outdoor media company.

clearchannel.co.uk

DentonWildeSapte...

Denton Wilde Sapte LLP is an international law firm with more than 600 lawyers and a network of offices across the UK, Europe, the Middle East, the Commonwealth of Independent States (CIS) and Africa. Its expertise spans the full range of commercial legal services and clients include many of the world's leading companies, with a particular expertise in four core sectors: energy, transport and infrastructure; financial institutions; real estate and retail; and technology, media and telecoms.

DentonWildeSapte...

Middle East

DentonWildeSapte...

The partners of Denton Wilde Sapte have great pleasure in inviting you to Ladies Day at Royal Ascot

Thursday 19th June
Royal Ascot Village

Agenda

11.00	Pimms & Champagne reception with canapes
12.00	Lunch is served
14.00	Royal procession
14.30	First race begins
15.30	Afternoon tea
17.30	Day draws to a close

RSVP

Sam Mason
T: 020 7320 3998
sam.mason@dentonwildesapte.com

Please advise of any special dietary requirements

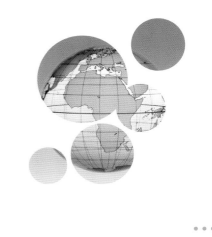

DentonWildeSapte...

Africa

Market

The last decade has been a time of consolidation within the UK's legal market with one third of the top 100 firms merging including Denton Wilde Sapte, created from the merger of Denton Hall and Wilde Sapte in 2000. This has resulted in a significant demand for brand building and differentiation.

While there are many ways of carving up the UK legal market, a generally agreed method is the Magic Circle (Clifford Chance, Freshfields, Linklaters and Allen & Overy); the Silver Circle (Herbert Smith, Ashurst, SJ Berwin, Berwin Leighton Paisner, Macfarlanes and Travers Smith); large City firms (Denton Wilde Sapte, Lovells, Simmons & Simmons, Norton Rose, CMS Cameron McKenna and Olswang); and the UK regional firms.

As a member of the City grouping, it has been important for Denton Wilde Sapte to demonstrate its viability as an alternative to the Magic and Silver Circle firms – offering

the same high-quality advice backed with comprehensive knowledge of the client's industry but at more competitive rates. Denton Wilde Sapte has also successfully established a reputation of excellence for work in a select number of high growth markets such as the Middle East, CIS and Africa.

Achievements

Denton Wilde Sapte's consistency in winning awards – being named Best Law Firm for Commodity, Trade and Structured Commodity Finance Deals by Trade Finance magazine for nine consecutive years, Best Trade Finance

Law Firm by Global Trade Review magazine and Best Law Firm for Trade Finance by Trade and Forfaiting Review magazine for many consecutive years – is testament to its success. Rather than being complacent, however, the company constantly strives to better itself; in 2008 it achieved Top Legal Employer status and the top ranking in the 2009 Chambers UK Guide for Trade Finance and Asset Finance: Rail, Construction and Real Estate.

The brand's pioneering approach has seen it spearhead a number of groundbreaking initiatives such as the creation of cross-departmental working groups (later implemented by other firms), the launch of its ambitious 'Ignite' project – to design and implement an integrated programme of business development training – and a customised cutting-edge pitch production system (EPIC). These latter programmes were commended by the Financial Times in 2008 for innovation in the legal market.

Product

Denton Wilde Sapte works strategically with many of the world's leading companies. Expanding relationships with existing clients through cross-selling work between practices has enabled the brand to develop a diverse and comprehensive product offering.

Alongside its sector expertise, Denton Wilde Sapte offers a full suite of legal services including banking advice; corporate and commercial; dispute resolution; European Commission and competition; employment and pensions; energy, infrastructure and project finance; insurance and reinsurance; real estate, including planning and public sector advice; taxation; and technology, media and telecoms.

The brand's commitment to service delivery is evident through its extensive range of value-added services such as secondments, onsite training, seminars and provision of consultancy services from non-fee earning staff.

Recent Developments

Denton Wilde Sapte's recent biannual client satisfaction survey, targeted at its major UK clients who account for more than 30 per cent of business, makes encouraging reading. In 2008 the key findings suggested that the brand's international high growth market focus has been a success. It achieved 42 per cent unprompted awareness among key clients who were considering instructing law firms for work in the African and Middle East markets; substantially ahead of competitor firms more than eight times its size. The survey also found that in addition to the majority of clients that were satisfied with client service, 25 per cent felt service levels had improved at Denton Wilde Sapte; this rose to more than 33 per cent among key clients – the recipients of focused brand building.

Future Plans

Denton Wilde Sapte prides itself on providing the highest quality service to its clients, made possible by an emphasis on staff retention, training and development. It works hard at maintaining an open and collegiate atmosphere, sharing ideas and working as a team towards shared objectives. Its strategic aim of providing the highest quality client service is built around a focus on client relationships through initiatives such as the creation of client service teams and a client

listening programme, a forum through which opinions and requirements can be expressed.

The brand's future plans look towards consolidating and developing these services in order to become clients' number one choice in the sectors and geographies in which it operates; annual satisfaction surveys help to identify areas that require further development.

Promotion

Over the past few years Denton Wilde Sapte has been working through a number of channels to improve the firm's public and internal image. In 2008, a 90-day profile-raising campaign resulted in more than 30 quotes in the national newspapers, including The Times, the Financial Times, the Guardian and The Daily Telegraph. By offering comment and opinion on prominent issues in the news, the brand is building its profile as an expert commentator and boosting staff morale. Notable success has been achieved in targeting comment at issues related to the financial crisis, which has highlighted the brand's expertise in insolvency work, financial regulation, employment, mergers, competition and other related subject areas.

In 2005 a 'creative laundry' was commissioned to evaluate the organisation, reviewing areas such as brand positioning, logo and marketing. As a result of the review, positive changes have been implemented that have improved overall brand perceptions.

Brand Values

Denton Wilde Sapte strongly believes that a brand is not just about a logo on a pen, a website, or a business card; it is an experience that stretches beyond the tangible, from how clients are treated when they walk into a reception area to the way in which partners or employees answer the telephone. Its brand values are evident throughout its work – clear, uncluttered and accessible – and it is these principles that filter through all aspects of its business dealings with clients and colleagues.

dentonwildesapte.com

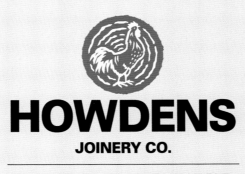

HOWDENS
JOINERY CO.

MAKING SPACE MORE VALUABLE

Howdens Joinery Co. was founded in 1995 in order to serve the needs of small builders undertaking routine joinery and kitchen installation work. By April 2008 it had become one of the UK's leading suppliers of kitchens and joinery products to the trade. Howdens has achieved this by creating a strong entrepreneurial culture within its depots, a close relationship with its customers and a range of kitchens specifically designed to meet the needs of modern living.

Market

Howdens operates within the trade or 'done for you' kitchen market, its core customer base comprising local builders and skilled professionals. The company has always believed that project management by the local builder is the best solution for installing a kitchen; they have experience in bringing together products, services and local trades in order to deliver a project on time, on budget and to a high standard. The introduction of additional legislation governing materials and services, combined with increasingly 'cash-rich, time poor' and design-savvy end-users, has seen this market grow dramatically.

Howdens helps builders to manage their businesses by guaranteeing product availability from local stock with rigid cabinets that are ready to install, saving builders time and money and allowing them to plan effectively. Its versatile and scaleable supply chain ensures its depots, and in turn the customer, receive a high level of service.

Specifically within the trade sector, key competitors are Jewson, Travis Perkins, Magnet Trade and Benchmarx.

Achievements

Since it was established in 1995, Howdens has demonstrated strong growth with a turnover nearing £750 million in 2007. In 13 years it has expanded from 14 depots to more than 450, supplying 234,000 building trade professionals and over 300 local authorities and housing associations with around 400,000 complete kitchens each year. In 2003 Howdens also set up Houdan Menuiseries in France with a further 11 depots.

In September 2007, a partnership between Howdens Joinery and Leonard Cheshire Disability was named Best Corporate Partnership at the Third Sector Excellence Awards. The research partnership aims to develop affordable, attractive and practical kitchen products for people with physical disabilities; in 2007, six kitchen activity centres

were created, donated and installed in Leonard Cheshire homes across the UK. It is an area with significant potential for ongoing product development and both Howdens and Leonard Cheshire Disability are committed to building their relationship in order to further benefit local communities. In addition, Howdens has developed a highly accessible kitchen collection called 'Inclusive Kitchens', which is sold through its depots.

Product

Howdens sells kitchens – encompassing appliances, accessories, handles, worktops, sinks and taps – and joinery, such as doors, flooring, stairs and hardware. A free survey and Computer Aided Design (CAD) service, which includes a site visit, is also available.

The company has the UK's largest kitchen range available from stock and ensures its portfolio remains informed by new product development. As all depots hold stock locally they are also able to offer local delivery when and where required.

Recent Developments

Howdens is continually seeking new ways to connect with customers and in May 2007, opened the Trade Expo Centre. The Centre's primary purpose is to provide an appointment-only facility where Howdens can engage with its customers, exploring their perception of the brand and their product requirements. The Centre also enables Howdens to raise

its profile as a supplier of kitchen and joinery products to the trade.

Since the autumn of 2007, the Centre's work has been amplified by a mobile display vehicle which highlights products aimed at the local authority and housing association market and showcases new items. The vehicle is able to travel to depots and customers' premises to create maximum impact and support localised marketing activities. In addition, the company's fleet of more than 400 delivery trailers has been redesigned to create further brand awareness.

Future Plans

In 2008, Howdens was awarded FSC and PEFC chain of custody certificates for a number of joinery products. In January 2009 this was extended to a selection of its complete kitchen ranges and work is underway to extend this in the future.

Product development will remain key to the company in order to ensure its continued growth. By offering products that are both affordable and in line with the latest design trends for the home, Howdens aims to meet changing market needs head on.

As consumers become ever more design conscious, increased emphasis will be placed on building brand awareness further, so that the Howdens name is recognised and recommended not only by builders but also by end-users themselves.

Promotion

Howdens puts the relationship between local depots and builders at the heart of its promotional strategy. As such its kitchen and joinery brochures, alongside other literature, are specifically designed to help builders in discussion with their own customers. Local marketing is key and the depots tailor their

promotional activity to meet the needs of their customers. Many depots also provide donations to local charities and community projects, including sponsorship of grassroots football and rugby teams.

More recently, Howdens has developed a website to showcase the company and its complete range of products, and for the first time in its history it has begun to undertake consumer and trade advertising campaigns. These ventures have been carefully considered to raise brand awareness and help the local depot and local builder in selling Howdens products to end-users.

Brand Values

Howdens is guided by an aim to provide small builders with kitchen and joinery products of the highest quality, at the best price and from local stock. The company attributes its success to the strength of the depots' relationships with their customers and the breadth of the market they serve; the quality and range of Howdens products; the ability to service customers from local stock; and the opportunity to streamline the business around supplying one customer, the small builder.

howdens.com

Landor

Landor Associates is one of the world's leading strategic brand consulting and design firms. Founded by Walter Landor (pictured below) in 1941, Landor pioneered many of the research, design and consulting methods that have become standard in the branding industry. Partnering with its clients, Landor drives business transformation and performance by helping to create brands that are more innovative, progressive and dynamic than their competitors.

Market

With an unrivalled network of more than 850 designers and consultants in 24 offices across 18 countries, Landor works to build its clients' brands and achieve business growth. Current and past clients include some of the world's most powerful brands including BP, Cathay Pacific, Citi, Danone, Diageo, Emaar, FedEx, Frito-Lay, the City of Hong Kong, HSBC, LG Group, Marriott Hotels & Resorts, Microsoft, Research in Motion, PepsiCo and Procter & Gamble.

Achievements

In recognition of its work, Landor has received many industry awards that acknowledge the central role that branding, strategy and design have on commercial success. A three-time winner of both Marketing magazine's Design Agency of the Year award and GRAMIA's Packaging Agency of the Year accolade, Landor has also collected 29 awards for its individual client work – bmi, BDO International, Cobra Beer, Gulf Air, Morrisons, Terry's Chocolate Orange, Traidcraft, Tropicana and Walkers Sensations to name a few.

In 2008, Landor's rebranding programme for Morrisons was rewarded with a GRAMIA award as well as a Gold at the DBA Design Effectiveness Awards which recognised its role in reversing Morrisons' market share decline, helping it to become one of the top five supermarkets in the UK.

However, Landor's achievements are not only limited to industry recognition and awards. Its annual ImagePower® Green Brands Survey has earned significant press coverage with the results published in national newspapers and leading industry magazines. Conducted in the UK and the US, as well as in China in 2008, the survey gives the people who engage with brands – the consumers – a chance to offer their opinions on green issues and products. The results inform clients as to how their brands and industries are perceived and indicate what they can do to bring about change.

Landor is also committed to a rigorous corporate social responsibility programme. Within the agency this includes recycling schemes and the purchase of an area of woodland in Kent, ensuring it is preserved for future generations. Furthermore, the agency contributes to WPP's carbon offset programme, aiming to reduce its carbon footprint by 20 per cent by 2011 through subsidising green energy farms in India and China. Landor also aims to engage its clients in ethical thinking. Examples include Ariel's 'Turn to 30°C' packaging design and its identity work for the non-profit organisation Traidcraft.

Product

Landor views a brand as an experience; the sum of all impressions formed by those interacting with it, whether in-store

or online, verbal or visual, or through personal interaction or product interface.

Its aim is to turn a brand into the driver of a business – with measurable financial results. It achieves this by helping clients identify a unique brand idea (a Brand Driver™) that they can own in the marketplace. The Brand Driver serves as a filter for strategic decision-making and a catalyst for change within an organisation. It becomes a platform for creating a compelling, multidimensional experience at every point of interaction with customers.

Recent Developments
A theme that Landor continues to place emphasis on is 'innovation', recognising it as the driver of the two hallmarks of brand strength – differentiation and relevance – and therefore its critical role in the growth and survival of brands and companies.

Landor approaches innovation by generating ideas that increase differentiation and relevance. Adopting an analytical approach to product and service categories, Landor determines which conventions consumers rely on to recognise a product or service category and which are purely traditional. Using this information, concepts are produced that aim to contradict or break category conventions, thus creating differentiation. To ensure relevance, it integrates the codes that consumers use to recognise a category.

Grounded in an understanding of market dynamics, global trends and consumer experience, Landor balances this generation

of creative ideas with a rigorous process that ensures that final concepts are also practical and actionable.

Future Plans
As brand messages continue to be communicated through an increasingly broad range of media touch points, Landor retains its 'medium agnostic' positioning, ensuring it is well placed to meet the future needs of its clients – both corporate and consumer – as their promotional strategies evolve.

Promotion
Landor makes use of numerous communication channels to encourage an interactive dialogue with its clients across the globe. Committed to taking a leading role in the conversation around

branding, its team of industry experts feature regularly in the media to offer an informed opinion on brands and branding issues. Industry issues are also addressed in 'Perspectives', a collection of thought leadership pieces derived from its global network.

The award-winning Landor.com website was relaunched in 2007 with a renewed focus on providing a dynamic news and content-rich website. It allows Landor to share its client work, media coverage, authored pieces and industry opinion with a global audience.

Brand Values
Landor is a leading global brand consultancy, partnering with major clients worldwide to deliver brand-led business growth. It combines unparalleled rigour with breakthrough creativity to transform the experience of brands. From strategy to action, from brand expression to behaviour, it aims to help transform business performance by transcending the competition and category conventions.

Landor is defined by: Experts – both in its field and in the brands and businesses it works with; Thinking Big – looking for the big opportunities to deliver brand-led business growth; Talented Team Players – operating as a single team across the globe; Change Agents – aiming to deliver real and significant improvement; and Lasting Impact – seeking to deliver measurable impact for the long term.

landor.com

Charities

On the pages that follow you will find details of some of the charities supported by the Business Superbrands and Brands to Watch featured in this publication.

Ascension Eagles Cheerleaders
www.ascensioneagles.com
Tel: 07866 612610
Registered Charity No: 1106766

From the 2012 London borough of Newham, Ascension Eagles Cheerleaders (AEC) are Britain's best cheerleaders. The AEC programme builds leadership, teamwork, citizenship and community integration while teaching championship level cheerleading. Founded in 1996 as a way to keep young people off the street, AEC trains 100 members (aged 6-24) twice weekly, and empowers them to lead outreach workshops that reach more than 2,000 other young people annually. Over the past decade, AEC has been recognised as one of the nation's most successful youth programmes, winning more than 300 trophies and entertaining over 200 million people at high profile events such as the FA Cup Final, UEFA SuperCup Final, Twickenham RFU, the London Marathon and the Olympic Flame Marathon.

From an outreach project in London's East End, to the top one per cent of cheer teams in the world, Ascension Eagles are record-breaking, history-making champions.

Supported by: ExCeL London

Believe in children
Barnardo's
www.barnardos.org.uk
Tel: 020 8550 8822
Registered Charity No: 216250 (England & Wales) and SC037605 (Scotland)

As one of the UK's leading children's charities, Barnardo's believes in children regardless of their circumstances, gender, race, disability or behaviour. We believe in the abused, the vulnerable, the forgotten and the neglected. We will support them, stand up for them and bring out the best in each and every child. We do this because we believe in children.

Barnardo's works directly with more than 100,000 children, young people and their families every year. We run vital projects across the UK, including counselling for children who have been abused, fostering and adoption services, vocational training and disability inclusion groups.

We use the knowledge gained from our direct work with children to campaign for better childcare policy and to champion the rights of every child. With the right help, committed support and a little belief, even the most vulnerable children can turn their lives around.

Supported by: Royal Mail

BRIDGES
TO UNDERSTANDING

Bridges to Understanding
www.bridgesweb.org
Tel: 001 206 925 5300

Bridges to Understanding is a Seattle-based non-profit organisation founded in 2001 by internationally renowned humanitarian photographer Phil Borges. Our mission is to use digital technology and the art of storytelling to empower and unite youth worldwide, enhance cross-cultural understanding, and build global citizenship.

Bridges connects students in the north-west region of the US with their peers in Africa, India, Guatemala, Peru and other countries around the world through teacher-guided online dialogues, curriculum-based programmes and the creation and sharing of digital stories.

Our programmes give teens from different backgrounds and cultures the opportunity to learn from, not just about, each other. By building relationships across global boundaries, students develop a sense of connection, an understanding of global problems from other points of view, and are empowered to act on issues that affect them, their families and communities.

Supported by: Getty Images

CABA
www.caba.org.uk
Tel: 01788 556366
Registered Charity No: 1116973

The Chartered Accountants' Benevolent Association (CABA) offers confidential financial, practical and emotional support to ACA students, current and former ICAEW members and their families residing in the UK and overseas.

Founded in 1886, CABA's prime purpose has been to provide financial assistance to members and their dependants experiencing difficult and challenging times. The development of additional services in recent years has enabled us to better meet the needs of members.

CABA now provides free stress management and well-being training courses, a free 24-hour advice and counselling helpline and support for those with caring responsibilities. Assistance has recently been extended to ACA students and staff of the Institute.

Our support is tailored to individual needs.

Supported by: ICAEW

Cancer Research UK
www.cancerresearchuk.org
Tel: 020 7242 0200
Registered Charity No: 1089464

Cancer Research UK is the world's leading independent charity dedicated to cancer research. We carry out scientific research to help prevent, diagnose and treat cancer, and we ensure that our findings are used to improve the lives of all cancer patients.

We have discovered new ways of treating cancer that together have saved hundreds of thousands of lives, and we work in partnership with others to achieve the greatest impact in the global fight against cancer. We help people to understand cancer by providing information to patients, their families and friends, and we run cancer awareness campaigns to help people reduce their risk of the disease. Our campaigning and lobbying helps keep cancer at the top of the political agenda.

One in three of us will get cancer at some point in our lives. Our groundbreaking work, funded almost entirely by the general public, will ensure that many more people survive.

Supported by: Flybe and Leyland Trade

CAF Charities Aid Foundation

Charities Aid Foundation
www.cafonline.org
Tel: 01732 520000
Registered Charity No: 268369

CAF (Charities Aid Foundation) is a registered charity and our aim is simple: to make charity donations go further. We make it easier for donors to give and for charities to manage their money. Making regular Gift Aided donations, setting up a charitable trust, donating shares, leaving money to charity in your will – we have lots of ways of helping you support the causes that matter to you.

A CAF Charity Account is an easy and flexible way to plan and manage all your giving needs: you can fund it regularly so that you always have a pot of money set aside for charity; it can be used to make donations to any UK-registered charities you like; and we reclaim the Gift Aid for you as soon as you put money in the account.

Visit www.cafonline.org/superbrands and find out how we can help you with your charitable giving.

Supported by: American Express

C☺MIC RELIEF

Comic Relief
www.comicrelief.com
Tel: 020 7820 5555
Registered Charity No: 326568 (England & Wales) and SC039730 (Scotland)

Comic Relief was launched on Christmas Day in 1985, live on BBC One. At that time, a devastating famine was crippling Ethiopia and something had to be done. That something was Comic Relief.

The idea was simple: Comic Relief would make the public laugh while they raised money to help people in desperate need. Red Nose Day soon followed with the first event in 1988 raising a staggering £15 million. To date, 11 Red Nose Days have raised more than £420 million.

A second major fundraising campaign, Sport Relief, takes place on alternate years and encourages people to actively participate in fundraising in order to help change lives.

Comic Relief uses all the money raised to make a difference to the lives of poor and disadvantaged people in the UK and across the world's poorest countries.

Supported by: Ryman

CRASH
www.crash.org.uk
Tel: 020 8742 0717
Registered Charity No: 1054107

CRASH is the construction and property industries' charity for homeless people. It is a practical charity addressing homelessness by harnessing the skills, products, talents and goodwill of the construction industry to improve buildings and premises for voluntary agencies working with homeless people, throughout the UK.

CRASH is a unique charity. Due to the way our core funding is covered by our generous Patron companies, all the donations received from our fundraising events go directly to projects that help individuals damaged by the experience of homelessness. Thanks to the generosity of the companies and individuals who support us, homeless people throughout the UK are helped to gain the confidence and skills they need to integrate back into society and achieve an independent way of life.

Supported by: British Gypsum

dreams come true

Dreams Come True
www.dctc.org.uk
Tel: 01730 815000
Registered Charity No: 800248

Dreams Come True was established more than 20 years ago with the aim of helping to fulfil the dreams of children with terminal and serious illnesses. The charity now fulfils around 400 dreams each year for children and young people aged 2-21 with conditions such as leukaemia, cystic fibrosis and muscular dystrophy.

The dreams are as varied as a child's imagination and recent dreams have included swimming with dolphins, taking a helicopter ride and meeting the pop group The Kooks.

Since the charity was founded, nearly 4,000 children have had their Dream Come True. With further support, we can help many more children.

Supported by: Mintel

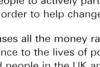 **FareShare**
community food network

FareShare
www.fareshare.org.uk
Tel: 020 7394 2468
Registered Charity No: 1100051

FareShare is the charity at the centre of two urgent issues facing the UK: food poverty and food waste. We address these issues by redirecting surplus food from the food industry to 500 community organisations that support disadvantaged people, improving the well-being of 25,000 people a day.

To tackle the root causes of food poverty, FareShare also provides training and education opportunities through our 'Eat Well, Live Well' programme. We teach safe food preparation and nutrition and provide innovative employability training that helps prepare vulnerable people for work.

Despite our considerable achievements so far, there is lots more work to do. As more and more people feel the effects of the economic downturn, access to affordable food is a huge concern. Please get in touch to find out how you can help FareShare lift thousands of people out of food poverty.

Supported by: Sodexo

 independence
Hollybank

Hollybank Trust
www.hollybanktrust.com
Tel: 01924 490833
Registered Charity No: 1043129

Hollybank Trust is a registered charity that cares for some of society's most vulnerable members. We provide education, care and often a home for children, young people and adults with profound physical disabilities and associated learning difficulties.

We have a commitment to lifelong care. A child may enter the school at five years-old and, if required, reside in our attached children's home. Upon reaching 18, the young adult will move to our on-site independence bungalow. At 25, a place will be found at one of our many homes in the community. We aim to equip those we care for with the knowledge, skills and confidence to become independent, making their lives as rich and fulfilling as possible.

Hollybank relies heavily on the support of individuals, organisations and companies, and we raise funds any way we can. Every penny counts.

Supported by: Leyland Trade

Leonard Cheshire Disability

Leonard Cheshire Disability
www.lcdisability.org
Tel: 020 3242 0200
Registered Charity No: 218186 (England & Wales) and SC005117 (Scotland)

Leonard Cheshire Disability exists to change attitudes to disability and to serve disabled people around the world.

We support more than 21,000 disabled people in the UK and work in 54 countries. We campaign for change and provide innovative services that give disabled people the opportunity to live life their way.

Our services in the UK support disabled people in the widest context, including through care homes, supported living, respite care, personal support and training and assistance for those looking for work.

In addition, we campaign locally, nationally and internationally on disability issues, helping to remove the barriers faced by disabled people each day. We also work to change public attitudes to disability, through our Creature Discomforts campaign.

Supported by: Howdens Joinery Co.

WE ARE MACMILLAN.
CANCER SUPPORT

Macmillan Cancer Support
www.macmillan.org.uk
Tel: 0808 808 2020
Registered Charity No: 261017

Cancer affects us all and two million of us are living with it today in the UK. Macmillan Cancer Support works to improve the lives of people affected by the disease. We provide practical, medical, emotional and financial support and push for better cancer care.

Macmillan is there for people living with cancer and their families every step of the way, from the moment they suspect they have the disease.

We fund specialist healthcare professionals and build cancer care centres. People need someone to talk to, so we listen, advise and share information though our CancerLine, website and support groups. People need help to cope with the extra costs cancer can bring, so we give benefits advice and financial grants.

We listen to people affected by cancer and work together to improve cancer care. We fight discrimination – from challenging unfair travel costs and insurance policies to improving the national benefits system.

Supported by: ExCeL London

Marie Curie Cancer Care
www.mariecurie.org.uk
Tel: 0800 716 146
Registered Charity No: 207994 (England & Wales) and SC038731 (Scotland)

Marie Curie Cancer Care provides free care to people with terminal cancer and other illnesses in their own homes and in the charity's hospices.

Every day, 410 people will die of cancer in the UK. Most (around 70 per cent) want to be cared for at home, close to the people and things they love, with a sizeable minority opting for hospice care. However, more than half of cancer deaths occur in hospital, the place people would least like to be.

This year, Marie Curie Cancer Care expects to care for more than 27,000 terminally ill people in the community and in its 10 hospices. But for every family the charity helps there are others that it can't.

Marie Curie Cancer Care is working to double the number of people with a terminal illness who have the choice to die at home.

Supported by: BSI

NSPCC
Cruelty to children must stop. FULL STOP.

NSPCC
www.nspcc.org.uk
www.childline.org.uk
NSPCC Helpline: 0808 800 5000
ChildLine Helpline: 0800 1111
Registered Charity No: 216401 (England & Wales) and SC037717 (Scotland)

The National Society for the Prevention of Cruelty to Children (NSPCC) is the UK's leading charity specialising in child protection and the prevention of cruelty to children.

The NSPCC's purpose is to see a society where all children are loved, valued and able to fulfil their potential. The society has 180 community-based projects and runs the NSPCC Helpline and ChildLine in the UK and the Channel Islands. Most of the NSPCC's direct work is with children, young people and their families, but they also work to achieve cultural, social and political change – influencing legislation, policy, practice, public attitudes and behaviours and delivering services for the benefit of young people.

Supported by: BMRB

Oxfam GB
www.oxfam.org.uk/corporates
Tel: 01865 472126
Registered Charity No: 202918 (England & Wales) and SC039042 (Scotland)

For over 60 years, Oxfam has been working with organisations around the world to find lasting solutions to poverty and injustice. Currently, we work in more than 70 countries and respond to an average of 30 emergency situations each year. Oxfam's work includes development, campaigning and advocacy at the highest level, lobbying international organisations and influencing governments. Because in a world rich in resources, there's enough to go around. Poverty isn't unfortunate, it's unfair.

We see working with the private sector as an opportunity to benefit us all. We'll use your contribution to help build schools, grow crops, protect livelihoods and stop climate change. In return, we'll help build your CSR strategy, grow your reputation, protect your donation and stop poverty in its tracks.

On our own we're only human. Together we're humankind.

Supported by: The Co-operative Bank and Weber Shandwick

ROSY
www.rosy.org.uk
Tel: 01865 848696
Registered Charity No: 1091570

It is sometimes difficult to contemplate, but some children are born with life limiting or chronic conditions and others develop them early in their young lives. Advances in medical science allow many of these children to be nursed at home where they can be with their loved ones and in familiar surroundings. This places an enormous burden on the families, a burden willingly undertaken and bravely born.

With the National Health Service's resources in huge demand, support for these families is often, understandably, limited. This is where ROSY comes in. We now pay the salaries of six nurses to provide additional respite support. We will buy any specialist equipment the families may need in the home to make their lives a little more bearable. We also provide psychological support where needed.

The administration of ROSY is sponsored so we can assure you that every penny entrusted to us will go to support those families who so need our help.

Supported by: British Gas Business

Save the Children
www.savethechildren.org.uk
Tel: 020 7012 6400
Registered Charity No: 213890

We are the world's independent children's charity. We are outraged that millions of children are still denied proper healthcare, food, education and protection. We are working flat out to get every child their rights and we are determined to make further, faster changes. How many? How fast? It's up to you.

Supported by: BSI

schoolfriendetc
education training childcare

Schoolfriendetc
www.schoolfriendetc.org
Tel: 0870 442 2287
Registered Charity No: 1112772

Schoolfriendetc provides affordable and high quality childcare in schools nationwide. Our After-school, Breakfast and Holiday clubs have been running since 2003 and assist schools in fulfilling the Extended Schools Agenda.

Clubs offer children the chance to participate in a wide range of activities including art, drama, sport, games and cookery. Children participate in the overall running of the club so that they take ownership of it and build their confidence and communication skills. They also have the chance to improve their numeracy and literacy skills using an online individualised learning programme, Schoofriend.com, which can be accessed in the club and at home. All clubs undergo Ofsted registration enabling parents to access Working Tax Credits.

We offer bursaries to children who could not otherwise afford to come and as a leading childcare organisation, we continue to lobby for childcare and extended schools services to be available and affordable to all.

Supported by: Sodexo

Shakespeare's Globe
www.shakespeares-globe.org
Tel: 020 7902 1400
Registered Charity No: 266916

Shakespeare's Globe has become one of the most popular visitor destinations in the UK, at the heart of the regeneration of London's Bankside. Shakespeare's Globe is a charity and receives no annual government funding.

Globe Education is one of the largest arts education departments in the country, and shares its creative approaches to the teaching of Shakespeare with more than 100,000 students a year – through workshops, courses and events. In addition, a major schools' project, 'Playing Shakespeare with Deutsche Bank', creates a production of a Shakespeare play for young people with free tickets for performances, workshops and web resources.

The Globe Theatre season plays in repertory from April to October and has gained an international reputation. Shakespeare's Globe Tour and Exhibition is open all year round and is London's only permanent exhibition dedicated to Shakespeare's theatrical career.

Supported by: Deutsche Bank

Shelter

Shelter
www.shelter.org.uk
Tel: 0845 458 4590
Registered Charity No: 263710 (England & Wales) and SC002327 (Scotland)

We are the fourth richest country in the world, and yet millions of people in Britain wake up every day in housing that is run-down, overcrowded or dangerous. Many others have lost their home altogether. Bad housing robs us of security, health and a fair chance in life.

Shelter believes everyone should have a home.

We help more than 170,000 people a year fight for their rights, get back on their feet, and find and keep a home. We also tackle the root causes of bad housing by campaigning for new laws, policies and solutions.

Our website gets more than 100,000 visits a month; visit www.shelter.org.uk to join our campaign, find housing advice or to make a donation.

We need your help to continue our work. Please support us.

Supported by: RIBA

SSAFA Forces Help
www.ssafa.org.uk
Tel: 020 7463 9297
Registered Charity No: 210760 (England & Wales) and SC038056 (Scotland)

The Soldiers, Sailors, Airmen and Families Association (SSAFA) Forces Help is the leading national charity committed to helping and supporting those who serve in our Armed Forces, those who used to serve, and the families of both.

We provide a reliable, caring and trusted service to more than 50,000 people each year through a network of professionally trained staff (approximately 700, including health and social work staff) and 7,000 volunteers. This includes practical and financial assistance, emotional support and a wide range of services to ensure that SSAFA Forces Help makes a real difference wherever there is a need and whenever anybody turns to us for help: 'One day's service. A lifetime of support.'

Supported by: Sodexo

StreetGames
www.streetgames.org
Tel: 020 7735 9800
Registered Charity No: 1113542

Launched in 2007, StreetGames is the only national charity dedicated to developing sport in disadvantaged communities and making sport accessible to all young people, regardless of their social circumstances. So far, the charity has generated over a quarter of a million sports attendances by kids up and down the country.

This is achieved by supporting and establishing local projects around the UK that deliver 'doorstep sport', i.e. positive activities provided to young people when, where and how they want them. StreetGames is also an active lobbying organisation with an ongoing objective of encouraging government to invest more money in sport for disadvantaged communities.

The charity also helps young people develop their sports coaching and community leadership skills via a national volunteering scheme, The Co-operative StreetGames Young Volunteers.

StreetGames is primarily funded by Sport England and The Football Foundation.

Supported by: The Co-operative Bank

STREET**SMART**
HELPING THE HOMELESS

StreetSmart
www.streetsmart.org.uk
Tel: 020 7292 5615
Registered Charity No: 1071657

StreetSmart aims to provide comfort and hope to homeless people living on streets close to restaurants in which patrons dine in style. Its pioneering brand of fundraising is innovative and effective: during November and December, a voluntary £1 per table is added to diners' bills at top-class restaurants in 18 UK cities. The donations are then collected by StreetSmart and distributed directly to charities, hostels and projects dedicated to helping the homeless in each respective city.

Since it was established in London in 1998 by entrepreneur William Sieghart of Forward Ltd and The Groucho Club's Mary-Lou Sturridge, the charity has raised in excess of £3,241,000 and has provided funding to 155 individual homeless organisations. The Deutsche Bank sponsorship of StreetSmart covers all of the administrative, production and promotion costs of the campaign, so that every single penny raised makes a direct difference to the homeless.

Supported by: Deutsche Bank

The National Autistic Society
www.autism.org.uk
Tel: 020 7833 2299
Helpline: 0845 070 4004
Registered Charity No: 269425

Over half a million people in the UK have autism, which is a serious, lifelong and disabling condition. The National Autistic Society (NAS) is the UK's leading charity for people affected by autism. We champion the rights and interests of all people with autism and aim to provide individuals with autism and their families with help, support and services that they can access, trust and rely upon and which can make a positive difference to their lives.

We were founded in 1962 by a group of parents who were passionate about ensuring a better future for their children. Today we have more than 18,000 members, 80 branches and provide a wide range of advice, information, support and specialist services to 100,000 people each year. A local charity with a national presence, we campaign and lobby for lasting positive change for people with autism.

Supported by: British Gas Business

The Prostate Cancer Charity
www.prostate-cancer.org.uk
Helpline: 0800 074 8383
Registered Charity No: 1005541

Prostate cancer is the most common cancer in men in the UK, with 35,000 diagnosed every year. In the UK one man dies of prostate cancer every hour. The Prostate Cancer Charity is the UK's leading charity in the field of prostate cancer. We fund research, provide support and information and campaign to improve the lives of men with prostate cancer.

The Prostate Cancer Charity aims to reach everyone affected by prostate cancer through our support services and information. We provide the only UK-wide prostate cancer helpline staffed by prostate cancer specialist nurses. The Prostate Cancer Charity aims to encourage, support and fund research into the causes, prevention and treatment of prostate cancer. Since 1994 we have invested more than £7 million in research.

The Prostate Cancer Charity has a vision of a world where lives are no longer limited by prostate cancer.

Supported by: Snap-on

The Scout Association
www.scouts.org.uk
Tel: 0845 300 1818
Registered Charity No: 306101 (England & Wales) and SC038437 (Scotland)

The Scout Association is the UK's largest co-educational youth movement, offering activities, adventure and personal development opportunities to 400,000 young people aged 6-25. Using volunteer adult leaders and basic facilities, Scouting helps young people from all backgrounds to develop universally valued qualities of trust, empathy, confidence, integrity and a spirit of adventure.

In Scouting, we believe that young people develop most when they are 'learning by doing'; when they are given responsibility, work in teams, take acceptable risks and think for themselves. Internationally, we have more than 28 million young people enjoying the benefits across 216 countries.

Scouting would not be possible without the efforts of our 100,000 adult volunteers. To find out how you can be part of it, visit www.scouts.org.uk/join or call 0845 300 1818.

Supported by: Chubb

Waste Watch
www.wastewatch.org.uk
Tel: 020 7549 0300
Registered Charity No: 1005417

Waste Watch is a UK environmental charity working to change the way people use the world's natural resources.

Waste Watch educates and supports people to make changes to their lives that will reduce their environmental impact and improve their quality of life.

We all have a part to play in tackling climate change and protecting the Earth's natural resources. Our vision is a world where people use resources effectively, live sustainably and make a positive contribution to the environment.

By changing the world around us – at home, at work, in school and in our communities – we can all make a big difference. Waste Watch exists to help people make that difference.

Supported by: The Co-operative Bank

York Against Cancer
www.yorkagainstcancer.org.uk
Tel: 01904 764466
Registered Charity No: 518478

Since 1987 York Against Cancer has made a significant difference to the lives of people affected by cancer. In addition to funding the Cancer Care Centre at York Hospital, we have funded important research with The University of York and education projects involving the local community.

Recently, we raised money for a mini bus to transport patients from York Hospital to St James's Hospital, Leeds for radiotherapy and chemotherapy treatments.

We have done all this with incredible support from local people – including local businesses. In the coming months we plan to focus our fundraising efforts on Give as You Earn schemes and other forms of corporate giving.

The phrase we use to sum up what we do is: Local people raising money to help local people affected by cancer.

Supported by: Portakabin (Shepherd Group)

York Minster Fund
www.yorkminster.org
Tel: 01904 557245
Registered Charity No: 252157

As with all ancient buildings, York Minster is in a state of constant restoration and conservation. The present project concerns the East Front. Decay caused by pollution and weather has meant that some 2,500 stones have to be replaced. This in turn has meant that the whole of the Great East Window, installed in 1408, and about the size of a tennis court, has to be removed. The cost of the project is around £23 million.

Support has come from many sources including the Shepherd Group and the Heritage Lottery Fund, but there is a never-ending need for money, and the Minster receives no direct help from either central government or the Church of England.

Supported by: Portakabin (Shepherd Group)

HR: the Antidote

**By Jonathan Cummings
Director
Start Creative**

We live in times of rapid structural change for all organisations, but particularly so for many of the global entities featured in this book. Even for the Business Superbrands, these are challenging times. The need to enhance competitive advantage, to find that magic that creates standout, is greater than ever. To help achieve that, it's time for businesses to brand their human resources. Or 'people' as we prefer to call them.

The Human Touch

In this age of thousands of media messages coming at us daily through an ever-increasing number of channels, an age of infinite consumer access to information and exponential growth in social networking, the role of 'people' in one's perception of a brand has never been greater. The experience we receive at any touchpoint in a customer journey, particularly a human one, hugely impacts our emotional connection to a brand. Likewise, brand advocacy from a trusted source is more powerful than any advert.

All brands need advocates. In tough economic times, we need our own people to be the greatest advocates of our brand; businesses need to ensure they recruit and retain the best talent and that this asset is operating at maximum efficiency and effectiveness. For that to happen, internal brand engagement is a fundamental part of the marketing mix. From recruitment to appraisal and reward, a brand needs to ensure that its people understand both the brand itself and their individual role within it.

The role of people as a critical tool in brand building is something that has been embraced by the Virgin brand, for example. The Virgin Group has created more than 200 branded companies worldwide and employs around

PEOPLE POWER!

50,000 people, across 29 countries, in sectors ranging from mobile telephony to transport, financial services, leisure, music, holidays, publishing and retail. And in its own words, Virgin aims to 'deliver a quality service by empowering [its] employees'.

Virgin set Start Creative a brief to develop the 'People Carrier': it was to be an engaging toolkit that could be delivered worldwide, online and offline, through hundreds of people managers for the benefit of tens of thousands of employees. Quite simply, it was to be the ultimate guide to a 'Virgin person' – a person that could become the embodiment of the brand, whatever their role within the Group.

The increasing importance of such an approach to internal branding and engagement was highlighted last year by the inclusion of the People Carrier in the Writing for Design section of the D&AD Annual 2008 – the definitive global guide to creativity in the commercial arena.

Yet however good the brand engagement programme may be, different people in different organisations will take a different length of time to change their behaviour – and to differing degrees. It is therefore essential that this thinking is not a one-off campaign, but that it is incorporated at the very heart of an organisation and consistent at every stage of the employee lifecycle – and that means it needs to be led from the very top but also developed and operated in a truly inclusive way throughout the organisation.

In the case of Virgin, the People Carrier reflects a long tradition of inside-out thinking within the Group. As its founder Richard Branson once said: "Convention dictates that a company looks after its shareholders first, its customers next and last of all worries about its employees. Virgin does the opposite."

But for many, the wider question still remains: Why has internal communication remained the poor relation of external communication for so long? At best, this is disrespectful; but in a world of increasing job mobility and diminishing loyalty, it's also short-sighted.

Long before graphic designers roamed the earth, a brand was a mark that you seared into livestock with a hot poker. Perhaps this explains why some companies still persist in blatantly bombarding consumers with their logo. It doesn't have to be like this. There are plenty of subtle ways to create a meaningful and lasting

impression. Environments, experiences, digital media and people (the most traditional medium of all) are all means that can be employed by brands wishing to build recognition.

Working for Change

In times of rapid change, the fastest way for big organisations to adapt is through their workforce. When companies are inventive with their internal communication budgets, the investment can pay back many times over in terms of hiring the right people quickly and cost-effectively, getting them operationally effective fast, retaining them and developing them as living, breathing brand advocates.

Of course, there are many ways in which people throughout an organisation affect a brand and, likewise, in which economic trends affect the way an organisation manages its people. Here are just a few of the current business themes that demand a fresh approach to communicating with the internal audience:

Globalisation

As businesses begin to extend their global tentacles, they not only face the challenge of people management on an international scale but also that of how they can nurture the free-flow of ideas across boundaries. Consumers and business customers experience brands across borders, so it's no use being parochial – the HR function needs to become a borderless business partner to make the most of opportunities. In this sense, the HR function

Love every second

The Virgin Trains
Feel Good
Awards

Win time and money for the things that make you feel good

Love every second

is as vital to the development of a global brand as the marketing department.

In the emerging economies of the East, it takes a certain dexterity to apply the communication strategies we're used to in the West. For example, at Start Creative we're currently working alongside a shopping mall developer in the Middle East to achieve differentiation through exceptional face-to-face customer service. In order to do this successfully we must ensure that specific cultural complexities are taken into account, reflecting both customer and staff profiles.

A shopping mall developer is, strictly speaking, a business to business organisation. All of its revenue comes from other businesses, namely retailers and advertisers. But to maximise its opportunity for success and to build a strong relationship with its customers, the experience of the end consumer is key. Visiting a shopping mall is very much a people business. Wayfinding, for instance, is a critical part of the experience. The majority of mall staff are contracted cleaners or security guards. It is vital that these individuals feel part of the team and understand the brand and the part they play in the company's success.

Outsourcing can add another layer of international complexity – when you sub-contract the task, how do you successfully export your brand values?

Marketing the Intangible

In his best-selling book, 'The Age of Access', Jeremy Rifkin identifies a transformational shift from ownership to access. "In the new era," says Rifkin, "markets are making way for networks, and ownership is steadily being replaced by access. Companies and consumers are beginning to abandon the central reality of modern economic life – the market exchange of property between sellers and buyers." He observes that in the network economy, both physical and intellectual property are more likely to be accessed than exchanged.

The trend can be seen in everything from private jet share schemes to online music retailing. Intellectual capital in particular, is closely held by the suppliers and leased or licensed to other parties for their limited use.

What's interesting is that the psychology of buyers hasn't essentially changed – they still crave a connection with the 'maker'. Given a choice, consumers prefer to find a qualified expert they trust. So there's still brand value in keeping it personal. An outstanding example is the Genius Bar in Apple's retail stores.

Front line staff naturally lead the way, but exposure to those behind the scenes is equally important. The engineer crafting the next generation of semi-conductor, the quality control specialist at an aircraft engine manufacturer, and so on. These people, individually and combined, reflect the values we want to see as customers. They provide that level of trust customers and end consumers search for and therefore are the best representation of the brand and its strengths.

Alongside real human contact, the interactivity of digital communication can take what Rifkin calls 'relationship bonding' to the next level.

But people and technology are far from mutually exclusive elements in the customer experience. Facilitating the seamless integration of man and machine to provide a stand-out experience is the challenge of every company in every sector.

From business banking to web-based procurement, and from corporate CRM to

effective sponsorship, technology is a great enabler. But it is the link with people that makes the difference.

Corporate Social Responsibility
Consumers are concerned about climate change along with wider social and environmental issues. Increasingly, we'll see their purchasing decisions influenced by which brands behave responsibly. While some companies continue to frame this as a marketing communications exercise, it's clear that 'greenwash' won't wash with the public. Quite rightly, many organisations are moving sustainability to the core of their brand thinking.

As with all the big commercial issues, there are no easy, off-the-peg answers. And no substitute for engaging your people in the solution. Authentic brand personality isn't something you can simply manage through guidelines – it's what your organisation exudes.

The complexities of modern business are reflected in the status of people specialists, many of whom are playing a fuller part in influencing strategy. "There has been a greater shift in HR in the past five years than in the previous 50," said Jeremy Tipper, managing director of Capital Consulting, in a recent interview. It's more strategic, more about adding value rather than just being a support function, and it's increasingly getting representation at board level.

The HR Health Check
All businesses must look at themselves and ask how well their HR function is aligned with the brand – rather than simply asking, is the right logo on the induction pack? Are all communications (internal and external) helping to recruit and retain talent? Have we identified what typifies an employee who embodies the brand through their work and have we embedded that into our recruitment process? Do our induction process, appraisal system, reward schemes and internal communications support the notion that our people are our most valuable brand asset?

It's time to give old-style HR the boot. If our people are not fully engaged with our brand and helping to create competitive advantage, it's time to change.

Start Creative
Start is an international design consultancy focusing on brand and digital services. Founded in 1996 by Mike Curtis and Darren Whittingham, it is now a top 10 independent agency in the UK and has offices in Mumbai, Dubai and Hong Kong. Brand design expertise includes strategy and management, identity design, literature design and brand engagement communications. Digital services include website design, online advertising, interactive television and mobile communications. Associate companies include brand environments specialist JudgeGill, events agency Anymedia and illustration agency Breed. Clients include adidas, Air Asia, the BBC, Bentley, Dubai World Trade Centre, Essar (India), figleaves.com, MBC (Dubai), MTS (Russia), Royal Mail, Schroders, Virgin (Atlantic, Galactic, Holidays, Management, Media, Mobile, Trains) and Warner Brothers.

startcreative.com

Innovate and Excite

By Paul Edwards
CEO, Research International UK

©istockphoto.com/minimil

market upswing. Innovation can be a powerful weapon in making others look slow-footed and off the pace.

Innovations that have done well during recessionary times include both the predictable (such as supermarket own labels) and the less predictable (airline loyalty programmes and soap operas). When times are changing it is time for brands to change as well. It is inevitable that customer needs will evolve – or at the very least people will believe they are evolving, their priorities will change and previously habitual decisions will provoke more thought – and brands will be credited with attention if they recognise this and change accordingly themselves.

Creating Innovation

At Research International we have found that innovation falls broadly into two types: renovation and true innovation. Renovation is largely the process of improving products and services to meet existing needs in a better way, while true innovation may meet or create new needs and will generally lead to new behaviours.

The Discman, for example, was an upgrade on the Walkman, providing better sound quality in the new CD format – but the consumer's behaviour did not need to change. The iPod, however, turned them into the editors of their own music, downloading selectively and choosing music from a large, stored repertoire rather than buying and playing an album created by an artist and record label.

True innovation may look more sexy and world changing but it is rare and there is plenty of opportunity in renovation – both routes should be considered as valid means to improved profitability.

But conventional wisdom tells us that innovation (of both types) is risky, with a huge proportion of projects deemed to be failures. This 'conventional wisdom' can have a negative effect on the product development process: often described as an 'innovation funnel', the standard method sees a lot of ideas gradually whittled down due to fear of failure. This feels to me like planning for

Uncertainty and Opportunity

Innovation is clearly one of the things that strong brands do. Whether strong brands are good at innovation, or innovation makes strong brands, is a good question and like most good questions, the answer is probably a bit of both. What is of more importance to us at the present time is: Should brands continue to innovate in an uncertain economy?

I believe strongly that they should. An uncertain economy creates both necessity and opportunity for innovation. It is a time of change; manufacturers and service providers cannot assume that things will go back to

being the way they were. Innovation is crucial to ensure that they are in a position to prosper in the new reality, facing potentially new customer needs. I am not advocating simple cost reduction; it is vital that products and services are refashioned to meet new needs (or to meet existing needs in a better way), which could result in either a more or less expensive product.

And it is a time of opportunity. Competitors may be holding back on innovation investment, or be in too weak a position to invest, allowing forward-thinking brands to gain market advantage in the post-uncertainty failure. In fact, the innovation failure rate remains high despite the 'precautionary' funnel approach being in use for many years. A strong focus is even more important in tight financial times; there is simply no spare money to waste on generating large numbers of ideas that have limited chance of coming to market.

Innovation is no different from any other marketing – it depends on the profitable anticipation of customer demand. Successful innovation occurs when a thorough knowledge and awareness of customer needs collides with a relevantly designed product or service.

I would argue that it is much better to invest time and money in making sure that customer needs are fully understood than in generating a large number of product ideas to fill a funnel. This small number of needs can then be socialised with research and development colleagues who can concentrate on developing a much smaller set of better solutions. More economical, more efficient and more likely to lead to success.

Evaluating Proposed Innovations
More than 40,000 innovations have come to Research International for testing before

launch. When it comes to evaluating them we concentrate on analysing two key dimensions: how likely are people to try the innovation (trial), and how unique is it perceived to be?

A high rating in both 'trial' and 'uniqueness' generally leads to success, while a low rating in both is a strong signal that we should abandon quickly and not invest further. Those ideas falling into 'Winning 'Me Too'' can be quite attractive providing we accept that they will probably require more marketing support to succeed in a competitive environment.

The 'Potential?' segment contains interesting innovations; they are different but do not show substantial appeal in terms of trial. There may be several reasons for this: it might be an innovation that is ahead of its time; it might be an innovation that has not been developed or explained properly; or it might just be a bit of a cranky idea. It is important to distinguish between these factors in order to determine whether it should continue to receive investment.

Generally speaking, a strong point of difference will drive a proposal to the right hand side of the chart and strong customer relevance will steer it towards the top of the chart. We have discovered that the key to

the coveted top right hand corner lies in the dimension of excitement. Excitement is used here in a relative sense, i.e. the innovation is more exciting than its competitors. For example, while it may be obvious to see how Virgin Atlantic can generate excitement with potential innovations, a more subtle view must be taken to recognise that an innovative insurance product can generate excitement among its target audience because it fulfils a real need in a new and meaningful way. Excitement is generated at the collision of a well understood need and a well crafted product or service designed to meet that need.

Exciting Times
At quite a simple level of meaning, excitement raises energy levels and in doing so drives people to action. It creates a change in the balance of a market, which can then provoke trial. It can cause the customer reassessment that is needed in order for anything new to be adopted.

Excitement provides the emotional push that gets innovations accepted. It can be very powerful in overcoming the rational objections that the new always evokes ("It's too expensive", "I don't know anyone who uses this", "Will it work?"). And remember we are talking about relative

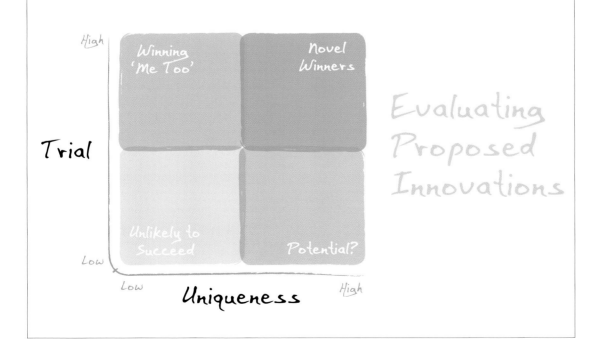

excitement – an attachment for a power tool that does something new that you really need is just as exciting in its context as the latest BMW is in its context.

So excitement is correlated with customers wanting to try an innovation and with them believing that it is different from other offerings. It has another advantage in that it is also linked to people wanting to talk about an innovation – they are proud of their discovery and want to pass it on. This is very good news for the innovation's long term chances of success – there is nothing better than personal recommendation. Those who have bought a new product are twice as likely to have first heard about it from someone they trust than people who are aware of it but have not purchased. Personal recommendation can assume even more importance when spending money is tight.

Think Knowledge, Not Numbers
Innovation is the lifeblood of a strong brand. It can be a disproportionate competitive advantage in difficult economic times. Great innovation is not the result of the quantity of ideas, but of really taking the time to understand your customers and how their needs are changing.

Evaluation of innovations is crucial before significant investments are made to bring them to market. We believe that there are a small number of consistent questions that should be asked of all innovations prior to launch. Understanding and interpreting the answers should play a vital role in deciding whether or not to launch the innovation into the market, and in deciding how to support it.

In uncertain financial times research is even more essential in order to make sure that resources are concentrated on the innovations or renovations that have the best chance of market success.

Innovation is an exciting process; success depends on ensuring that your innovations are the ones that create excitement.

RESEARCH INTERNATIONAL

Research International
Research International stands for 'Insight, Inspiration and Innovation'. A global market research company with offices in more than 50 countries across the world, it has a history dating back to the 1960s and is now part of the WPP network of companies.

Working across most types of research – from qualitative to segmentation to service measurement – its main focus is now innovation, offering a full service from idea generation to market potential forecasting. Research International has more than 40,000 innovation tests in its database, giving it the experience and resource to truly indicate what really is 'good' rather than simply the best of the bunch.
research-int.com

Events Made Well

By Debora Smith
Managing Director
Anymedia

When I was asked to contribute to the Business Superbrands book this year, I contemplated what I could tell you that you didn't already know… after all, organising events is easy, isn't it? But it's frightening how the minority can ruin it for the majority by producing bad experiences, thus creating a negative image of events.

Often the fun of organising an event overtakes the fundamental objectives that should clearly be at the forefront of any valuable budget spend. Here I have highlighted three critical areas that should be given consideration before embarking on an event.

Integration
Events have always played their part in the marketing mix. But now more than ever, the value of developing long term relationships through effective face-to-face interaction has never been greater.

Why is it then that events are still considered tactical rather than a key part of an integrated strategy? All too often they are found on the periphery, working in splendid isolation from other marketing activity, and/or as a finite opportunity with little consideration of how

to ensure longer term communication. Yet in these times of fierce competition, fluctuating markets and increasingly aggressive sales negotiations, building real creative and commercial dialogue with your clients isn't a 'nice to have' but an absolute 'must have'.

Over the past few years we have seen a decline in exhibition or group-run event investment – for a very good reason. Quite simply, the formats

are not focused or niche. Nor are they fluid enough to evolve at a pace more akin to that of the markets they represent. The result is that they rarely deliver critical ROI. They are expensive and lumpy – effectively a one-stop-shop that cannot and does not fit all.

Before the fun creative ideas, you need a robust strategy that has been pulled apart and put back together again. Creativity will only be born

out of knowing and believing in your end goal, and the message you wish to convey in order to get you there. What are your objectives? – Market/brand alignment? Lead generation? Data capture? – What are your follow up mechanisms? What are you promoting and is the event you are planning really the right format for this message? Do your objectives stack up financially against budget spend?

Relationships
In the B2B sector, the role of the individual frequently gets overlooked. People buy from people, it's as simple as that. Yet how can you effectively do this if you have no tangible relationship to leverage?

Greater emphasis needs to be placed on developing relevant face-to-face experiences that engage and inspire audiences. The requirement should be to create connections that are inclusive not exclusive and which add real value to your brand strategy and bottom line. It's no longer about numbers through the door but about the quality of the people you are engaging with and the level of interaction you are able to offer.

Developing a programme of events (either own or jointly branded) enables brands to build relationships, talk directly to the people that matter, demonstrate products and entertain and engage with their audience. Properly integrated events can provide real hooks to ensure contacts become buyers rather than browsers. During both good and bad times, mass marketing will not deliver you comparable leads.

Interaction
Creating memorable experiences with a point of differentiation and which actively involve your audience, or deliver something they

didn't know they wanted or needed, is the way forward in order to develop the client relationship over the long term.

Increasingly, smart brands are looking at alternative initiatives to demonstrate their products. Pop-up stores (such as KIN, pictured left), roadshows and even temporary/mobile venues are just some of the routes that Anymedia has taken to help its clients create differentiation.

Targeted audience demographics that pinpoint specific towns – such as university towns and festivals for 18-25 year-olds – are a perfect way to get straight to the heart of your target market. 'Here today, gone tomorrow' temporary shops and venues create an impact for any brand and motivate the consumer to try or purchase because they know the opportunity to do so is limited. And although this may be a B2C example, the same creative initiative applies to B2B.

We all like a good event, but ask yourself not just what your event can do for you, but what it can do for your guests. The two should be mutually inclusive, not exclusive.

TOP TIPS FOR CREATIVE BRAND EXPERIENCES

Create activities that are scalable. Less is often more when it comes to events which are specifically devised to build relationships.

Re-purpose. There is no need to spend time and money on reinventing the wheel. If you have a proven winning formula, simply roll it out to other locations. In times of tight budgets, travel is often one of the first things to be cut – so why not take the mountain to Mohammed?

Don't hide online. There are many benefits to online activity but not when you are trying to engage with your audience in open dialogue. Webcasts and seminars are not engaging in a physical sense; they require very little commitment from an audience and it's all too easy to get distracted and log out.

Create a point of differentiation. Get creative – wow the audience with something they weren't expecting but will talk about for weeks or months afterwards. It's this that will make sure your message is heard and remembered.

Use professionals. Find specialist suppliers who are willing to pass on their industry-preferred rates to you for venues, production, AV, and so on. A successful event for you is a successful event for them and we know how powerful word-of-mouth can be; it's their reputation on the line as well.

Keep dialogue going. Use technology or adopt alternative strategies for event follow up mechanisms. Spend time nurturing each contact with relevant messaging. In down times we all need to feel a little more special.

Anymedia
Anymedia is a creative live events agency as well as Superbrands' exclusive event partner.

Anymedia forms part of the Start Group of companies, a collective of agencies specialising in brand and digital creation, live events, experiential retail design and strategic direction. Collectively they assist brands worldwide including adidas, the BBC, Bentley, Dubai World Trade Centre, figleaves.com, O2, Post Office®, Royal Mail and Virgin.

The best ideas are born out of thinking and working together. Anymedia is passionate about differentiation and creating experiences that engage and inspire.

anymedia.co.uk

The Centre for Brand Analysis

The Centre for Brand Analysis (TCBA) manages the research process for all Superbrands programmes in the UK. It compiles the initial brand lists, appoints each Expert Council and manages the partnership with YouGov, whose panels are used to access consumer opinion.

About TCBA

TCBA is dedicated to understanding the performance of brands. There are many ways to measure brand performance. TCBA does not believe in a 'one size fits all' approach, instead offering tailored solutions to ensure the metrics investigated and measured are relevant and appropriate.

Its services aim to allow people to understand how a brand is performing, either at a point in time or on an ongoing basis, as well gain insight into wider market and marketing trends.

Services fall into three categories:

Brand perception – measuring attitudes among customers, opinion formers, employees, investors, suppliers or other stakeholders.

Market insight – providing intelligence, trends and examples of best practice.

Marketing analysis – reviewing brand activity, including: campaign assessment; image/brand language assessment; marketing/PR review; agency sourcing and roster review; and ROI analysis.

TCBA works for brand owners and also provides intelligence to agencies and other organisations. It utilises extensive relationships within the business community and works with third parties where appropriate, to access pertinent opinions, data and insights.

tcba.co.uk

Business Superbrands Selection Process

The entire selection process is administered by The Centre for Brand Analysis (TCBA). The key stages of the selection process are as follows:

TCBA researchers compile a list of the UK's leading business to business brands, drawing on a wide range of sources from sector reports to blogs. From the thousands of brands initially considered, a list of just over 1,100 brands is created.

These brands are scored by the independent and voluntary Expert Council, which is assembled and chaired by TCBA's chief executive. Bearing in mind the given definition of a Business Superbrand, the council members individually award each brand a rating from 1-10. Council members are not allowed to score brands with which they have a direct association or are in competition to. The lowest-scoring brands (approximately 40 per cent) are eliminated at this stage.

The remaining brands are voted on by more than 1,500 individual business professionals – defined as those who have either purchasing or managerial responsibilities. These individuals are accessed via a YouGov panel.

Taking the views of the experts and the business professionals into equal account, a combined score is produced for each brand. This score determines its position in the official league table; only the top 500 brands in that table are deemed to be Business Superbrands.

Definition of a Business Superbrand:

When voting on the brands, both the expert council and the business professionals consider the following definition of a Business Superbrand:

'A Business Superbrand has established the finest reputation in its field. It offers customers significant emotional and/or tangible advantages over its competitors, which customers want and recognise.'

In addition, the experts and professionals are asked to judged brands against the following three factors:

Quality. Does the brand represent quality products and services?

Reliability. Can the brand be trusted to deliver consistently against its promises and maintain product and service standards at all customer touch points?

Distinction. Is the brand not only well known in its sector but suitably differentiated from its competitors? Does it have a personality and values that make it unique within its market place?

Brands to Watch Selection Process

The Centre for Brand Analysis analysed the past three years of Business Superbrands voting data and identified just 73 Brands to Watch. To qualify, each of these brands had to fulfil the following criteria:

Consistent year-on-year improvement in the official 2007-2009 Business Superbrands voting; **AND**

A ranking between 501 and 750 in the official 2009 Business Superbrands voting.

Expert Council 2009

Stephen Cheliotis
Chairman,
Expert Council
& Chief Executive,
The Centre for
Brand Analysis

Stephen began his career at Brand Finance, where he advised companies on maximising shareholder value through effective brand management. In addition, he produced key studies including comprehensive reports on global intangible assets. His annual study of City Analysts was vital in understanding the importance of marketing metrics in forecasting companies' performance.

In 2001 Stephen joined Superbrands UK, becoming managing director in 2003 and overseeing two years of significant growth. Given a European role in 2005, his expertise was used across 20 countries.

He has been a freelance consultant since 2006 and in 2007 set up The Centre for Brand Analysis, which is dedicated to understanding the performance of brands and is contracted to run the selection process for Superbrands' three annual programmes in the UK.

He speaks regularly at conferences and also comments for international media on branding and marketing, with frequent appearances on CNN, the BBC and Sky.

Jaakko Alanko
Managing Director
McCann Erickson
Business
Communications

Jaakko merged his independent business to business agency, Anderson & Lembke, with McCann Erickson in 2001 and established McCann Erickson Business Communications as a division of McCann's London base. His focus is on Enterprise Branding, which is based on the belief that an organisation whose people are emotionally connected and behaviourally aligned has a sustainable competitive edge.

Apart from managing the operations of McCann Business, Jaakko advises the agency's key clients: the Carbon Trust, Sony Professional, HP, SABIC, Nestlé Professional, Kimberly-Clark Professional* and iSOFT.

A native of Finland, Jaakko joined McCann Erickson in Helsinki having graduated from the Turku School of Economics. He worked on the agency's network accounts, Esso, Unilever, Coca-Cola and General Motors, and later progressed to McCann's World Headquarters in New York as an international client co-ordinator with responsibility over Goodyear and Exxon. After moving to London, Jaakko entered the world of business to business as an entrepreneur.

Chris Bailey
Regional Creative
Director (Western
Europe)
Saatchi & Saatchi

Chris is an honours business graduate, with more than 16 years' experience in marketing and communications, both nationally and internationally. He has worked as a copywriter, creative director and strategic creative director for BBDO, JWT, Euro RSCG, Grey, Porter Novelli and Saatchi & Saatchi.

Currently regional creative director (Western Europe) for Saatchi & Saatchi, Chris has worked on both B2C and B2B brands, covering FMCG, retail, transport, recruitment, technology, healthcare, finance, corporate and professional services. He has helped to plan, create and execute integrated concepts and campaigns for a wide variety of brands including: BA, Hewlett-Packard, Shell, TNT, Maersk, Yahoo!, BI Pfizer, Novo Nordisk, ADT, AstraZeneca, Regus, SpinVox, Randstaad, Snickers, Pepsi, Uncle Ben's, Foot Locker, Canon, Nokia and Vodafone. He has written several thought leadership pieces on creating and integrating 'Big Brand Ideas' across multiple channels.

Prior to his career in advertising and PR, Chris worked in radio as a presenter, producer and comedy writer.

Gary Brine
Founder & Ex-CEO
Gyro International

Gary left Gyro International in 2008 after leading the business for 17 years.

He established the full service integrated marketing communications agency in 1991; it now encompasses offices in 11 countries and employs 400 people. Named as 'One to Watch' by The Sunday Times, it is the UK's largest and fastest-growing B2B agency.

Before founding Gyro, Gary was an account director at a leading integrated shop (CGA London), prior to which he was a professional ice hockey player and represented his country more than 20 times.

In 2008 Gary was a London finalist for the Ernst & Young Entrepreneur of the Year award.

Richard Bush
Founder & Managing Director
Base One Group

Richard's military background provides not only shrewd strategic insight, but also ensures a rigorous sense of discipline is instilled in his troops. The driving force behind the success of the Base One Group, Richard has guided the agency from its beginnings as a small business advertising specialist in 1997 to its current form as a multi-disciplined agency group, offering strategic brand consultancy as well as both online and offline campaign implementation; that Base One was awarded the accolade of Agency of the Year by B2B Marketing in 2007 is largely his work.

Richard is also a regular presenter at the Institute of Direct Marketing and writes and speaks frequently for a number of industry publications and institutions, including B2B Marketing, the Internet Advertising Bureau and the Association of Business to Business Agencies.

Steve Cooke
Marketing Director
BMRB

For the past 10 years, Steve's responsibilities have been in corporate and service marketing. In his current role he is responsible for developing the communications strategy for BMRB. Steve manages all central aspects of brand development which includes advertising, PR, corporate events, conferences, website, internal comms and marketing collateral. He recently headed up a rebranding programme, resulting in the launch of a new identity for BMRB.

Steve has a wealth of experience in business to business marketing and market research, gained from his current role and previous positions at television sales house TSMS and media independent BBJ. He holds a postgraduate diploma in marketing.

Nadia Cristina
Partner
Practice Management
International LLP

Nadia is a partner in Practice Management International LLP, an organisation which encourages professionalism in marketing and management in professional service firms worldwide through founding and organising influential trade associations. To this end, it runs the Managing Partners' Forum (MPF) and the Professional Marketing Forum (PM Forum). She joined the organisation 15 years ago and has been instrumental in its growth and direction.

Nadia's main focus is Professional Marketing, the worldwide magazine for marketing professional services from the PM Forum. She is the managing editor, responsible for commissioning, editing and design, a role which she continues to enjoy immensely.

Jonathan Cummings
Director
Start Creative

Jonathan joined Start Creative in early 2007 after four years as marketing director of the Institute of Directors (IoD). A top 10 independent UK brand and digital design agency, Start's clients include Virgin, adidas, figleaves.com, the BBC, Royal Mail, Bentley, Hertz and Hilton among others. In January 2009, Jonathan became managing director of Start Creative Hong Kong, a new venture for the group following development of business in Russia, India and the United Arab Emirates.

At the IoD Jonathan was responsible for the marketing of its diverse range of activities; from top-end hospitality to publishing and from business information and advice to director-level training. Jonathan sits on various advisory boards and collaborative bodies and presents regularly on brand and digital marketing issues. A key theme for Jonathan is to communicate the benefits of a holistic brand engagement strategy, and the importance of ensuring that every stakeholder in an organisation truly understands the brand and their influence on it.

Paul Edwards
CEO
Research
International UK

Paul worked at Bartle Bogle Hegarty on a range of FMCG and retail accounts, before a spell as head of planning at Young & Rubicam and Still Price Lintas. He then became chairman and chief executive of The Henley Centre, working on future strategic direction for a wide range of blue-chip clients and developing new working techniques for management groups. While at Henley, Paul was a frequent commentator on TV and radio on branding, consumer and new media matters. More recently he was the group chief executive for Lowe & Partners and the chairman of the London agency, taking particular responsibility for serving clients' integrated marketing needs.

After a year avoiding corporate life, consulting for a bewildering range of clients (from Sugar magazine to Challenger tanks), he joined Publicis in October 2004 as chief strategy officer. In August 2007 Paul moved to Research International UK, the company he had joined as a graduate trainee many years previously.

Pamela Fieldhouse
Managing Director
Edelman UK

Pamela is managing director of Edelman UK, the world's largest independent PR consultancy. She is a senior communications consultant with more than 18 years' experience in corporate reputation, issues and crisis management, brand strategy and business communications.

She provides strategic counsel to senior executives from both the public and private sector and currently advises clients across a wide range of industry sectors including technology, retail and construction. Over the years she has worked with some of the world's best-known brands including Microsoft®, Levi Strauss Europe, UPS and Mitsubishi Electric.

After graduating from Queen's University Belfast with an honours degree in psychology, Pamela began her career with Charles Barker in 1989 as a graduate trainee; by 1999 she had progressed to managing director of the agency. Pamela went on to become deputy chief executive of BSMG Worldwide UK (now Weber Shandwick) and a principal of the global organisation before joining Edelman in 2005.

Carlos Grande
Editor
WARC Online

Carlos is currently editor of WARC Online, a unique resource that brings together a range of case studies, research, best practice guides, consumer insight and marketing intelligence on leading companies and brands. The content is relied upon by a core audience comprising creative and media agency networks, market research companies and media owners.

He began his journalism career as a news and features writer at the Western Morning News, moving on to become deputy editor of New Media Markets, the FT's specialist weekly for cutting-edge multimedia. Further roles at the FT followed, including e-business correspondent, editor of Creative Business, media correspondent and marketing correspondent.

Richard Groom
Head of Consultancy
Groom Associates

With a strong background in brand development, Richard has worked in leading marketing roles for more than 15 years with companies such as United Biscuits, Délifrance and McCain Foods.

In 2004 he co-founded Groom Associates, a brand and design agency. Based initially in Leeds, it now has offices in San Francisco and Beijing.

As head of consultancy at Groom, Richard's role has seen him work with an extensive national and international customer base across a wide variety of sectors, with clients such as Gulf Oil, National Grid, the Chartered Institute of Marketing, C Group International and 3663.

Joanna Higgins
Senior Editor
BNET UK

Joanna is senior editor at BNET UK, the new UK business and management website owned by CBS. Previously, as group editor of the Institute of Directors' publications, Joanna led a highly praised and radical redesign, launched the website, oversaw the development of new editorial products and in 2004, spun out leisure and lifestyle publication After Hours – now a successful quarterly title.

Joanna has sat on the judging panel for a number of prestigious business awards for organisations including Business in the Community, Working Families, the Scottish Institute for Enterprise, Shell and Sage. She is frequently asked to comment on issues relating to the small and medium-sized enterprise sector, business leadership, and enterprise in Britain.

Jason Karaian
Deputy Editor
CFO Europe

Jason joined CFO Europe, a magazine for senior finance executives published by The Economist, in 2002. He covers a wide range of beats, edits the publication's news pages and manages the European channel of CFO.com. He also oversees the magazine's original research activities, including the quarterly Business Outlook Survey, a widely-followed indicator of economic confidence among finance chiefs.

In addition to the CFO titles in Europe, Asia and the US, Jason's work has appeared in other group outlets, including Economist.com, Intelligent Life and the Economist Intelligence Unit's wire services.

Before joining CFO Europe, Jason was an economist at a boutique consulting firm in Chicago and occasional contributor to Barron's. He studied economics at Northwestern University and the London School of Economics.

Darrell Kofkin
Chief Executive
Global Marketing Network

Darrell began his career in marketing management with London Underground and InterCity before entering a career in professional education and development. In 2002 he combined his passion for marketing and teaching and founded premier marketing college, London School of Marketing. Between 2002 and 2005 he led this to become one of the leading providers of professional marketing education programmes in both the UK and Russia. He subsequently sold his stake in the company in 2005.

In 2007 he launched Global Marketing Network, the professional body for marketing professionals. He has since led its expansion into India, Nigeria and Sri Lanka.

Passionate about getting more people engaged in the marketing profession and putting marketing at the heart of the boardroom agenda, Darrell speaks regularly at conferences and business schools and in the media.

Mark Lanigan
Partner
Ogilvy

Mark has worked at Ogilvy for more than 20 years and now leads Ogilvy Primary Contact's Interactive Group.

He began his career at the FT in the financial advertising department before moving to Ogilvy Primary Contact, working on a wide variety of business brands including BP, BT, Bayer, DHL, Intel and SriLankan Airlines.

Mark is passionate about using established branding and direct marketing techniques across both traditional and new media channels to build enduring customer relationships. He believes that B2B demands specialist skills and sits on the IDM B2B Marketing Council, promoting training and education in the area.

Mark divides his spare time between computing, cooking and travel in the Far East.

Kate Manasian
Managing Director
Saffron Consultants

Kate is a director and owner of Saffron, a brand consultancy formed in 2001 by Wally Olins. Before joining Saffron, she worked at Wolff Olins for 12 years where she was a partner and owner.

Starting out in branding more than 20 years ago at a small design firm in Chiswick, Kate's early career also encompassed freelance speechwriting and work for various design journals such as Design Magazine and Interior Design.

Her experience is wide and varied – retail design, packaging and corporate design for industries including automotive, oil, food retailing and telecoms as well as NGOs and professional service organisations. Clients have included Unicef, Cadillac, Tesco, PricewaterhouseCoopers, Co-operative Retail Services, House of Fraser, AOL, BP, Shell, BT, Weil Gotshal, Smith & Nephew, Thames Water, Mitsubishi and Nissan.

Kate launched Wolff Olins' American business in 1998 and is now leading Saffron's US business.

Ruth Mortimer
Editor
Brand Strategy

Ruth is editor of Brand Strategy magazine, the leading global monthly title for senior marketers. In addition to this role, she is a contributing editor and guest columnist for Marketing Week and a regular contributor to Design Week. She often appears on CNN, Sky and the BBC as an expert on business issues and is currently editing two books about marketing effectiveness for publisher Wiley.

A regular speaker at conferences including the Marketing Week Brand Summit and the MIDEM music marketing conference in Cannes, Ruth has also acted as a judge for awards such as the BT Digital Music Awards. Before becoming editor of Brand Strategy, she was a freelance journalist working for both business and consumer media such as Channel 4.

Ruth trained initially as an archaeologist, graduating from Manchester University with a first class degree and working in the Middle East for several years before retraining as a journalist.

Marc Nohr
Managing Partner
Kitcatt Nohr
Alexander Shaw

Marc is managing partner at DM Agency of the Year Kitcatt Nohr whose clients include Waitrose, Lexus, Citroën, John Lewis, NS&I, Britannia, the NSPCC and WWF.

Marc is a fellow of the Institute of Direct Marketing, and one of its most popular speakers. He also contributes regularly to debates on marketing in the media, and was one of the founding columnists in the FT's Creative Business supplement. He now has a column in the leading DM monthly title, Marketing Direct and was recently named Number One in its DM Power 100.

Phil Nunn
Partner
Trinity

Phil launched the media company, Trinity, in September 2007 with two partners Simon Timlett and Amy Lennox. Trinity now has 15 clients including New Look, TalkTalk and Majestic Wines. The business focuses on unifying communication solutions across digital, brand and direct channels.

Phil has spent a total of 18 years in media, starting at BBC Worldwide and moving on to Publicis' Optimedia. There he launched Interactive@Optimedia in 1998, running accounts including Hewlett-Packard, Allied Domecq, COI, BA Holidays and MBNA.

He joined Manning Gottlieb OMD in 2003, going on to become managing partner. He was responsible for – and actively involved in – John Lewis, Virgin Media's launch, and all new business delivery.

His new venture Trinity is proving a huge success. One of the youngest media agencies to be recognised by the IPA, the company's work has been nominated for awards by Marketing Week, DMA and New Media Age.

Andrew Pinkess
Strategy Director
Rufus Leonard

Andrew has 20 years' experience in brand and marketing consultancy. His specialisms include: brand strategy and development; digital strategy; integrated communications; and internal communications as a catalyst for organisational change. His client experience spans business to business, business to consumer and the public sector.

He joined brand and digital media consultancy Rufus Leonard in 1998, and key clients include the BBC, British Council, BT, COI, Foreign & Commonwealth Office, Identity & Passport Service, Lloyds TSB, Morgan Stanley, Royal Mail, Royal Bank of Scotland, Save the Children, Shell, UK Trade & Investment, and the Wellcome Trust. Before joining Rufus Leonard, he was planning director at financial services advertising agency CCHM and managing consultant at P Four Consultancy.

His early career was spent in international marketing and the travel industry. Andrew is an Oxford graduate with an MBA from Warwick University.

Shane Redding
Managing Director
Think Direct

Shane is an independent consultant with more than 20 years' international business to business and consumer direct marketing experience. She provides strategic direct marketing advice and practical training to both end-users and DM suppliers; clients include Dennis Publishing, Advertising Standards Authority, the IoD and Royal Mail. Specialising in direct and digital data, databases and analysis, Shane enjoys helping large and small businesses use direct marketing to significantly improve the bottom line.

In addition to her consultancy business, Shane also holds a number of non-executive directorships and board advisory roles including Livingstone Partners Cyance Ltd and Total Hotspots.

Shane was recently awarded an honorary fellowship of the Institute of Direct Marketing (IDM). Furthermore, she has held a number of association roles including chair of the IDM's B2B Council, vice chair of FEDM and past DMA UK board member.

Matthew Stibbe
Writer-in-Chief
Articulate Marketing

Matthew is writer-in-chief at Articulate Marketing. His clients include HP, Microsoft®, eBay and HM Government. He helps them talk to non-techies about technology and also writes the popular blog, BadLanguage.net.

Before starting the agency in 2005, he worked as a freelance business and technology writer and was a regular contributor to Wired, Popular Science and Director. He also reviewed business jets for The Robb Report and still flies for fun; but in much smaller and cheaper planes.

In 1992 Matthew started a computer games company which has developed over 20 games for publishers such as EA, Sony and LEGO®. He ran the business until 2000 when he sold it to his management team. Prior to this, he read Modern History at Pembroke College Oxford.

Morvah Stubbings
Managing Director
BPRI

Morvah began her career at Frank Small and Associates in Melbourne, Australia's largest locally owned Market Research Company at the time. Here she specialised in service industry research for blue-chip clients in the airline, banking and telecommunications industries. Joining Nett Effect – the division set up to focus on customer service and satisfaction offers – at its inception, she helped develop and package proprietary methodologies for use within the wider group.

Later she joined TNS in Sydney, ultimately running the Business Services division. Leaving to set up the Asia Pacific office of BPRI, Morvah travelled extensively helping international clients understand and respond to regional challenges. Moving back to the UK in 2003 with BPRI she is now a managing director. BPRI is the specialist B2B brand within Kantar – WPP's research, insight and consultancy arm.

Giles Thomas
Chief Operating Officer
Branded

Giles is currently COO of brand consultancy Branded, where he has been advising a broad range of clients across many markets and countries for the last eight years. His clients include Orange, Yahoo!, EA, Channel 4, and Transport for London.

He is an experienced international marketer, having earned his credentials as marketing director at MTV Networks Europe and European marketing director at Sega.

At MTV Networks Giles ran marketing across 26 territories, including launching VH1 to music fans across Europe. While at Sega, he directed the launch marketing of the Dreamcast console and all games titles in Europe.

Giles spent the first seven years of his career in advertising at Young & Rubicam, Chiat Day, and Banks Hoggins O'Shea.

Richard Williams
Founding Partner
Williams Murray Hamm

A graduate of The London College of Printing, Richard worked as an in-house designer at Sainsbury's before moving into design management with Allied International Designers. In 1986 he co-founded Design Bridge and grew it into one of Europe's largest independent design firms. He left the company in 1996 and founded Williams Murray Hamm with Richard Murray.

A fellow of The Royal Society of Arts and a member of the Design Council, Richard often acts as a spokesman for the design community, appearing on Radio 4's 'Today' programme as well as speaking at Ashridge Management College, Warwick Business School and New York's FUSE.

He also works on behalf of the Design Council on its Designing Demand initiative, visiting manufacturing and marketing businesses across the UK, interrogating their use of design and helping them make better use of the discipline.

He was the Design Council's nominated judge on the panel for the Prince Philip Designer's Prize 2007.

Chris Wilson
Managing Director
Loewy Brand Communications

Chris has spent 14 years in business to business marketing – both client-side and agency. His agency career has been spent working with organisations primarily in the technology and telecommunications sectors, such as Fujitsu, IBM, HP, BT, T-Mobile, Cisco and Oracle. Chris helps B2B organisations define their brand proposition and then communicate this effectively to their target audience, both internally and externally.

He is a member of the Association of Business to Business Marketing and the Chartered Institute of Marketing, as well as author of 'Punching Above Your Weight' – a guide to B2B marketing within the IT/Telco sectors.

Andrew Worlock
Director
Insidedge

Simon Wylie
Founding Partner &
Managing Director
Xtreme Information

Andrew heads up the UK IPG agency Insidedge, a specialist internal communications consultancy based in London. Working with multinationals and blue-chip organisations across Europe, he advises those facing the eternal dilemma of how to maximise resource and budget in order to achieve corporate goals internally.

Before joining Insidedge, Andrew worked primarily in the telecommunications, automotive and IT sectors across EMEA, focusing on performance improvement and brand engagement. A stint at TNS, working within a research environment, gave Andrew sound experience in strategic planning and insight, while his time as a European director for both Omnicom and Maritz instilled in him an in-depth knowledge of brand engagement and internal communications across consumer, employee and channel partners.

Simon is a founding partner of Xtreme Information, the leading media intelligence source of global advertising, and has more than 20 years' experience within the field of advertising, media intelligence, research and insight. Throughout this period he has worked with major global brands such as Coca-Cola, P&G, IBM, Microsoft®, HP, Ford and GM, as well as a number of European NGOs, the European Commission and other regulatory bodies.

During his leadership at Xtreme, the company has experienced consistent growth through expansion into new markets and the launch of key initiatives such as the European Media Digest, a summary of media expenditure data across Western Europe; Xtreme Insight, an advertising and media insight consultancy; and Contagious, an intelligence and consultancy service examining future facing media and brand/consumer engagement.

Simon also works with the Newspaper Marketing Agency and WARC to provide consultancy on media intelligence and advertising matters.

The YouGov Vote

YouGov

YouGov is an international, full service research company. Primarily using online panels, it provides quantitative and qualitative research across a range of specialisms including consumer markets, financial services, technology and telecoms, media, politics and the public sector. YouGov's full service offering spans added value consultancy, syndicated product offers, omnibus and field and tab services.

YouGov operates a high quality panel of more than 200,000 UK members representing all ages, socio-economic groups and other demographic types, with excellent response rates. YouGov also specialises in growing and maintaining dedicated panels of specialist consumer and professional audiences.

YouGov has developed an extensive business to business offering, owing to its ability to access thousands of business decision makers on its panel, which have been profiled to determine individuals' sectors and responsibilities. In addition, The YouGov Small Business Omnibus allows clients to quickly and cost-effectively interview 500 decision makers of small businesses every month.

YouGov dominates Britain's media polling and is one of the most quoted research agencies in Britain. Its well-documented track record demonstrates the accuracy of its survey methods and quality of its client service work.

YouGov and Superbrands

YouGov has worked with the Superbrands organisation over the past few years, conducting online elections for all three of its UK programmes – Superbrands, Business Superbrands and CoolBrands. The survey for Business Superbrands 2009 was conducted online.

Online research has proved to be the best medium for quantifying the perception of Business Superbrands; the stimulating process is intuitive, so it can be quick and enjoyable for participants and is non-intrusive as the questionnaires are completed by invitation.

Fieldwork for the Business Superbrands 2009 election took place in the summer of 2008; interviews were conducted with 1,667 business professionals of management or board level.

The final scores were incorporated with the scores given to the brands by the Expert Council (see selection process details on page 136).

Tim Britton
Chief Executive UK

YouGov®

www.yougov.co.uk
info@yougov.co.uk
+44 (0)20 7012 6000

The Business Superbrands Results 2009

By Stephen Cheliotis
Chairman, Expert Council
& Chief Executive,
The Centre for Brand Analysis

Top Performers

It is now three years since the methodology for selecting the Business Superbrands was amended and it is the second year in which search engine giant Google has emerged from the process in the top spot. Maintaining its number one position, the American giant has reaffirmed its credentials not only as the UK's leading consumer brand, but as the leading business to business brand.

In total, five of last year's top 10 brands once again make this group, showing their strength while simultaneously demonstrating the difficulty faced by other brands wishing to challenge the top tier. Rolls-Royce Group, one of Britain's largest engineering concerns and one of the few majors to remain UK-owned, has improved its position and enjoys a four place rise; its second consecutive year improving. From 2007 to 2008 it rose from ninth to sixth place, while 2009 sees it climb into second place. Despite, perhaps, being less topical or exciting than Google, the brand may have a serious chance of taking the top spot next year.

Microsoft® has had a slightly less solid year, although it remains firmly entrenched in the top 10; it falls from second place (a position that it held for two years) to fourth.

Sony, Nokia, Michelin and Bupa are all new entries to the top 10, reaffirming the positive halo effect that brands which operate in both the business to business and business to consumer arenas can enjoy. The other new entry to the top 10 is London Stock Exchange, which has successfully withstood a number of hostile takeovers in recent times. With the turmoil on the markets worsening since this research was conducted, it will be interesting to see how the brand fares in 2010.

GlaxoSmithKline falls one place to sixth this year while BP drops from third to ninth. Those brands completely falling out of the top 10 are BBC Worldwide (the commercial arm of the

BUSINESS SUPERBRANDS TOP 10

Rank	2008	2009
1	Google	Google
2	Microsoft®	Rolls-Royce Group
3	BP	Sony
4	BBC Worldwide	Microsoft®
5	GlaxoSmithKline	Nokia
6	Rolls-Royce Group	GlaxoSmithKline
7	FT	London Stock Exchange
8	British Airways	Michelin
9	FedEx Express	BP
10	Hertz	Bupa

BBC), the FT, British Airways, FedEx Express and Hertz. The BBC, criticised by some for being too commercial, suffers as BBC Worldwide drops to 15th place, while fellow media brand the FT falls to 31st. FedEx Express and Hertz fall to 19th and 28th respectively.

Arguably the most high profile brand dropping out of the 10 is British Airways. After another turbulent year in which it had to contend with fuel price fluctuations, a range of high profile corporate activity and the disastrous opening of Heathrow Terminal 5, the brand has fallen to its lowest position in any Superbrands survey, dropping 28 places to 36th. In third place two years ago, it fell fractionally to eighth last year.

Aside from Michelin's incredible performance to reach the top 10 (rising from 63rd in last year's results), fellow tyre manufacturers have also steered a successful course with Goodyear in 18th and Pirelli in 20th position. For both brands this is a significant improvement on their previous performance; Goodyear sat in 98th place in 2008 while Pirelli was 85th.

Other brands in the top 20 include Apple, staying in 11th position; Chubb, which has

risen from 57th to 12th; Boeing, which goes from 20th to 13th; Visa, climbing two places to 14th; Shell, which improves by one position to sit in 16th; and PricewaterhouseCoopers which drops three places to 17th.

Movers and Shakers

More widely there are 102 new brands in the top 500, showing that while the top of the league experiences relative calm, overall volatility remains and brands have to fight hard to feature in the table. The list of new entrants includes five that have effectively been rebranded since last year's research. For example, the newly merged Thomson Reuters secures 85th position; previously Thompson Financial sat in 407th position and Reuters as a standalone was in 13th.

Some of these can perhaps be defined as the 'yo-yo brands'; having qualified in 2007 they fell out of the top 500 last year but have managed to regain their position in 2009. The best performers within this group are Norton in 129th place and Cable & Wireless in 136th.

The highest new entry in the top 500 is Yale, which has achieved an impressive 57th

position. Nokia Siemens Networks, the joint venture between the two electronic giants, also enters the list strongly in 127th while ceramics manufacturer Armitage Shanks joins at 137th.

New entrants just sneaking into the top 500 include aerospace company Bombardier in 494th position, studio owner Pinewood Shepperton in 491st, Rackspace in 486th and Whitehead Mann Group in 484th place. In total, six of the last 10 positions in the top 500 are occupied by new entries.

The biggest year-on-year riser within the top 500 is Investors in People which has risen an incredible 207 places to sit at 210. Other fast risers include engineering behemoth ThyssenKrupp which improves by 186 positions, Eurotunnel which climbs 162 positions, and London City Airport whose traffic increase has been matched by its brand improvement, rising 154 places. The previously troubled catering blue-chip, Compass Group, also improves its position by 144 places to reach 270.

Expert Council vs. Business Professionals

As always, there are both similarities and significant differences between the views of the Expert Council and those of the wider business professionals surveyed as part of the selection process. The views of the two audiences share equal weight in producing the total score that is allocated to each brand. This score determines each brand's final position.

In terms of the largest bias toward the experts – i.e. the brands rated significantly higher by the experts than by the professionals – it is perhaps no surprise that marketing organisations feature. For example, advertising agency BBH is ranked a full 510 places higher by the experts, many of whom hail from the marketing industry – it secures 72nd place in the expert vote compared to 582nd in the professional vote. The difference can perhaps also be attributed to the brand's adoption of the BBH acronym; in previous years the established Bartle Bogle & Hegarty name attracted a higher rating from the professionals.

Other brands securing considerably higher ratings from the experts include Glue London

TOP 10 YEAR-ON-YEAR CLIMBERS

Brand	2009 Rank	2008 Rank	Rise
Investors in People	210	417	207
ThyssenKrupp	213	399	186
Fairtrade	126	304	178
Eurotunnel	140	302	162
London City Airport	261	415	154
McAfee	159	305	146
Dunlop	53	197	144
Compass Group	270	414	144
Hogg Robinson Group	267	410	143
Wolff Olins	330	473	143

PROFESSIONAL BIAS TOP 10

Brand	Professional Rank	Expert Rank	Bias
BAE Systems	35	596	561
Stagecoach	163	716	553
Cable & Wireless	83	570	487
National Express	101	567	466
Arriva	272	728	456
Europcar	236	684	448
Bank of America	289	725	436
Exxon Mobil	73	494	421
Thames Water	282	687	405
Scottish Power	241	641	400

EXPERT BIAS TOP 10

Brand	Professional Rank	Expert Rank	Bias
BBH	582	72	510
Glue London	719	237	482
ABB	696	215	481
Rackspace	672	193	479
Stopgap	729	259	470
Powwow	738	290	448
TBWA\London	682	235	447
Spencer Stuart	627	190	437
RKCR/Y&R	715	303	412
Etihad	683	271	412

(482 places higher), ABB (481 places higher), Rackspace (479 places higher), and Stopgap (470 places higher). The rationale for such difference of opinion, however, is not always as obvious as in the case of BBH.

Conversely, brands gaining much higher positions within the professional vote include defence giant BAE Systems; it tops the professional bias table by virtue of securing 35th place with business professionals compared to 596th place among the council, a difference of 561 positions.

In addition, three transport conglomerates in the form of Stagecoach, National Express and Arriva feature in the professional bias top 10, with a difference in position of 553, 466 and 456 places respectively. Whether this is a result of high awareness levels among business professionals, due to these all being UK consumer facing brands, or of the experts not viewing them as particularly innovative in marketing terms is debatable.

Equally, the question can be raised as to whether the issue of ethics is one that is more acutely considered by the experts. Aside from the merits of each brand, it is interesting that a defence company, three transport companies and two power companies feature in the professional bias table – it does at least raise that debate. They include oil giant Exxon Mobil which despite being ranked 73rd by professionals, occupies 494th place in the expert vote – a difference of 421 positions.

If we were to compare the top 10s of the expert council and the business professionals, we would find that only two brands feature in both: Nokia and Sony. Nokia performs slightly better in the expert vote (sixth vs. ninth) while Sony finds more favour with the professionals (fifth vs. seventh). In 2008 only Google and Microsoft® made both top 10s, but 2009 sees Google fall to 11th place in the professional vote while Microsoft® falls to 11th in the expert vote.

Brands that have made the professional top 10 but not that of the experts are Rolls-Royce Group, Microsoft®, Michelin, London Stock Exchange, Chubb, Bupa, GlaxoSmithKline and BP. Conversely, the expert council places

PROFESSIONAL TOP 10

Rank	Brand	Category
1	Rolls-Royce Group	Aerospace & Defence
2	Microsoft®	Software & Computer Services
3	Michelin	Automobiles & Parts
4	London Stock Exchange	Financial - Exchanges & Markets
5	Sony	Electronic & Electrical Equipment
6	Chubb	Support Services – Security & Fire Protection
7	Bupa	Healthcare Equipment & Services
8	GlaxoSmithKline	Pharmaceuticals & Biotech
9	Nokia	Electronic & Electrical Equipment
10	BP	Oil & Gas

EXPERT TOP 10

Rank	Brand	Category
1	Google	Media – Marketing Services – Advertising Solutions
2	Apple	Technology – Hardware & Equipment
3	FT	Media – Content Creators/Owners
4	BlackBerry	Electronic & Electrical Equipment
5	The Economist	Media – Content Creators/Owners
6	Nokia	Electronic & Electrical Equipment
7	Sony	Electronic & Electrical Equipment
8	eBay	Media – Marketing Services – Advertising Solutions
9	Goldman Sachs	Financial – Banks
10	McKinsey & Company	Support Services – Consultancies

Apple, the FT, BlackBerry, The Economist, eBay, Goldman Sachs and McKinsey & Company in its top 10.

Sectors

The most heavily represented sector in the top 500 by some margin is the Technology – Hardware & Equipment category. Headed by Apple it features 30 brands this year, down one from last year. Coming a considerable distance behind is Construction & Materials – Tools & Equipment. Lead by Bosch it has 19 brands, up from 17 in 2008. Other categories in the top five by volume of brands included in the top 500 are Financial – Banks, which we suspect might not perform as well next year, Construction & Materials and Retailers – Office Equipment & Supplies.

The least represented sector is Travel & Leisure – Airline Charter & Fractional Ownership with only NetJets in the top 500. A further five categories have just two brands in the top 500.

The worst performing segments year-on-year are Automobiles & Parts and Travel & Leisure – Airlines, both of which lost seven representatives this year. In the case of the former, however, the car manufacturers from that segment were removed from the process this year.

For all of the sectors, bar two, representation within the top 500 has altered by no more than five brands year-on-year. Aerospace & Defence is the most improved sector; it increases its representation from nine brands to 14 to become one of the most represented sectors by volume. Four categories gain three representatives this year.

If we look at sectors another way – by the average position achieved by a sector's brands in the top 500 – we can see that two Media – Marketing Services sub-categories sit at the bottom of the table: Media Agencies and PR Agencies. The categories have just three and four representatives respectively and average positions of 470 and 466, revealing that the few brands that did make the grade only just scraped in.

The most successful categories by average position attained are Electronic &

TOP CATEGORIES BY VOLUME

Category	Number of Brands in 2008	Number of Brands in 2009
Technology – Hardware & Equipment	31	30
Construction & Materials – Tools/Equipment	17	19
Financial – Banks	22	19
Construction & Materials	17	17
Retailers – Office Equipment & Supplies	21	17
Support Services – Associations & Accreditations	13	16
Software & Computer Services	13	15
Aerospace & Defence	9	14
Pharmaceuticals & Biotech	13	14
Support Services – General	10	14
Travel & Leisure – Business Hotels	17	14

Electrical Equipment (averaging 91st), Telecommunications – General (averaging 79th) and topping the table, Financial – Credit Cards (averaging 49th); we have already highlighted that this research was conducted before the full extent of the credit crunch became evident.

Category Winners

In terms of categories, almost all see the 2008 sector leaders maintain their position again this year. For example, Eurostar remains in pole position in the Travel & Leisure – Train & Bus Operators sector; in the overall rankings it improves its position, rising from 67th in 2008 to 52nd this year. NEC Birmingham retains top position in Conference Centres (another Travel & Leisure sub-category) despite only rising by two places in the overall rankings. ExCeL London, meanwhile, rises one place in the sector to take second – in the overall rankings it jumps significantly from 280th to 176th place.

Other brands maintaining their sector leadership include Hilton, Hertz, Apple, Chubb, Linklaters, AA, McKinsey & Company, HSBC, Nokia, JCB, Rio Tinto, Saatchi & Saatchi, BP, GlaxoSmithKline, Microsoft®, PricewaterhouseCoopers and London School of Economics and Political Science. While the extent of the leadership gap has narrowed in some cases this year, it remains a powerful indication of the dominance and strength of the market leaders – a situation that is likely to be exacerbated by the current economic downturn, with market leaders expected to extend their competitive position.

In fact only a handful of brands have lost the converted number one slot in their sector. In the Utilities sector, British Gas Business is beaten by npower (third in the category in 2008). British Airways falls in the rankings, losing its top position in the Travel & Leisure – Airline sector to rival Virgin Atlantic. Reuters, following its merger with Thompson Financial,

loses the top position to FTSE in Support Services – Information Providers.

Conclusion

As always, it is important to congratulate all the brands featuring in the top 500; the variety of sectors covered and the sheer number of brands analysed means that even breaking into the 500 is an achievement. Invariably the top 10 and top 20 draw most attention, but the reality is that year-on-year this elite group often remains the same. Of course it is not totally static, as we have seen, with notable falls for the FT, Hertz and British Airways. Nevertheless compared to the wider list, and some of the more significant swings up and down within it, the top brands tend to perform consistently in the tables. What is also notable is that category leaders are hard to displace and the majority have been able to retain their top position.

Special praise should go to those brands making the grade for the first time and those that have re-entered the table after an absence. As always, a long, varied and often illustrious list of brands just failed to make the grade; these include (in no particular order) Ryder, ABB, PR Newswire, Inmarsat, Business Link, Brakes, EADS, Rexam, SanDisk, Swissport, Westfield, Misys, Kelly Services, the Business Design Centre and Oxford Instruments, to name but a few.

We look forward to seeing what happens next year; with the economic situation likely to continue throughout 2009, it is probable that both at a sector and individual brand level the 2010 results will show greater change than has been evident over the previous three years. Which of these brands will last the distance, which will continue to invest in themselves and build their equity and which will slip, what will happen between individual competitors and how will whole sectors perform? All will be revealed in February 2010...

Qualifying Business Superbrands 2009

3
3663
118 118
3COM
3M
AA
ABBEY
ABBOTT MEAD VICKERS
    BBDO
ABN AMRO
ABTA
ACAS
ACCA
ACCENTURE
ACCOUNTANCY AGE
ACER
ACNIELSEN
ADECCO
ADMIRAL GROUP
ADOBE
ADT
AGA FOODSERVICE GROUP
AIG
AIM
AIRBUS
AKZONOBEL
ALAMO
ALLEN & OVERY
ALLIANZ
ALLIED IRISH BANK (GB)
ALSTOM
AMD
AMEC
AMERICAN EXPRESS
ANGLO AMERICAN
APPLE
ARCHITECTS' JOURNAL
ARMITAGE SHANKS
ARRIVA
ARUP
ASHRIDGE BUSINESS
    SCHOOL
ASK.COM
ASTRAZENECA
AUTOCAD
AVERY
AVIS
AVIVA
AVON
AXA
AXA PPP HEALTHCARE
B&Q
BACS
BAE SYSTEMS
BAIN & COMPANY
BAKER TILLY
BALFOUR BEATTY
BANHAM ALARMS
BANK OF AMERICA
BANK OF SCOTLAND
BARCLAYCARD

BARCLAYS
BASF
BASILDON BOND
BAYER
BBC WORLDWIDE
BBH
BDO STOY HAYWARD
BG GROUP
BHP BILLITON
BIFFA
BISHOP'S MOVE
BLACK & DECKER
BLACKBERRY
BLOOMBERG
BLUE CIRCLE
BLUETOOTH
BMI
BMRB
BNP PARIBAS
BOC
BOEING
BOMBARDIER
BOSCH
BOSTIK
BOSTON CONSULTING
    GROUP
BP
BRIDGESTONE
BRISTOL-MYERS SQUIBB
BRITISH AIRWAYS
BRITISH ENERGY
BRITISH GAS BUSINESS
BRITISH GYPSUM
BRITISH LAND
BRITISH RETAIL
    CONSORTIUM
BROOK STREET
BROTHER
BRUNSWICK
BSI
BT
BUDGET
BUPA
BURSON-MARSTELLER
BUSINESS WEEK
CABLE & WIRELESS
CALOR
CAMBRIDGE JUDGE
    BUSINESS SCHOOL
CAMPAIGN
CANARY WHARF GROUP
CANON
CAPGEMINI
CAPITA
CARBON TRUST
CARILLION
CARPHONE WAREHOUSE
CASIO
CASTLE CEMENT
CASTROL
CATERPILLAR

CAZENOVE
CB RICHARD ELLIS
CBI
CHUBB
CIMA
CITIGROUP
CITY & GUILDS
CLIFFORD CHANCE
CNBC
CNN
COMPASS GROUP
CONQUEROR
CONTINENTAL
CORBIS
CORUS
COSTAIN
CRANFIELD SCHOOL OF
    MANAGEMENT
CREDIT SUISSE
CROWN
CROWNE PLAZA
D&B
DATAMONITOR
DE LA RUE
DE VERE VENUES
DEWALT
DELL
DELOITTE
DESIGN WEEK
DEUTSCHE BANK
DEUTSCHE POST
DHL
DOLBY
DOW CHEMICALS
DOW CORNING
DRAPER
DRESDNER KLEINWORT
DTZ
DULUX
DUNLOP
DUPONT
DYMO
E.ON
EASYJET
EBAY
EDDIE STOBART
EDF ENERGY
ELI LILLY
EMIRATES
ENTERPRISE
EPSON
ERICSSON
ERNST & YOUNG
EUROPCAR
EUROSTAR
EUROTUNNEL
EVERSHEDS
EXCEL LONDON
EXPERIAN
EXXON MOBIL
FAIRTRADE

FEDEX EXPRESS
FIREFOX
FIRST
FLIGHT INTERNATIONAL
FLYBE
FRESHFIELDS BRUCKHAUS
    DERINGER
FT
FTSE
FUJITSU
FUJITSU SIEMENS
G4S
GALLUP
GARMIN
GATWICK EXPRESS
GE
GENERAL DYNAMICS
GETTY IMAGES
GFK NOP
GKN
GLAXOSMITHKLINE
GOLDMAN SACHS
GOODYEAR
GOOGLE
GRANT THORNTON
GREAT PORTLAND ESTATES
GREEN FLAG
GULFSTREAM
HANSON
HAPAG-LLOYD
HARRIS
HARROGATE
    INTERNATIONAL CENTRE
HAYS SPECIALIST
    RECRUITMENT
HEATHROW EXPRESS
HENLEY BUSINESS SCHOOL
HERBERT SMITH
HERTZ
HEWLETT-PACKARD
HILL & KNOWLTON
HILTON
HISCOX
HITACHI
HOGG ROBINSON GROUP
HOLIDAY INN
HONEYWELL
HOOVERS
HSBC
HSS HIRE
IBIS
IBM
IBM BUSINESS CONSULTING
    SERVICES
ICAEW
ICC BIRMINGHAM
IDEAL STANDARD
ING
INGERSOLL RAND
INITIAL
INTEL

INTERBRAND
INTERCONTINENTAL
INTERLINK EXPRESS
INVESTEC
INVESTORS IN PEOPLE
IOD
IPSOS MORI
ISTOCKPHOTO
JANES
JARVIS
JC DECAUX
JCB
JEWSON
JOHN LAING
JOHNSON & JOHNSON
JOHNSON MATTHEY
JOHNSTONE'S
JONES LANG LASALLE
JP MORGAN
JWT
KALL KWIK
KIER GROUP
KIMBERLEY-CLARK
    PROFESSIONAL*
KING STURGE
KITEMARK
KNIGHT FRANK
KORN/FERRY INTERNATIONAL
KPMG
LAFARGE
LAND SECURITIES
LAZARD
LEGAL & GENERAL
LENOVO
LETTS
LEXMARK
LEYLAND TRADE
LG
LINKLATERS
LLOYD'S
LLOYDS TSB
LOCKHEED MARTIN
LOGICA CMG
LOGITECH
LONDON BUSINESS SCHOOL
LONDON CITY AIRPORT
LONDON METAL EXCHANGE
LONDON SCHOOL OF
    ECONOMICS AND
    POLITICAL SCIENCE
LONDON STOCK EXCHANGE
LYCRA
LYNX EXPRESS
M&C SAATCHI
MAERSK
MAKITA
MALMAISON
MANAGEMENT TODAY
MANCHESTER BUSINESS
    SCHOOL
MANPOWER

MARKETING
MARKETING WEEK
MARRIOTT
MASSEY FERGUSON
MASTERCARD
MCAFEE
MCCANN-ERICKSON
MCKINSEY & COMPANY
MEDIACOM
MERCER
MERCK
MERRILL LYNCH
MICHAEL PAGE
  INTERNATIONAL
MICHELIN
MICROSOFT
MILLENNIUM & COPTHORNE
MILLWARD BROWN
MINTEL
MONSTER.COM
MOODY'S
MORGAN STANLEY
MOTOROLA
MSN
NATIONAL
NATIONAL EXPRESS
NATIONAL GRID
NATWEST
NEC
NEC BIRMINGHAM
NETGEAR
NETJETS
NOKIA
NOKIA SIEMENS NETWORKS
NOMURA EUROPE
NORTEL
NORTHROP GRUMMAN
NORTON
NORTON ROSE
NOVARTIS
NOVELL
NPOWER
O2
OFFICE ANGELS

OGILVY
OLYMPUS
ORACLE
ORANGE
OXFORD BLACK N' RED
OXFORD SAID BUSINESS
  SCHOOL
OYEZ STRAKER
P&O
PA CONSULTING
PALM
PANASONIC
PAPERMATE
PARCELFORCE WORLDWIDE
PARCELINE
PAYPAL
PC WORLD
PEARL & DEAN
PFIZER
PICKFORDS
PILKINGTON
PINEWOOD SHEPPERTON
PIRELLI
PITMAN TRAINING
PITNEY BOWES
PORTAKABIN
PORTMAN TRAVEL
PRATT & WHITNEY
PREMIER INN
PRESS ASSOCIATION
PRICEWATERHOUSECOOPERS
PRONTAPRINT
PRUDENTIAL
QATAR AIRWAYS
QINETIQ
QUARK
RAC
RACKSPACE
RADISSON EDWARDIAN
RAYTHEON
REED
REED ELSEVIER
REGUS
RENTOKIL

RESEARCH INTERNATIONAL
REXEL
RIBA
RICOH
RIO TINTO
ROCHE
ROLLS-ROYCE GROUP
RONSEAL
ROYAL & SUN ALLIANCE
ROYAL BANK OF SCOTLAND
ROYAL MAIL
RYMAN
SAATCHI & SAATCHI
SAGE
SAINT-GOBAIN
SALVESEN
SAMSUNG
SANOFI-AVENTIS
SAP
SAVILLS
SCHERING-PLOUGH
SCHRODERS
SCOTTISH POWER
SCREWFIX
SECURITAS
SERCO
SEVERN TRENT WATER
SHANKS GROUP
SHARP
SHELL
SHERATON
SIEMENS
SINGAPORE AIRLINES
SIR ROBERT MCALPINE
SKANSKA
SKYPE
SLAUGHTER & MAY
SMITH & NEPHEW
SMITHS
SNAP-ON
SODEXO
SOIL ASSOCIATION
SONY
SONY ERICSSON

SPENCER STUART
STAEDTLER
STAGECOACH
STANDARD & POOR'S
STANDARD LIFE HEALTHCARE
STANLEY
STAPLES
STRUTT & PARKER
SUN MICROSYSTEMS
SWISS
SWISS RE
SYMANTEC
TARMAC
TDK
TEFLON
TETRA PAK
THALES
THAMES WATER
THE BANKER
THE CO-OPERATIVE BANK
THE DAILY TELEGRAPH /
  THE SUNDAY TELEGRAPH
THE ECONOMIST
THE GROCER
THE GUARDIAN /
  THE OBSERVER
THE LAW SOCIETY
THE LAWYER
THE OPEN UNIVERSITY
  BUSINESS SCHOOL
THE QUEEN ELIZABETH II
  CONFERENCE CENTRE
THE TIMES / THE SUNDAY
  TIMES
THE WOOLMARK COMPANY
THISTLE
THOMSON DIRECTORIES
THOMSON REUTERS
THYSSENKRUPP
TICKETMASTER
T-MOBILE
TNS
TNT
TOMTOM

TOPPS TILES
TOSHIBA
TOTAL
TRAFFICMASTER
TRAVELEX
TRAVELODGE
TRAVIS PERKINS
TWYFORD BATHROOMS
UBS
UNICHEM
UNISYS
UNIVERSITY OF
  STRATHCLYDE BUSINESS
  SCHOOL
UNIX
UPS
VELCRO
VELUX
VENT-AXIA
VEOLIA ENVIRONMENTAL
  SERVICES
VERISIGN
VIKING
VIRGIN ATLANTIC
VIRGIN TRAINS
VISA
VODAFONE
WALES MILLENNIUM CENTRE
WALKER MEDIA
WARWICK BUSINESS
  SCHOOL
WD-40
WEBER SHANDWICK
WHITEHEAD MANN GROUP
WICKES
WOLFF OLINS
WOLSELEY
XEROX
YAHOO!
YALE
YELLOW PAGES
YKK
ZENITHOPTIMEDIA
ZURICH

Qualifying Business Brands to Watch 2009

ABB
ABBOT
ACCOR SERVICES
ADDLESHAW GODDARD
ALCATEL-LUCENT
BERWIN LEIGHTON
  PAISNER
BIBBY LINE GROUP
BOEHRINGER INGELHEIM
BRAKES
BUILDING
BUSINESS PAGES
BUSINESS POST GROUP

BYWATERS
CASS BUSINESS SCHOOL
CEMEX
CHARTERED MANAGEMENT
  INSTITUTE
CLEAR CHANNEL OUTDOOR
CLOSE BROTHERS
CUSHMAN & WAKEFIELD
CWT
DENTON WILDE SAPTE
DIGITAS
DLA PIPER
EADS

EDELMAN
EGON ZEHNDER
ETIHAD
EURONEXT.LIFFE
FREUD COMMUNICATIONS
GENERAL HEALTHCARE
  GROUP
GLUE LONDON
GVA GRIMLEY
HAMMERSON
HEATHCOTES
HEIDRICK & STRUGGLES
HELLA

HEWDEN
HOTELS.COM
HOWDENS JOINERY CO.
INMARSAT
IRIS
JARDINE LLOYD THOMPSON
  GROUP
KIDDE
KINGSTON SMITH
LACIE
LANCASTER UNIVERSITY
  MANAGEMENT SCHOOL
LANDOR ASSOCIATES
MANCHESTER CONFERENCE
  CENTRE
MAXTOR
MORGAN CRUCIBLE
NICEDAY
NIPPON EXPRESS
NOVO NORDISK

PINSENT MASONS
PKF
PSION TEKLOGIX
RIDGEONS
RKCR/Y&R
RYOBI
SAFFREY CHAMPNESS
SIMMONS & SIMMONS
SJ BERWIN
SMURFIT KAPPA
SOPHOS
STARCOM
STOPGAP
SUN CHEMICAL
SWISSPORT
THE BALTIC EXCHANGE
TRANSGLOBAL EXPRESS
UK COAL
WILLIAMS MURRAY HAMM
WYETH